MARIJUANA

Not Guilty As Charged

CAUTION-DISCLAIMER

MARIJUANA

Not Guilty As Charged

DAVID R. FORD

GOOD PRESS
Sonoma, California

Published by Good Press, P.O. Box 1771, Sonoma, CA 95476,
drford@vom.com

Distributed by Access Publishers Group, 1-800-507-2665

Library of Congress Cataloging-in-Publication Data
Ford, David R.
Marijuana: not guilty as charged / David R. Ford; foreword by Tod H. Mikuriya, M.D.
p. cm.
Includes bibliographical references and index.
ISBN 0-9655932-5-8

1. Marijuana—United States. 2. Marijuana—Law and legislation—United States. I. Title
HV5822.M3.F67 1997 615'.323962
QBI97-40104
LC 97-70795

Manufactured in the United States of America.

Dedication

This book is dedicated to those courageous victims of cancer, AIDS, glaucoma, spasms, and other illnesses who risk prison and worse for using marijuana, a nontoxic medication, to achieve a better quality of life.

To the open-minded research scientists and physicians who are not deterred by government pressure to withhold the fact that marijuana is a precious medicine.

To Keith Stroup, founder of the National Organization for the Reform of Marijuana Laws (NORML).

To the millions who are convinced that marijuana is evil, addictive, and poison, but who will evaluate *Marijuana: Not Guilty As Charged* and be open to change their minds over "potphobia."

And to President Bill Clinton, with the optimism that he will read this book—and when marijuana is legalized, inhale!

In Memory of Eleanor

On January 18, 1997, a memorial service was held for one of my dearest friends, Eleanor Nazarek. Eleanor died from the brutal effects of cancer.

Eleanor was a former teacher who instructed and loved thousands of children. She retired in 1991 as assistant principal of Santa Rosa High School in California.

For seven months, even with her five prescribed medications for nausea, pain, depression, appetite, and sleep, Eleanor's suffering did not cease. She frequently found sleep unattainable.

As a former cancer patient myself, I suggested she try marijuana. "It would be difficult, Dave," she explained. "For so many years I've taught children what I had been taught—that marijuana is a dangerous drug and has no medical value."

The effect of her chemotherapy caused such terrible nausea that Eleanor frequently threw up her medications. Her weight dropped from 135 to nearly 70 pounds. I finally convinced this dear 72-year-old law-abiding lady to try marijuana. I put some bud into a water pipe so that it would not irritate her throat. It was good, strong marijuana. After only two inhales and five minutes, Eleanor fell into a peaceful sleep. I sat by her bedside for two hours. Then her beautiful blue eyes opened. She looked up at me, smiled, and said, "I'm hungry! That marijuana did all the things those five capsules were supposed to do."

Sadly, however, it was too late. Eleanor actually died of starvation. She hadn't been able to eat for more than one month.

Eleanor read the manuscript for this book and gave me encouragement before she ever tried smoking marijuana. I felt that she was just being the loving teacher she always was. Then, within a week of her death, she said, "Dave, your book has a very important and honest message. Get your book out there. Marijuana is indeed medicine."

Dearest Eleanor, and all people who are in pain or dying, this book is for you.

Foreword

by Tod H. Mikuriya, M.D.

IN 1967, I WAS HIRED TO START UP A MARIJUANA RESEARCH program by the National Institute of Mental Health (NIMH) Center for Narcotics and Drug Abuse Studies. In the course of that work, I learned things I would rather have not. The research had already been done by the military and Central Intelligence Agency (CIA) contractors, and public policy was dependent upon what was politically correct "on the Hill." The information from that research was then classified. So was a mountain of clinical and scientific data on the use of cannabis preparations published prior to the 1937 Marihuana Tax Act. Additionally, the CIA's labyrinthine functioning precluded contact with the outside world unless clearance was obtained from the Secretary of Health, Education and Welfare. Where public policy and reality are arbitrary and politically driven, science and fact fall victim to censorship and institutional denial.

Little did I know at the time how impossible was my mission. Some twenty years after my NIMH experience, I learned that the CIA contractors (who were also influential in official drug research policy) got unrestricted support for their secret research while blocking public research on the drug. Notwithstanding efforts of physician researchers to declassify vital medical rediscoveries, the hostile climate toward medical applications has prevented their development.

In this book, David Ford brilliantly conducts us on a tour through the "Malice in Blunderland" of American marijuana policy. He presents tales of viciousness, hypocrisy, and ignorance, facilitated by realities constructed by self-serving special interest groups. He draws from authoritative documents, news clippings, and personal stories—including his own.

The reader cannot keep from feeling a rising sense of outrage at the harmful effects of current laws and policies that intrude ever more on the citizen. Drug testing, loyalty oaths, drug-sniffing dogs, helicopter flyovers, property forfeiture, and surveillance of electric bills, cash transactions over $10,000, and laboratory equipment—these are just some of the more glaring harms of marijuana prohibition.

Prohibition, the American disease, is a form of populist persecution seen in the Salem witch burnings and in lynchings in the southern United States of the 1930s. Prohibition nationwide for alcohol from 1919 to 1933 was the culmination of a movement that started in 1869 and gradually took over America. In 1922 the attorney general took over control of drug policy from the surgeon general. Physicians were purged from that function. In America, the police now tell doctors which drugs they can and cannot prescribe. Presidents refuse to even read exhaustive studies commissioned by the federal government.

Ford describes numerous tragedies of our American alcohol/nicotine society, in which special pressure and ignorance combine to persecute, kill, and sicken consumers. He chronicles the willful deception of the alcohol and tobacco industries as they disingenuously encourage marijuana prohibition while promoting their own products, which are more dangerous by an order of magnitude.

Through bringing these issues to public political debate, it is hoped that there can be a meaningful dialogue. Instead of the usual bipartisan agreement (and collaboration by the press) to sweep it under the rug, it would be constructive to bring all the true facts out in the marketplace of free ideas. From the ensuing authentic discussion, a functional democratic process would produce policy that embodies fair play and cost effectiveness.

For we wrestle not against flesh and blood, but against principalities, against powers, against the rulers of the darkness of this world, against spiritual wickedness in high places.

(EPHESIANS 6:12)

Contents

Preface: The Inside Information

THE AMERICAN MEDICAL ASSOCIATION and numerous other groups only recognized the medicinal botanical marijuana by the name of cannabis, or hemp. The legal term is *cannabis sativa.* Marijuana is a mongrel name that came from Mexico and means "the weed that intoxicates." The government and the media encouraged calling it marijuana because they felt it would frighten the public. It did.

Today, as in 1937, few people are aware that marijuana *is* cannabis. If members of the U.S. House of Representatives had known that when the Marijuana Tax Act of 1937 came before them for approval, the probability is that the bill would never have been passed, and cannabis would have remained legal. A congressman asked, "What is the bill?" A House member stated, "It has something to do with something called marihuana. I believe it is a narcotic of some kind." The bill passed.

News stories included such erroneous federal government employee statements as "marijuana is the most violence-causing drug in the history of mankind." The media repeated such prohibitionist propaganda because anything supporting the war on drugs sells newspapers.

In reference to marijuana, many books, magazine articles, and news stories use "marijuana," "cannabis," and "hemp." At times, all three are used in the same story and generally mean the herb marijuana. This is confusing to the reader, who questions which is which. Let's accept the now-popular name—marijuana—and embrace it for its medical value, as well as its additional extraordinary applications.

There are male and female marijuana plants. The males are practically useless for medical or recreational use because they have virtually no "drug" in them. They are generally pulled up and discarded. The medical and euphoric plant is the female.

The female has "flowers." Sometimes they are referred to as "buds" or "colas." It is this part of the plant that provides medicine and also the "high." When the buds are trimmed for selling purposes, a portion of them break up. Those small pieces are called "shake." Sometimes just the leaves of the female plant are sold. They contain far less of the drug. They are referred to as "leaf."

An individually rolled marijuana cigarette is generally about half the size of a nicotine cigarette. When marijuana is used for medicinal or religious purposes it is frequently called "sacred herb." When used for relaxation and socially it is referred to as pot, joint, bud, reefer, weed, smoke, the kind, Maui-wowi, Kona-gold, pakalolo, giggle-weed, grass, happy-grass, herb, dope, and many other names.

To avoid confusion between marijuana and cigarettes in this book, tobacco will be referred to as "nicotine," which is the addictive toxic drug in cigarettes. Marijuana does not contain nicotine, and there is no record of marijuana or any of its preparations ever destroying life.

Alcohol will be mentioned in comparison to marijuana and considered a drug. Ninety percent of alcohol users do not abuse alcohol. However, the contrasting point being made is that marijuana is a drug that reduces aggressive tendencics while alcohol produces warlike behavior in various people.

Tetrahydrocannabinol (THC) is the active ingredient in marijuana—the "drug." It is sometimes referred to as delta-1-THC, delta-9-THC, or merely THC. We will simply use THC when referring to marijuana's psychoactive ingredient, which is generally 3 to 4 percent THC.

Hemp is not marijuana, nor is it smoked or used medicinally. It does not produce a high, since it contains only approximately 0.3 percent THC, not enough for even a slight buzz. However, it resembles marijuana. "Hemp" is used when referring to the plant put to use for commercial purposes. The hemp plant is an economically and environmentally valuable source of fiber, oil, pulp for paper, and fuel. It provides nutritious food, such as a gruel, which can be produced for third world countries (and our own country) for pennies. It's a complete source of vegetable protein. Its versatility includes the fiber for the manufacture of the finest rope, insulating building materials, clothing, and biomass for clean methanol fuels. There are literally thousands of other articles that can be manufactured from hemp. It is estimated that one acre of hemp can save four acres of timberland used for paper.

Hemp also offers competition to patented products such as nylon and other synthetics. Consequently, it was demonized and outlawed along with marijuana in 1937.

Note: "Marijuana" is also spelled "marihuana" by some writers. The author will use the spelling "marijuana," unless quoting another source.

1

My Introduction to Marijuana

HAVE YOU EVER LOVED SOMEONE UNEQUIVOCALLY? Have you believed in someone's honesty, integrity, and caring so completely that you would have risked your life for that person?

As a youngster, that's how I felt about my family and my country. If Uncle Sam asked me to risk my life for my country, I was prepared to do it, no questions asked.

Newspapers taught me that Nazi Germany burned history books, as well as books that were considered culturally decadent. Citizens who didn't agree with Hitler's politics were tortured, imprisoned, and raped. Some died at the hands of other prisoners, others at the hands of their government. Some committed suicide. Cruel and unusual punishment was the norm in certain foreign countries. I was sure that such atrocities never occurred in the United States.

One day in the fifth grade, a schoolmate revealed that his parents smoked marijuana cigarettes. And when they did, they laughed and played with him a lot. He said when they drank liquor, they laughed at times, but they also argued, and sometimes his dad hit his mom. But never when they smoked "happy grass"—he said that's what they called it.

My mom and dad also argued a lot, so I asked Pop why they didn't smoke that happy grass stuff also called marijuana. His face turned a scary red. "Harry Anslinger heads our Federal Bureau of Narcotics, and Mr. Anslinger said that '*Marijuana is the most violence causing drug in the history of mankind. It turns people into criminals, and many marijuana users go insane!*'"

Dad paused to pour another splash of bourbon into his glass. I heard his familiar "Aaaah," and I knew he wasn't finished with me. He turned and glared at me. He said that Commissioner Anslinger not only made that statement before the Congress of the United States but also speaks to parent-teacher groups, police, judges, and even the Federal Bureau of Investigation (FBI). Dad said, "We read his speeches in the newspapers and hear them on the radio, so you better believe what he says is true!" Dad emptied his glass of bourbon, then took a deep drag of his Camel cigarette. The subject was closed.

I came to believe the shocking stories that began appearing more frequently in the newspapers about "the killer weed." We were told that some people fly into an insane rage and that because the drug makes people irresponsible, they may commit violent crimes. I later read that Harry Anslinger said marijuana is more dangerous than heroin or cocaine.

One news story reported that a young person who smoked marijuana used an ax to slaughter his family.[1] We children were startled; our parents were terrified.

Dad never forgot those reports, and neither did I. He repeated them to me from the time I was nine all the way through my graduation from San Rafael High School, whenever I mentioned the word "marijuana."

In high school, some of the students who experimented with "pot" were caught by their parents and soundly thrashed. One of my best buddies was found trying marijuana. His father—a heavy drinker—told him that he would turn him over to the police if he was ever again discovered with those "violence causing cigarettes." My friend eventually became an alcoholic. He died at age 42.

My Education in Marijuana

During high school, I had my own live teenage radio show, *Junior Jamboree*, which was broadcast throughout northern California on KTIM in San Rafael. I interviewed various celebrities, including vocalist Frankie Laine and actors Humphrey Bogart and Lauren Bacall. Consequently, I was invited to parties where marijuana was openly smoked.

At first I was shocked. "Aren't you afraid of becoming violent and going insane?" I asked the marijuana users. They laughed and tried to educate me. "You feel happy, not violent. Believe us, it's far less harmful than other drugs, including alcohol and nicotine." I never did see anyone become violent or mean from marijuana use—although I saw plenty of that from alcohol drinkers. I became intrigued about why we were bombarded with sinister information about marijuana.

The first time I used marijuana I was seventeen. It was 1945. I was with my friend Fae McNally, who was a fabulous piano player and a featured pianist on my radio show. One night while going over the following week's show with Fae, he suggested that I enter the Lions International Public Speaking contest for California and Nevada. "There are only 12,000 in the contest so you have a chance," he chuckled. "Thanks for your confidence, Fae," I said, "but I just don't have the time to research and practice for such an event."

Fae lit up a marijuana cigarette, which he referred to as a "joint," took a drag, and handed it to me. The setting was comfortable and I trusted my friend. My years of curiosity got the best of me, and I followed his inhaling technique of holding one's breath. Fae had explained the feelings I could expect, which was wise of him. I soon found myself in a pleasant relaxed state in which ideas began to flow freely, and I experienced a feeling that time slowed down. Fae mentioned the required speech title for the contest and handed me paper and pen.

Within an hour I had written a speech, with a sense that I was humoring my friend. Ironically, the title was "Can youth by local leadership strengthen the responsibility of government?" I won first place, a scholarship toward the college of my choice, and various other prizes.

Even though I have gone a year or more at a time without smoking marijuana, my experiences with it have taught me to be far more relaxed, to have increased empathy toward others, and not to take life so seriously.

Over the years I have learned that not only is marijuana comparatively harmless, but it also offers various medical benefits—including dramatically effective and proven medical uses for patients suffering from cancer, AIDS (Acquired Immune Deficiency Syndrome), glaucoma, and other ailments. Still, our government goes out of its way to broadcast and print misinformation and to brainwash the media into believing marijuana is evil. It hides the positive facts—even from medical doctors, who have had to learn of the many benefits from their patients!

A Short History Lesson

I have learned that marijuana is not evil; tyrannical government is. Falsely instilling fear into the hearts of its citizens is immoral. Withholding medical marijuana from patients is criminal.

The *abuse* of any drug is wrong, of course, but let's not confuse *use* with *abuse.* It is important for us to be able to count on our government to give us the truth about the positive findings, not just the fictitious negative stories.

During World War II, the Japanese cut off our supplies of hemp (which yields fiber) from the Philippines. Hemp was desperately needed by our military for rope, thread for boots and shoes, fire hoses, parachute webbing, tents, and backpacks. Suddenly it was perfectly safe for children in 4-H clubs to grow at least a half-acre but preferably two acres of hemp each. Our hypocritical government dubbed this effort "Hemp for Victory!"[2] When the war ended, nonintoxicating hemp again became a "deadly drug."

More hypocrisy was evident between 1948 and 1950, during the height of the communist scare when we were told that marijuana caused its users to become pacifistic. The communists could use it to weaken our military personnel so they would become passive and lose their will to fight. This idea was the total reverse of what we had been told before.

Some segments of the federal government do not feel compelled to tell the truth—perhaps it's because of their ignorance. For over fifty years, I have spoken with hundreds of marijuana users about their experiences and learned firsthand about marijuana's therapeutic applications.

It's time for Uncle Sam to face the truth about marijuana. If he can do that, marijuana will be legalized. It's hypocritical to ban this relatively harmless drug, which has never caused one death in thousands of years of historical use, and leave genuinely dangerous drugs—alcohol and nicotine—legal. We are entitled to a choice between alcohol and marijuana—and the honest facts.

Marijuana Became My Medicine

In January 1991, I left for a two-week trip to Indonesia. Shortly after I arrived in Jakarta, the Gulf War began. Newspaper, television, and radio reports of children and other civilians being killed by American bombings caused many of the people of the region to become antagonistic toward Americans. I came close to being physically attacked.

In addition to becoming emotionally distraught over the war myself, I began to feel physically ill and elected to return home early. Was it just because of all the stress caused by the war? No. Within six months of my return to the wine country of Sonoma, California, I learned that I had cancer.

It was after my second surgery that I experienced marijuana's medical magic. I received anonymous little "care" packages from acquaintances in Hawaii, where I had lived for 30 years. (I doubt that there is a marijuana grower who isn't aware of the medicinal benefits of the plant.) Marijuana accomplished almost as much for pain control as my prescribed morphine, Demerol, Vicodin, and other toxic drugs. Pot allowed me to relax, which eased the pain. This relatively harmless drug also helped to induce sleep even if I was in pain. I still have an old prescription for Vicodin that was never filled.

No argument—all the drugs prescribed for me were tremendously helpful. However, at times I found the pain so severe that regardless of how strong the addictive painkillers were, my body frequently remained tense; and at those times my pain turned to agony.

Several hours after that second surgery, the pain was unbearable. I asked for another shot of morphine. This time it didn't release the cramping agony. My body couldn't relax.

Having learned from my previous surgery that morphine doesn't always stop the pain, I had put a "joint" and a cigarette lighter in a zipper storage bag in my jacket, which hung in the closet of my hospital room. I had already told my surgeon that I smoked marijuana on occasion to relax and sleep. He's a fine surgeon and a caring man. He gave a little understanding nod. No doubt he already knew that marijuana produces relaxation and eases pain, but he couldn't sanction anything illegal. The federal government has jeopardized free speech. Most physicians are afraid to talk openly with their patients about the medical benefits of marijuana. Classifying marijuana along with heroin is dishonest and unfair to those who are ill or dying.

Still connected to an intravenous (IV) tube and a urinary catheter, I got out of bed and almost collapsed from weakness. I made it to the closet where my jacket hung and removed the zipper storage bag. I hauled the IV tower and urine bag into the bathroom. By now I was dizzy. Perspiration dripped from my face. Pain and nausea overwhelmed me. I thought I was going to pass out, yet I was afraid to press the "Nurse" button on the wall.

I lit the joint and inhaled. Good Lord, I thought, how embarrassing if I pass out in here and they find me with a joint in my hand! I was terrified. Would they call the police? I took another puff. Then a miracle came to pass. A feeling of peace enveloped me. I stopped sweating. My body relaxed. The pain faded. I felt drowsy.

I returned the partly smoked marijuana cigarette to its zipper storage bag and put it back into my jacket pocket. I waited for the exhaust fan to draw out the smoke before attempting my journey back to bed. This time it was easy—and almost painless. I fell into a deep, recuperative sleep—marijuana is nature's tranquilizer. Since I'm a private airplane pilot (until the media began using helicopters in the late 1980s, I flew network cameramen over the volcano eruption site on the Big Island of Hawaii), I dreamed that I was back in Hawaii flying my plane with the engine throttled back. I was exhilarated—gliding around the silvery cumulus clouds. The ocean below was sparkling blue, and there was a vivid rainbow circling the plane and reflecting on the shimmering, sapphire blue sea.

I awoke three hours later as a food tray was placed before me. I was hungry and ate ravenously!

Synthetic Pot

Marinol is the brand name of the synthetic pot capsule. It mimics the psychoactive effects of natural marijuana. Physicians may legally prescribe Marinol for the nausea associated with chemotherapy and AIDS. However, taking tetrahydrocannabinol (THC, the active ingredient in Marinol and marijuana) in capsule form is far less effective for suppressing nausea and vomiting than smoking it because smoke cannot be thrown up. Federal agencies guaranteed a market for Marinol to Unimed Pharmaceuticals. The federal government produces synthetic THC for five cents a dose. Unimed markets that product for up to eight dollars a capsule.[3] Taking Marinol can cost thirteen thousand dollars a year.

Isn't it interesting that Marinol is a Schedule Two drug and can be legally prescribed, yet natural marijuana is illegal medicine?

Marijuana is competition for some very profitable drugs. It's cruel and deceitful to allow Marinol to be prescribed for suffering patients while refusing a patient access to organic marijuana, which can be grown at little or no cost but cannot be patented.

John Morgan, M.D., professor of pharmacology at City University of New York Medical School, puts it this way:

> The government allows some patients to use a synthetic version of THC—marijuana's primary psychoactive component—which does not work as well for many. This is analogous to allowing vitamin C tablets but making possession of orange juice a felony!

Dr. Ronald Siegel, pharmacologist with the UCLA School of Medicine, is among the growing group of experts who say the quest for altered consciousness is a force as natural as the drive for water, food, or sex. It is referred to as the "fourth drive."[4] As proof they point to the animal world, where creatures from birds to cats, from elephants to jaguars, seek out mind-altering plants.[5]

Human history is filled with accounts of drug use from Sumerians, who 5,000 years ago used alcohol, to South American Indians, who have chewed coca leaves for thousands of years. In the Philippines and other South Pacific islands, people drink kava, an intoxicating mixture made from the root of the pepper plant *(Piper methysticum)*.[6] Every civilization has some method for its citizens to get "high." Our country has chosen alcohol, caffeine, and nicotine. Ninety percent of alcohol drinkers do not abuse alcohol. The same is true of users of other drugs.

We must keep an open mind and seriously consider the use of marijuana, especially when it offers amazing medical benefits.

The world has been deceived for too long regarding "the assassin of youth." Thousands of nonviolent marijuana "criminals" are in prison in this country. Marijuana gardeners receive longer mandatory sentences than many convicted murderers, rapists, and child molesters. Many have lost their homes, jobs, children, and life savings. Some have committed suicide after being raped by sex-starved inmates.

I do not condone the use of any drug that is illegal by preteen or teenage youths, including marijuana. Young people should not use marijuana except in connection with chemotherapy treatments, to prevent vomiting, or for other demonstrated medical benefits.

The marijuana debate is primarily a conflict between an older generation that views marijuana as evil (because of sixty years of untrue marijuana propaganda) and a younger generation that finds its effect nonviolent—which frequently is not the effect of alcohol.[7]

The Latest Propaganda—True and False

During the 1996 presidential campaign, Republicans, eager to demonstrate President Clinton's permissive attitude toward drugs, said that Clinton's administration had not called for increased penalties for drug use and that teen drug use was out of control. Let's pause for a reality check: Nationwide, 1995 saw the greatest number of marijuana arrests in history. FBI figures show that nearly six hundred thousand Americans were arrested on marijuana charges. This brings the total number of marijuana arrests under the Clinton administration to 1,450,751. (More than 83 percent of those arrests were for simple possession.)[8] President Clinton soft on drugs? Hardly. He's just not educated on the least harmful drug. If he were, he wouldn't be wasting billions of our tax dollars imprisoning peaceful marijuana users. Had he been pot educated, he would have inhaled when he experimented with marijuana.

News reports claim that teen drug use doubled between 1992 and 1995. Not so. The 1995 National Household Survey showed that 90 percent of teens didn't use any mood-altering drugs in the month prior to the survey. Of the 10 percent who did, the overwhelming majority used milder drugs such as marijuana.

Only 1 percent of youths indulged in cocaine or heroin. Drug Abuse Warning Network's (DAWN) newest survey shows that four-fifths of those hospitalized for drug abuse were over the age of twenty-five. But forget the facts—young teens don't get to vote. Using the phrase "kids on drugs" scares parents and causes adults to vote for more punitive attacks against marijuana users—and perpetuates an already lost drug war. In Los Angeles County, where 1 million teenagers live, not one person 13 to 19 years old died from any kind of drug overdose in 1994, compared to 552 adults.[9]

Teens are getting the blame for drug abuse when it's the adults who far more frequently misuse alcohol and other drugs. Long-term studies demonstrate that occasional pot smoking, which accounts for most teenage drug experimenting, does not lead to problems later in life. Many teens who smoke pot never go on to use alcohol or smoke death-dealing nicotine.

Nicotine is so deadly and so addictive. I've seen people with smoking-caused larynx cancer who had to have total laryngectomies. After surgery, some were so desperate for a nicotine "fix" they inhaled cigarettes through their tracheotomy openings.

Politicians publicly decry tobacco. Still, our country's highest leaders continue to accept money from and attend lavish parties thrown by tobacco companies. They do so in exchange for continuing to subsidize tobacco with our tax dollars and keeping it legal.

On September 16, 1996, Bob Dole, speaking before law enforcement officers in Villanova, Pennsylvania, vowed to cut teen drug use in half—while doubling current spending on state prison construction. (Dole, who has received hundreds of thousands of dollars from the tobacco industry, shys away from mentioning the most harmful of all drugs, nicotine.) President Clinton, not to be outshined, promised more prisons and tougher treatment of juvenile offenders.

There are times when one wonders if the war on drugs could possibly be a camouflage for our pathetic war on the national debt or other White House frustrations. If it were truly a war on drugs, wouldn't tobacco and alcohol be the primary targets? They are the two most commonly used and abused drugs in America and unquestionably the cause of more harm to the user and to society than marijuana. A dangerous drug is one that can cause physical addiction and death—like nicotine or alcohol. Marijuana causes neither.

The war on drugs has become a war on marijuana smokers—and the Constitution.

On February 14, 1996, Fairfax Police Chief Jim Anderson was one of the latest officials to speak out in favor of California's medical marijuana initiative. Anderson has been employed in law enforcement since 1964 and has been a police chief for fourteen years. He is also a member of the U.S. Army Reserve with the rank of lieutenant colonel. Chief Anderson said, "I believe there is adequate unbiased and scientific evidence that marijuana does have medicinal benefit. Even if there are no other benefits than relief of pain or stimulation of appetite, there appears to be a legitimate place for marijuana in the wide array of legally prescribed drugs."[10]

Even though the majority of California voters were supporting the medical marijuana initiative, on August 4, 1996, state narcotics agents, at the direction of California Attorney General Dan Lungren, raided the Cannabis Buyers' Club of San Francisco. The club sold marijuana to AIDS, cancer, and other patients, some terminally ill.[11]

We must try to educate those in politics, the "justice" system, the media, and the general public who believe marijuana is not medicine. Not only is marijuana medicine, but also, compared to alcohol and nicotine and dozens of other drugs, "grass" is the mildest and safest euphoric available. Let's stop the cruel and unusual punishment of those who "just say no" to corrupt laws.

Thirty-five million Americans, 15 percent of the population, currently smoke marijuana. Seventy million have tried it. Those figures are from the National Organization for the Reform of Marijuana Laws, NORML, and were echoed on the ABC news show "America's War on Drugs—Searching for Solutions," which aired on April 7, 1995. It has been demonstrated time and again that punishment does not curb drug use. *Honest* drug education can, as has been proven with worthy nicotine cigarette education.

Based on projections from the U.S. Justice Department arrest statistics since 1965, the ten millionth marijuana arrest took place on July 20, 1995. Another takes place every fifty-four seconds.

On November 5, 1996, the voters of California and Arizona legalized marijuana as medicine when its use is deemed appropriate by a physician. The passage of Proposition 215 in California and Proposition 200 in Arizona clearly demonstrated that Americans, in spite of years of government hysteria, have found that marijuana *is* medicine.

It didn't take the federal government long to exert its power to crush the will of the people who had triumphed over sixty years of government oppression. On December 30, 1996, President Clinton approved a plan to combat the new state laws legalizing marijuana for the ill and dying. The federal government is threatening doctors who recommend marijuana with the loss of their Drug Enforcement Administration (DEA) certification, preventing them from prescribing medicines.

Marijuana will remain *federally* illegal until our "coin-operated" politicians stop accepting money from corporations that do not want competition from legalized marijuana. Since our government leaders know the deadly effects of alcohol and nicotine, how long will they continue to accept money from companies whose products are proven killers?

On February 16, 1997, it was reported that the Democratic and Republican parties received an unprecedented $263.5 million in "soft-money" donations for the 1996 election. The largest contribution to the Democrats was $1.3 million from Joseph F. Seagrams & Sons. Not to be outdone, the Republicans received over $2.52 million from Philip Morris.[12]

On February 25, 1997, President Clinton proposed spending $175 million for a national television blitz targeting drug use by our country's youth. Matching funds from the private sector will be sought (from liquor, nicotine, and pharmaceutical producers, no doubt). Clinton said, "If a child does watch television—and what child doesn't—he or she should not be able to escape these messages."[13]

I hope the president realizes it is crucial that scare tactics not be used. The effort to frighten children away from illegal drugs has publicized and consequently popularized the drugs attacked. Such publicity has been not only ineffective but also counterproductive. Warnings act as a lure. You may recall the ad campaign against glue sniffing. It wasn't long before all stores were out of glue! It's like telling youngsters not to put beans up their noses.

Now it's time to learn more about marijuana as medicine—and the *real* reasons why the federal government wants to keep marijuana and hemp illegal.

2

Marijuana—Medical Miracle Herb

IMAGINE A DRUG THAT reduces nausea, prevents vomiting, and increases appetite in people with cancer, anorexia, and AIDS; reduces eye pressure in glaucoma patients, preventing blindness; and controls muscle spasms in people with cerebral palsy and multiple sclerosis. Some patients with epilepsy enjoy substantial improvement when they combine marijuana with their prescribed medications to control seizures. Marijuana reduces many forms of chronic pain; decreases anxiety and depression; eases withdrawal from alcohol, cocaine, nicotine cigarettes, and heroin; and reduces the pain of childbirth and premenstrual syndrome (PMS). Now reflect that this drug, which can be grown at home for free or purchased for pennies a dose, has fewer side effects than over-the-counter drugs, including aspirin. Also consider that it is supported for healing use by medical experts and prestigious scientific organizations. Now stamp that drug "illegal" and brand its users as criminals.

The amazing botanical capable of these myriad medical uses is marijuana. For thousands of years this now endangered species was recognized medicine.

Early Uses of Marijuana as Medicine

The magic of marijuana as medicine began in China. Then the knowledge spread to India, Persia, the Arab countries, Europe, Africa, and finally the Americas.

In the cradle of civilization, archaeologists discovered pottery dating back to the Stone Age imprinted with marijuana, which had been pressed into the clay while it was still wet. That pottery was created more than 10,000 years ago in Taiwan, off the coast of mainland China.[1]

Chinese Emperor Shen-Nung, in about the twenty-eighth century B.C., experimented with various herbs. He found that marijuana aided people with menstrual fatigue, malaria, rheumatism, gout, beriberi, or other ailments. Shen-Nung was glorified as the father of Chinese medicine.

Renowned Chinese surgeon Hua T'o is reported to have performed major surgery during the second century A.D. He created an anesthetic made from marijuana resin and wine. His painless surgery included organ grafts, resectioning of intestines, laparotomies (incisions into the loin) and thoracotomies (incisions into the chest).[2] Hebrew University scientists excavated a family tomb near Jerusalem and studied the remains of a girl who died in childbirth about A.D. 400. They found traces of marijuana in a vessel. Evidently, the marijuana was burned and administered to the girl as an inhalant to reduce pain. Although this seems to be the first physical evidence of pot used as medicine, reports of such use appear in an Egyptian papyrus dating from the sixteenth century B.C.[3]

By 1621 marijuana was suggested in England as a therapy for depression. *The New English Dispensary* stated in 1764 that boiling marijuana roots and applying them to the skin reduced inflammation. This had been accepted practice in eastern Europe for centuries. In addition, this type of poultice was used to dissolve deposits in people's joints as well as to dry up tumors.

Surgeon William O'Shaughnessy, employed by the British East India Company, was a professor of chemistry at the Medical College of Calcutta. In 1843 O'Shaughnessy discovered that patients using marijuana reported a reduction in the pain of rheumatism, a "remarkable increase of appetite," "great mental cheerfulness," and a feeling of aphrodisia. The doctor also found that marijuana reduced the agony associated with rabies and reported that his patients experienced relief from the symptoms of cholera, tetanus, and epilepsy. Marijuana was also prescribed for migraine headaches, pain reduction, and involuntary twitching and as a sleep aid and an aid in withdrawal from morphine and alcohol addiction.

Dr. John Grigor of England, alluding to the obstetrical use of marijuana, wrote, "it is capable of bringing the labor to a happy conclusion considerably within half the time that would otherwise have been required, thus saving protracted suffering of the patient, and the time of the practitioner."[4] Another eminent English physician who administered marijuana to his patients was Dr. J. R. Reynolds, doctor of medicine to Queen Victoria.

By 1854, the *United States Dispensatory* began including marijuana as medicine. The Ohio Medical Society in 1860 catalogued some of the illnesses aided by marijuana: neuralgia, rheumatism, mania, asthma, convulsions, palsy, hysteria, withdrawal from alcohol, and loss of appetite. Physicians noted:

> An overdose has never produced death in man or lower animals. Not one authentic case is on record in which marijuana or any of its preparations destroyed life—marijuana does not seem capable of causing death by chemical or physiological action.[5]

In 1887, physician H. A. Hare prescribed marijuana to subdue restlessness and anxiety and distract terminally ill patients. He stated, "The patient, whose most painful symptom has been mental trepidation, may become more happy or even hilarious."[6]

Universally, doctors prescribed marijuana for relief from labor pains, menstrual cramps, depression, insomnia, headaches, epilepsy, vomiting, and neuralgia and as an accelerated treatment for asthma. Oil from the seeds was used as medication for earache. Boiled roots were used for easing cramped joints.

Marijuana in the 1990s and Beyond

Our government in all its (lack of) wisdom will not permit those who suffer from nausea, pain, spasms, and other marijuana-alleviated symptoms to get relief legally. In fact, the government puts its bureaucratic head in the sand and pretends not to see this drug's medical uses—despite documentation from every front. How can it ignore all the evidence?

Cancer and AIDS

Cancer patients undergoing chemotherapy experience severe nausea and vomiting after each treatment and often become sick at the sight or smell of food for days afterward. They often can't keep food down. People with AIDS, similarly, waste away from the debilitating nausea and loss of appetite caused by the illness and the toxic drug AZT. In both cases, loss of appetite is more than unpleasant—it's life threatening. It's no secret to doctors that many of their cancer and AIDS patients clandestinely and routinely find dramatic relief by smoking marijuana, nature's gift to those suffering from cancer, AIDS, and anorexia (where the patient must eat or die).

No doubt you've heard of pot causing the "munchies"; even plain foods become savory. Patients can eat and regain strength in order to fight their diseases. Psychologically, they can regain determination and optimism when they're "winning" the battle against nausea, pain, and weight loss. The healthful effects of a positive outlook are well documented. AIDS patients state that marijuana also helps in reducing their fear of death.

In 1988, while undergoing chemotherapy for cancer of the colon, Jo Daly, a former San Francisco police commissioner, discovered that a few puffs of a marijuana cigarette stopped the treatment's hideous nausea and pain. "I can't explain to anyone how violently ill you can become after chemotherapy," she said. "You lose control. It's like a nuclear implosion inside your body. The word nausea doesn't even come close. But with the marijuana—a tiny bit—it went away almost instantly."

"I tried Marinol," says John Wilson of San Francisco, who has AIDS. "I went through five pills before I was able to keep one down. They're real expensive, about $6 to $8 a pill, and believe me, I was not about to reach into the toilet and try to get them back. When I did manage to keep one down, it took a long while to take effect and only worked for about half a day. Two or three inhales on a joint help me immediately."

Smoking marijuana accomplishes more than any toxic medication. Notice I say *smoking* marijuana. Attempting to swallow THC in capsule form is virtually impossible when one is gagging with gut-wrenching nausea.

In the February 1996 issue of *High Times*, Peter Gorman interviewed Ralph Seely, a forty-six-year-old Washington attorney with terminal chordoma bone cancer. Seely gives an excellent comparison between Marinol and marijuana. One of Gorman's many questions was, "Did you find Marinol effective?"

> *Seely:* No, so it didn't take much to get from there to smoking marijuana, because I started throwing up those pills. And this is something so fundamental it just astonishes me that people don't seem to get it. When you're throwing up you can't keep the damned capsules down. You have to understand that chemotherapy-induced nausea is not an upset tummy. It is absolutely debilitating. I would be curled up in a fetal position on the floor of a bathroom at the University of Washington, covered with my own vomit. . . . I mean, it is such a violent action that you just completely lose control and you can't stop: You just keep heaving and heaving and heaving, and your system just erupts. You can't control your bowels, and—Jesus, it was awful!"
>
> *Gorman:* How long does the nausea last?
>
> *Seeley:* I would be getting these chemicals pumped into my veins on Friday night, and I would go home on Saturday. And on Saturday and Sunday and sometimes into Monday or even Tuesday, this nausea just comes on, there's no warning.

> You get a minute or two of feeling a little nauseous, and the saliva starts working in the back of your jaws, and then bam, you're just retching and you can't stop. And you take one of the damn tablets and it just comes right back up. And they don't seem to understand that all these new drugs that they have, that they're no good to you because you can't get 'em into your system.
>
> Worse, I found that when I got a tablet down, if it finally kicked in, then I'm debilitated for 12 to 14 hours. If I take one of those god-damn things at like 10 o'clock or midnight, I go to work the next day and I'm losing an argument with the doorknob. It's a severe high. *You don't get moderately high on five milligrams of Marinol. It makes you very, very high and unable to concentrate and unable to do your work.*
>
> *Gorman:* And the difference when you smoke cannabis?
>
> *Seeley:* Now, you smoke a little marijuana, first of all, you get relief within two or three minutes. And secondly, you don't have to get that super dose. You put a little piece of bud in a pipe and you light it and take it down in two tokes, and you wait 10 minutes. And usually that's it. You feel a little bit high, the nausea recedes, it's like a visible wave going away. It's like a weight coming off your shoulders.[7]

Our thanks to NORML for permission to reprint many of the letters that appear throughout this book from those who have benefited from medical marijuana—and also from people, well and ill, who have suffered from the hand of the law. Here is a letter from Mae, the mother of Keith, a cancer patient.

> Before (marijuana use), Keith would go to his chemotherapy, come home and rush upstairs. He would shut himself in his bedroom and stuff towels under the door to keep out the smell of dinner cooking. He would not join us for dinner and would remain in his room or the bathroom, vomiting for the rest of the evening. The cancer and chemotherapy made Keith act like a wounded animal—timid and retiring. He would have intense hot and cold flashes, his joints became swollen and painful, his hair fell out and he felt sick all over. The anti-

cancer drugs were so toxic that Keith could pull off large pieces of skin where the chemotherapy injections had been given.

Smoking marijuana dramatically changed all of this. Immediately before chemotherapy Keith would smoke one marijuana cigarette. Following chemotherapy he would smoke all or part of a second (marijuana) cigarette if he felt queasy.

On good days Keith didn't have to remain in the hospital after his chemotherapy treatments. When we got home, Keith would stay in the living room and talk with his brother and father. He would join the family for dinner, where he would eat more than his share. He became outgoing and talkative. Keith became part of our family again because marijuana controlled the debilitating symptoms of his chemotherapy.

Glaucoma

Another striking medical use of marijuana is treating glaucoma, a disease of the eye. Excessive fluid accumulates, causing increased intraocular pressure and distorted vision. This increased pressure within the eyeball can damage the optic nerve and lead to partial vision loss and, eventually, blindness. This ailment affects more than two million Americans thirty-five years of age and older. There are some 300,000 new cases each year.

Glaucoma medications such as pilocarpine and epinephrine, manufactured by pharmaceutical companies, have side effects that include skin rashes, kidney stones, gastric ulcers, drug fevers, abrupt mood swings, hypertension, respiratory or cardiac failure, and even death.[8] However, a medical regimen of smoking marijuana can effectively reduce intraocular pressure into the safe range.

Muscle Spasms

Muscle spasticity is the loss of muscle control due to spasms. People with multiple sclerosis (MS) lose mobility and independence when muscle spasticity disables them. With MS, the normal functioning of nerve fibers in the brain and spinal cord is disrupted by the destruction of myelin, the protective covering of the nerve fibers. Painful muscle spasms, loss of coordination and balance, and weakness or paralysis are common.

Smoking marijuana significantly reduces the intensity of spasms and may, in fact, allow the person to temporarily regain coordination and control.

Many quadriplegics and paraplegics routinely smoke marijuana to control muscle spasms, a therapy that is acknowledged by their physicians. Because of their medications and lack of exercise, many wheelchair patients also have little appetite and become dangerously thin. Marijuana brings on hunger, encouraging these patients to eat.

NORML estimates that 65 to 75 percent of people in wheelchairs are smoking marijuana to reduce muscle spasms. People with cerebral palsy and those who have had some types of strokes also find relief with marijuana. This therapy is illegal and therefore much more expensive and risky than it would be if marijuana were legal.

Greg was diagnosed with multiple sclerosis. He was placed on an intensive form of steroid therapy, involving a drug named ACTH, to slow the effects of the disease. At the end of three months of ACTH therapy, there was no improvement in Greg's condition, and because of serious side effects his doctor discontinued the therapy. It was later resumed for another three months, and the side effects continued to worsen. Once, a life-threatening potassium deficiency sent Greg to the emergency room nearly comatose. After six months of therapy, Greg related this story:

> I had lost all control over my life. I was bedridden. On rare, good days I could shuffle across my bedroom by leaning against the wall and on my wife, using a walker or a cane.
>
> One evening some old friends came to visit and we smoked some marijuana. When my friends got up to leave, I stood up to say good-bye. Everybody in the room suddenly stopped talking and looked at me. At first I could not understand what was wrong. Then I realized I was *standing*—I was stunned.

I went through a series of trial-and-error tests. I quickly discovered that when I did not smoke marijuana, my condition worsened. I suffered more frequent spasms, and the spasms were more intense. When I smoked marijuana my condition stabilized, then dramatically improved.

For the past seven years my MS has been well controlled. The only time I experience spasms or other serious symptoms is when I run out of marijuana and cannot find and/or afford more. My doctor has been astonished by my tremendous recovery. While most MS patients grow progressively weaker and more crippled, I have gone in the opposite direction. I can actually run!

I do not like breaking the law. I do not like being forced to pay terribly inflated prices for an unregulated, uncontrolled product. I do not like having to purchase marijuana from drug dealers and I do not like having to use marijuana without medical supervision. However, I do like to walk, talk, write, read, and see. Marijuana allows me to do these simple, human things by controlling the symptoms of my MS.[9]

Schedule One? Schedule Two?

Under the U.S. government's Controlled Substances Act, drugs are "scheduled" according to the potential for abuse and knowledge of the drug's effects and therapeutic applications. Schedule One drugs are the most tightly controlled and are defined as having a high potential for abuse and no accepted medical use, a good example being heroin. Schedule Two drugs, such as morphine, may be prescribed for medical use.

In a judgment call that remains a mystery to those who understand marijuana's medical benefits, the government classifies marijuana as a Schedule One drug. Cocaine and morphine are Schedule Two substances and are classified as less dangerous than marijuana.

THC alone is classified as Schedule Two, which allows it to be prescribed for medical use—but not in cigarette form. Doctors can prescribe Marinol, synthetic THC, but not marijuana cigarettes. (Home-grown medicine is, of course, virtually free; pharmaceutical companies don't like the idea of your getting something for nothing.)

Since 1972, NORML has fought in the courts to have marijuana removed from Schedule One and moved to Schedule Two, making it available medically. The criteria for Schedule Two drugs are that they have "accepted medical use in the United States" and that the drugs are "safe for use under medical supervision." Placement in Schedule Two would allow physicians to prescribe marijuana for their patients for legitimate therapeutic purposes without violating federal law. The government is forcing medical doctors to only prescribe medicines it approves of.

In 1979, the federal government's Department of Health, Education, and Welfare (HEW) advised the DEA that marijuana should remain in Schedule One. NORML again petitioned the U.S. Court of Appeals.

In 1986, the Drug Enforcement Administration asked its own Administrative Law Judge, Francis L. Young, to hold hearings on NORML's petition. There was great apprehension that Young would rule that marijuana was useless as medicine, supporting the DEA's deceit in proclaiming that marijuana has no medical value. There was also great hope that if the DEA's own judge really looked at the evidence and acknowledged marijuana's medical value, the DEA would have to accept his findings and reclassify marijuana as Schedule Two.

People dying of AIDS and cancer would be able to relieve their suffering without breaking the law, without sneaking and hiding, without paying exorbitant street prices for their medicine, and without going to prison. Insurance companies won't pay for marijuana used as medicine. So it should have been obvious that patients would be loath to risk obtaining it if it didn't offer real relief.[10]

Judge Young read hundreds of pages of documentation, then listened to fifteen days of testimony from dozens of patients and medical doctors. In 1988, he ruled, "Marijuana has accepted medical use in the United States and is safe for use under medical supervision." Moreover, rather than calling it the dangerous drug the DEA proclaimed it to be, Judge Young decreed, "Marijuana in its natural form is one of the safest therapeutically active substances known to man."

Judge Young recommended rescheduling marijuana and making it legally available for some medical purposes, including treatment of cancer patients. He wrote, "It would be unreasonable, arbitrary and capricious for the DEA to continue to stand between those sufferers and the benefits of this substance in light of the evidence in this record."

The judge cited medical researchers from Harvard, New York University, and other leading medical schools as well as a number of medical experts and patients. His conclusion: marijuana's medical use is "clear beyond any question." Judge Young added that smoking marijuana was far more effective than taking pills with synthetic THC, the active ingredient in marijuana.

He found similar benefits for using marijuana to control muscle spasms suffered by patients with multiple sclerosis, spasticity, and hyperparathyroidism, a painful hormonal disorder that causes bone spurs.[11]

Judge Young related the story of a three-year-old child's marijuana medicine:

> In late 1980, a three-year-old boy was brought by his parents to a hospital in Spokane, Washington. The child was diagnosed as having cancer. Surgery was performed. Chemotherapy was begun. The child became extremely nauseated and vomited for days after each chemotherapy treatment—several standard available anti-emetic agents were tried by the child's doctors. None of them succeeded in controlling his nausea or vomiting.
>
> Learning of the existence of research studies on THC and marijuana, the parents asked the child's doctor to arrange for their son to be the subject of such a study so that he might have access to marijuana. The doctor refused, citing the volume of paperwork and recordkeeping detail required in such programs and his lack of administrative personnel to handle it. The child's mother read an article about marijuana smoking helping chemotherapy patients. She obtained some marijuana from friends. She baked cookies for her child with marijuana

> in them. She made tea from marijuana. When the child ate these cookies or drank this tea in connection with his chemotherapy, he did not vomit. His strength returned. He regained lost weight. His spirits revived.
>
> The parents told the doctors and nurses at the hospital of their giving marijuana to their child. None objected. They all accepted smoking marijuana as effective in controlling chemotherapy-induced nausea and vomiting, and were all curious about the cookies.
>
> Soon the child was riding a tricycle in the hallways of the Spokane hospital shortly after his chemotherapy treatments while other children there were still vomiting into pans, were tied to intravenous bottles in an attempt to rehydrate them, to replace the liquids they were vomiting up. Parents of some of the other patients asked the parents of this "lively" child how he seemed to tolerate his chemotherapy so well. Of those parents who began giving marijuana to their children, none ever reported back encountering any adverse side effects. In the words of the mother,
>
> "When your kid is riding a tricycle while his other hospital buddies are hooked up to IV needles, their heads hung over vomiting buckets, you don't need a federal agency to tell you marijuana is effective. The evidence is in front of you, so stark it cannot be ignored."
>
> Marijuana cigarettes have an important, clear advantage over synthetic THC capsules in that the natural marijuana is inhaled and generally takes effect more quickly than the synthetic capsule.

Judge Young concluded: "The overwhelming preponderance of the evidence (in the record) establishes that marijuana has currently accepted medical use in treatment in the United States for nausea and vomiting resulting from chemotherapy treatments in some cancer patients."[12] (See Appendix II for more excerpts from Judge Young's ruling.)

For young cancer chemotherapy patients, brownies or cookies containing marijuana are the best bet. Despite Judge Young's findings, the DEA rejected NORML's petition "in all respects." On December 30, 1989, DEA Administrator John Lawn ordered that marijuana remain listed as a Schedule One narcotic, "having no known medical value." Obviously, the DEA is in denial.

As of 1997 only eight patients have been allowed to use marijuana legally in the United States.

The Investigational New Drug (IND) program for marijuana was canceled in 1992. This program was authorized by the U.S. Food and Drug Administration (FDA) and offered wider access to investigational therapies for patients with immediate life-threatening or otherwise serious diseases for which there was no satisfactory alternative treatment.

Do we believe the DEA or the thousands of patients who with their own eyes and bodies see and feel the benefits from marijuana? Would three- and four-year-old cancer patients lie about the benefits of marijuana when they didn't know what medicine was in their cookies?

Calling Dr. Dean Edell

On the night of February 12, 1991, I phoned the well-known radio and television personality Dr. Dean Edell. He was doing his phone-in *House Calls* show on the ABC affiliate, KGO television, in San Francisco. Dr. Edell has dispensed medical advice via radio since 1978. He has the second-highest-rated radio call-in show in the country and is heard on more than 300 stations. He courageously tells the truth about marijuana.

"Medically speaking, which drug—alcohol or marijuana—causes more violence, and which of those drugs is more physically addictive?" I asked Dr. Edell.

Here's what television viewers heard him answer:

> There's no question. The answer to that: alcohol kills 60,000 to 100,000 people a year. There has yet to be a death, a single death, from marijuana. As far as violence is concerned, you just don't see people who smoke marijuana going at each other with knives. Alcohol, of course, is associated with mayhem, homicide, violence, to a very sad degree. And overall, when you look at the legal drugs, there are about 500,000 deaths a year in this country from alcohol and tobacco.

> All illegal drugs combined, and a couple of legal ones, add up to less than 5,000. So it's a 100-to-1 ratio between legal and illegal. Abuse of either is bad, plain and simple.
>
> I think—and this my personal opinion—I think there is a way to responsibly use these drugs. Alcohol for instance—most people who drink alcohol are not alcoholics. And I think the same probably is true of marijuana. Most adults use it responsibly.
>
> It is illegal though, and you can wind up in jail over something like that. So that's important to take into consideration. Medically speaking though, I don't think there is any comparison."[13]

An ill or dying person with AIDS, cancer, or other illness who uses marijuana to relax muscles, free him from pain, and create appetite is hardly a threat to society. Those patients who are obtaining marijuana in order to reduce their symptoms are not going to be dope sellers. They are not junkies. It is a draconian law that prohibits a relatively mild substance and claims it has no medical benefit.

Thousands of ill people who illegally use marijuana never used it prior to their illness. They would not risk the loss of their homes and possibly years in prison for using marijuana to ease their pain—or to be physically and emotionally aided—if other medications provided the same virtually nontoxic relief. Thus, legions of people feel that it's all right to break the law in pursuit of a greater justice.

Who Has Been Helped by Marijuana as Medicine?

Bill Anderson, 37, Coloma, Michigan: Sustained head injuries in a 1985 car crash (hit by drunk driver) resulting in amnesia, chronic pain. Since 1987, marijuana has alleviated the agonizing pain in his head. His medicine is illegal.[14]

Karen Boehnke, 40, Margate, Florida: Has suffered from cataracts and glaucoma since childhood. Since 1992, marijuana has halted the progress of the disease and alleviated the pain. Her medicine is illegal.[15]

Danny Burgess, 41, Louisville, Kentucky: Vietnam veteran; paraplegia from broken back. Since 1991, marijuana has alleviated chronic pain and spasticity. Arrested in 1992; served time for using medicine.[16]

Bryan Clark, 21, Portland, Maine: Hemophiliac; contracted HIV (human immunodeficiency virus) from blood transfusion at age fourteen. Since age sixteen, marijuana has alleviated nausea and prevented extreme weight loss. His medicine is illegal.[17]

Etienne Fontane, 25, Berkeley, California: Suffered shattered knee cap and "Desert Storm Syndrome" during 1991 Gulf War. Since 1991, marijuana has alleviated pain. Discharged from the army in 1992 for positive results on urine test. Now a full-time volunteer for the Cannabis Action Network (CAN). Has traveled through forty-seven states advocating marijuana relegalization. He has said, "I'd rather die on my feet than live on my knees."[18]

Russell Hokanson, 51, Colebrook, New Hampshire: Paraplegia from back broken in a 1965 car crash. Since 1966, marijuana has alleviated pain and spasticity. Arrested in 1993 and convicted of cultivating marijuana; had property seized.[19]

Margaret Lang, 42, Winnipeg, Manitoba, Canada: Rheumatoid arthritis since age nine. Since 1981, marijuana has mitigated the pain and increased agility. Her medicine is illegal.[20]

Todd McCormick, 24, San Diego, California: Cancer; ten lesions since age two. Since age nine, marijuana has alleviated the nausea caused by chemotherapy. His medicine is illegal.[21]

Shelley Mitchell, 29, York, Pennsylvania: Migraine headaches. Marijuana decreases the pain. Arrested in 1993 for possession of her medicine; served two months.[22]

Darrell Paulsen, 24, St Paul, Minnesota: Cerebral palsy since birth, now confined to wheelchair. Since 1989, marijuana has eased the pain and spasticity. His medicine is illegal.[23]

Jackie Rickert, 43, Mondovi, Wisconsin: Muscles, tissue, and bones deteriorating due to Ehlers-Danlos Syndrome and reflex sympathetic dystrophy; diagnosed at age nineteen, unable to walk since 1990. Discovered marijuana lessens chronic pain and increases agility. His medicine is illegal.[24]

Tom Stephenson, 29, Ogden, Utah: Grand mal seizure disorder since age twelve; discovered medicinal marijuana in 1992; no seizures since. Arrested October 23, 1994, for possession and cultivation of his medicine.[25]

Richard Brookhiser, senior editor of the *National Review*: Marijuana helped relieve the nausea caused by the chemotherapy treatments he received during his bout with testicular cancer in 1993. "None of my doctors or nurses discouraged me from using it."[26]

Hundreds of thousands of patients who derive pain reduction from marijuana say the same thing: "Stop arresting sick people!"

More People Join the Marijuana Revolution

Consider the following statements from patients and medical doctors.

"We're refugees of the war on drugs." (Robert Randall, glaucoma patient)[27]

"It [marijuana] was a dream come true. We had tried six different legal drugs and nothing stopped the nausea. The criminal justice system isn't a place for sick people." (Kenny Jenks, AIDS patient)[28]

"Physicians . . . should also be allowed to prescribe marijuana to supplement cancer therapy, AIDS and eye treatments." (Ivan J. Silverberg, oncologist)[29]

"Marijuana has been shown to be safe and effective, particularly for nausea, in people being treated for cancer, AIDS, and other serious illnesses." (Center for AIDS Prevention Studies, University of California, San Francisco)[30]

"People suffering from cancer or HIV should be spared pain." (Art Agnos, former San Francisco mayor)[31]

"Don't let narrow-minded politics interfere with good medicine." (Jo Daly, retired San Francisco police commissioner and cancer patient)[32]

"Let physicians alleviate suffering. The American Medical Association testified against the federal prohibition of marijuana in

1937, predicting that it would lead to an elimination of its availability as medicine." (Tod Mikuriya, M.D.)[33]

As of October 1994, thirty-six states—including California, Texas, New York, and Florida—had issued letters to President Clinton asking him to change federal policy, which currently prevents states from decriminalizing marijuana even for medical use. Opponents make such statements as, "Approval would send a message to youngsters that it's okay to smoke pot."[34]

If that's the case, one might say providing morphine to those in pain sends a message to the young that morphine is okay to use recreationally. It will take decades, if it ever happens, for the pharmaceutical industry to synthesize nontoxic drugs that accomplish all the things that natural marijuana does safely.

How Dangerous Is Marijuana in Comparison to Other Substances?

Number of American deaths per year that resulted directly from the following selected causes nationwide, according to world almanacs, life insurance actuarial (death) rates, and the twenty years of U.S. Surgeon Generals' reports from the federal government's Bureau of Mortality Statistics and the National Institute on Drug Abuse (as of 1988):

Tobacco	340,000 to 425,000
Alcohol (Not including 50% of all highway deaths and 65% of all murders)	150,000+
Aspirin	180 to 1,000+
Caffeine (Stress, ulcers and triggering irregular heartbeats, etc.)	1,000 to 10,000
"Legal" drug overdose	14,000 to 27,000
Illicit drug overdose (From all illegal drugs)	3,800 to 5,200
Marijuana	0

Marijuana users also have the same or lower incidence of murders and highway deaths and accidents as the general nonmarijuana using population. (Crancer Study, UCLA; first and second Jamaican Studies, 1968 to 1974; Costa Rican Studies, 1980 to 1982.)

One hundred percent of the studies done at dozens of American universities and research facilities show that marijuana toxicity does not exist. Medical history does not record anyone dying from an overdue of marijuana (UCLA, Harvard, Temple, etc.).

Source: *The Emperor Wears No Clothes,* 1991.

3

Marijuana Prohibition—Sham!

Marijuana prohibition has seduced millions of well-intentioned Americans into supporting actions that undermine all of their basic values: truth, individual freedom, limited government, and even the integrity of the family. Children are encouraged to turn in their parents for using marijuana. By demonizing marijuana and dehumanizing the marijuana user, this process has set in motion an escalation of violence in which the end has come to justify the means. Marijuana prohibition is not only an unjust failure but also counterproductive because it aggravates America's substance abuse problems.

Every escalation in the war on marijuana has been followed by an increase in alcoholism and dangerous drug use. The crack cocaine epidemic, with much accompanying violence, is only one example of this cost of marijuana suppression. Crack has become easier to obtain and less expensive than marijuana. Crack is physically addictive. Marijuana is not.

The Harrison Narcotic Act

Prior to the Harrison Narcotic Act of 1914, drug users and addicts were free to purchase their drugs legally through registered suppliers or with physicians' prescriptions. Originally, the Harrison Act was merely drug recordkeeping. It was basically a taxing measure with emphasis on drugs produced outside of the United States, such as opium and cocaine. The law did not prohibit possession of such drugs; they were available for purchase on the open market. They were uncontaminated and could be purchased literally with pocket change. There was virtually no disorder because of the low price of legal narcotics. It was unnecessary to steal or rob or turn to prostitution in order to purchase drugs. The word violence was rarely heard in connection with drug use during those pre-illegal drug years. There were no gangs, no killings over turf, no underworld drug lords.

Business in the Bureau of Narcotics was slow during the early 1920s, other than for alcohol prohibition, which bureau staff knew would come to a jolting end because citizens refused to accept it any longer. During those depression years, the bureau's budget was cut by some $200,000, a goodly amount of money in those days, and the number of agents reduced. To justify their existence and to add to their job security, those in the bureau influenced Congress to expand the Harrison Narcotic Act to make drug users criminals.

Drugs became criminalized with encouragement from women's groups, such as the Anti-Saloon League and the Women's Christian Temperance Union. Such support was welcomed by the Bureau of Narcotics, which presumably concluded, or led the public to believe, that making drug users criminals would cause them to stop desiring drugs.

How Propaganda Succeeds

The government sanctioned a campaign of deception to create public hysteria against all drug users who generally were well-behaved. When drugs were legal, there was no need to spend millions of dollars on thousands of police to go after users of drugs. Nor were there hundreds of thousands of generally peaceful drug "criminals" imprisoned at a cost of billions of our tax dollars each year. The illegality of drugs has had the sole result of protecting the black market in drugs, artificially inflating prices, and keeping drug profits fantastically high.

More violence and killings took place after drug prohibition than ever took place when drugs were legal. Alcohol prohibition caused more violence than the country had ever known. This should have been a barometer to the bureau that its intention to make certain drugs illegal would cause violence. Was the motive altruistic, or was the action a selfish grab for power and job security?

Since the Harrison Act was expanded, some drug addicts have been forced to commit crimes to pay for their addiction. Those addicted to drugs are now criminals and face prison, whereas alcohol addicts are seen to have a disease and treated medically.

It was simple to change the public's perspective of a drug addict, who previously had been seen as someone caught up in problems caused by a personal defect, someone who held down a full-time job and paid taxes. The bureau developed techniques for manipulating people's attitudes. Negative news stories began to appear. Now the user was a criminal. It then became easy to create stories that would teach the public to see drug use as a moral epidemic, a disease that destroys the spirit, leaves the body in decay, and unleashes the vicious animal that had never been visible before.

The propaganda began with publicizing the evils of narcotics. The public was "educated" to believe that our country was on the verge of a drug-induced moral collapse, children were being victimized, narcotics were lethal and enslaving, and drug users were criminals and depraved bloodsuckers. There were more stories charging that "addicts" were committing crimes (and with the soaring cost of illegal hard drugs, the bureau-created propaganda began to come true).

Now the public was willing to believe that mind-altering drugs of *any* sort transformed normally law-abiding citizens into violent criminals. *This belief was the planned precursor to declaring the illegality of marijuana.*

Prior to 1937 marijuana was legal and was used primarily by poor minority groups. They used marijuana (because it cost practically nothing) for its medicinal value, for relaxation, and in religious ceremonies—while other segments of the population used alcohol.

Mexican immigrants were rapidly moving into the United States. For a time they were employed, as blacks have been, because of the meager wages they would accept. During the depression of the 1930s, the American economy was ravaged. The few available jobs were in demand by white Americans. Mexican Americans and African Americans became the scapegoats and were often accused of being provoked to violence by marijuana.

On November 25, 1992, Benson B. Roe, physician and professor emeritus of surgery at the University of California at San Francisco, stated:

> The propaganda that illegal drugs are "deadly poisons" is a hoax. There is little or no medical evidence of long-term ill effects from moderate consumption of uncontaminated marijuana, cocaine, or heroin. If these substances, which have been consumed in enormous quantities for decades, were responsible for any chronic, progressive or disabling diseases, they certainly would have shown up in clinical practice and/or on the autopsy table. But they simply have not![1]

On an ABC news show that aired on April 7, 1995, the announcer mentioned marijuana and other drugs. Former Director of National Drug Control Policy William Bennett, a guest on that show, stated, "This is a deadly and poisonous activity. People should be imprisoned for long periods of time for doing it."

Harry S. Anslinger's Role in Marijuana Legislation

Andrew Mellon owned the Mellon National Bank of Pittsburgh and was the financier for the DuPont company. The same

Andrew Mellon was secretary of the treasury under President Herbert Hoover, as well as under Presidents Harding and Coolidge. In 1930, Mellon selected his future nephew-in-law, Harry S. Anslinger, to head the federal Bureau of Narcotics and Dangerous Drugs.

Anslinger learned well from the bureau how it had achieved its goal of turning the public against hard drug users. It didn't take long for him to use the same duplicity to destroy marijuana and those who used it. Anslinger used the Bureau of Narcotics' blueprint of the "drug-inspired violence" campaign to create his own agenda for power and to triumph in outlawing marijuana. One of his first deceptions was achieved when he succeeded in grouping marijuana along with heroin.

The propaganda against marijuana included the following advertisement supported by the Federal Bureau of Narcotics in what it called its "educational campaign describing the drug, its identification, and evil effects."

> BEWARE! YOUNG AND OLD—PEOPLE IN ALL WALKS OF LIFE! THIS (photo of marijuana cigarette) MAY BE HANDED TO YOU BY *THE FRIENDLY STRANGER*. IT CONTAINS THE KILLER DRUG "MARIJUANA"—A POWERFUL NARCOTIC IN WHICH LURKS MURDER! INSANITY! DEATH![2]

(The above advertisement can be purchased in placard form in some poster shops.)

Such dishonest representations expanded the government's lack of credibility among young people. Those who believed such chicanery were candidates to use cocaine, heroin, or other, more harmful drugs. Perhaps they figured, "At least those other drugs don't cause insanity!"

The bureau's propaganda worked well. Each year its budget was increased. It succeeded so well that its budget is now in the hundreds of millions of dollars. Then, as today, it did not succeed in reducing drug use one iota.

Anslinger had to prove that there was a *new* drug menace threatening the country, one that required immediate federal intervention, one that the bureau could deal with if its budget was increased further. Anslinger didn't want marijuana to be included in the original Harrison Narcotic Act, which didn't prosecute users of drugs. He felt that stiff penalties would get people off drugs and that users should be heavily fined and imprisoned.

During alcohol prohibition, Anslinger contended that if it had been up to him, the alcohol laws would have included severe punishment. Most people continued using alcohol, even though it was illegal. Like marijuana users, they felt what they did in the privacy of their own homes, or in "speakeasies," was their business, not the government's. For illegal alcohol use, Anslinger would have had half the adults in the United States incarcerated. (And no doubt many youngsters.)

If his office (now the DEA) using the same philosophy, caught and convicted all who have tried marijuana, estimated at 70 million people, there wouldn't be many people occupying their homes.

When will our country face up to the truth? Imprisonment doesn't stop drug use any more than does punishing a person who wets his bed. Longer sentences and more prisons have not affected the level of drug use. Will even more savage policies turn the population, many who use marijuana medically, spiritually, creatively, or socially, into "good citizens"?

Anslinger felt it was necessary to create a media campaign of horror stories. He relied on reports of how the use of marijuana drove young people into depravity. He brought in the racist angle. And the campaign worked. Most of the stories were not based on actual events, but rather were stories produced by Anslinger and fed to the news media as fact.

Propaganda enabled Anslinger to prepare the nation to accept the marijuana ban. He acquired a partner on his superhighway of conspiracy and hoax, publisher William Randolph Hearst, head of a nationwide newspaper chain. Hearst joined up with the king of chicanery to publish propaganda damning marijuana.

Anslinger deserved the "Pinocchio" award for being the country's greatest shameless perjurer. Almost single-handedly he convinced law enforcement, newspapers, and the country to believe that marijuana was a deadly narcotic.

Hearst and other newspaper publishers jumped at the opportunity to increase circulation by printing unconfirmed horror stories about marijuana. The misrepresentation rivaled the reporting in any of today's grocery store tabloids. (William Randolph Hearst III is an ethical and honest editor, cable executive, and newspaper publisher who in no way continues the unethical practices of his grandfather.)

Racism in Drug Propaganda

Fanning the fires of racial prejudice and stereotypes was a giant leap toward the goal of terrifying parents. Sadly, those stereotypes loom today, a result of the fabrication of yesterday. If fiction is printed and broadcast long enough, people believe it.

How could racial lies help cause marijuana to become illegal in 1937? Hearst's newspapers and the tabloids excelled in perpetuating the fantasy of "lazy marijuana-crazed Negroes raping white women."[3] The propaganda portrayed blacks as "frenzied beasts" under the influence of marijuana, using their voodoo-satanic music (also known as jazz!) to inflict "disrespect" on white people. This included stepping on white men's shadows, looking at a white woman twice, looking white people directly in the eye for three seconds or more, laughing at white people, and similar ludicrous portrayals.[4]

For such "crimes," hundreds of thousands of Hispanics and African Americans spent years in prison and on chain gangs. The country wasn't concerned when those minorities spent up to twenty years in prison for pot "crimes." (Punishment lessened in the 1960s, when legislators' youngsters were caught with pot.)

With such monstrous punishment, could government have been afraid that the black population was gaining power, in spite of many whites doing their damnedest to keep them suppressed? Perhaps they thought blacks might not take orders and be our "slaves" much longer. How much have things improved? The government may subconsciously resent African American males, owing to the conventional idea of their superior physical attributes.

Anslinger felt that by guiding racism—making it public and showing that certain "types" were preventing our good white people from obtaining jobs—it would be easier to obtain the passage of the 1937 Marijuana Tax Act. Tragically, he was correct. Some legislators, always seeking to pass bills that would get them votes, jumped on this vehicle of deception.

A Texas police captain claimed that under marijuana's evil influence, "Mexicans become very violent, especially when they become angry, and will attack an officer even if a gun is drawn on them. They seem to have no fear. I have also noted that when under the influence of this weed they have enormous strength and that it will take several men to handle one man, while under ordinary circumstances one man could handle him with ease."[5]

Joseph F. Taylor, Los Angeles chief of detectives, referring to Hispanics, stated, "In the past we have had officers of this department shot and killed by marijuana addicts and have traced the act of murder directly to the influence of marijuana with no other motive."[6]

During the depression years, labor groups and anti-foreigner groups such as the American Coalition demanded that California's legislators drive the Mexicans out of California on grounds that marijuana was undermining our morality. C. M. Goethe, spokesman for the coalition, stated, "Marihuana, perhaps now the most insidious of our narcotics, is a direct by-product of unrestricted Mexican immigration. Easily grown, Mexican peddlers have been caught distributing sample marihuana cigarettes to school children. Bills for our quota against Mexico have been blocked mysteriously in every Congress since the 1924 Quota Act. Our nation has more than enough laborers."[7]

More whites than blacks use marijuana and other drugs, but more blacks are continually arrested. In Chicago each day, Judge Oliver Spurlock goes through the dozens of drug cases on his docket. Most all of the faces he sees are young, male—and black. A court should be the melting pot of a city, but there's no sign of a rainbow in U.S. courtrooms. The few white people in the room are on the other side of the law: attorneys, police officers, or bailiffs. The war on marijuana and other drugs has ravaged black communities and sent thousands of men to court, to jail, and to dead-end lives. Most of them were not really criminals to begin with, but they come out of prison equipped to be.

Why do blacks make up an overwhelming majority of the drug cases in the criminal justice system when most of the nation's drug users are white? Many experts blame it on the drug war emphasis: on the streets of the inner cities, where dealing is blatant, crack is cheap and plentiful, and arrests are fast and easy. Destroying black communities is bigoted and ineffective.

It's past time to be honest. If these were high school and college students from middle-class white communities, would they be the ones arrested and shipped off to prison? Hardly. Then we'd be talking about youngsters who were just experimenting with drugs, and we don't want them to have a police record to spoil their future.

Nationally, blacks account for 12 percent of the population. Yet, of the more than 760,000 drug arrests in 1991, 41 percent involved blacks. The proportion of blacks arrested for these crimes increased sharply in the last decade, while the share of whites charged has declined just as dramatically.[8]

Conspiracy against Blacks?

According to a report by Miller's National Center on Institutions and Alternatives, a nonprofit group that promotes effective options to prison, blacks accounted for 91 percent of juvenile drug arrests. Once arrested, these juveniles find the courts a particularly hostile environment.[9]

"The lives of young white men are valued more than young black men," argues Angela Jordan Davis, director of the Public Defenders Service in Washington, D.C. "A white prosecutor is going to empathize more with someone who looks like their son or brother rather than a black kid from a poor environment." The racial disparity that exists for juveniles is no different for adults.[10]

A 1990 California study may offer a clue as to why this disparity exists. It found that 70 percent of those sent to prison for drug offenses were black, while *two-thirds of drug treatment slots went to whites.*[11] When young black men, or any man or woman regardless of color, are put behind bars with the knowledge that they were unfairly sought out and imprisoned, what is accomplished, other than delivering back to the community socially crippled, angry young men, with an understandable interest in "getting even" with the society that wronged them?

Drug courts can save money and lives. Nonviolent offenders, rather than being sent to prison, which wastes money and lives, should be offered treatment programs. A Ventura County judge recently said that state taxpayers save $7 for every $1 spent on drug and alcohol abuse treatment. The drug court would act as judge, counselor, cleric, and social worker. This system would present an opportunity for nonviolent offenders to receive humanity, understanding, and education, rather than prison punishment.

Respected "Cannabis" Changed to Frightening "Marijuana"

"Cannabis" had been a respected medical term, but William Randolph Hearst coined a new name: "marijuana." This helped to hide the recognized and proven medical benefits of cannabis. The unfamiliar name, marijuana, began to terrify the country. "Hemp" was also cast out. Cannabis and hemp were now joined together as marijuana. In changing the names from cannabis and hemp to marijuana, Hearst and Anslinger knew the public would not realize that not only had a natural medicine and exalted industrial resource been outlawed, but also the correct names had been erased from our language!

In 1937, Anslinger testified before Congress: "Marijuana is the most violence-causing drug in the history of mankind." He followed this testimony up with an account of two Black students at the University of Minnesota impregnating a white coed. The congressmen of 1937 gasped when they heard that marijuana seemingly caused white women to eye black men with passion.[12]

All of this propaganda paved the way for the Federal Marijuana Tax Act of 1937. The connection between marijuana and minority groups intensified the panic over what the 1936 movie called *Reefer Madness.*

Hearst slanted news stories to help spread panic. If a marijuana "roach" (less than half of a smoked marijuana cigarette) was found in a car that was involved in an accident, the story made front-page headlines. Alcohol-related auto accidents were found on the back pages. Hearst directed such front-page headlines as "Marihuana makes fiends of boys in 30 days: hashish [dried marijuana resin] goads users to blood lust."[13] More than anyone, Hearst and Anslinger caused marijuana to be seen as a violent drug throughout the United States.

During the mid-1930s, Anslinger traveled around the country giving speeches to parent-teacher groups, judges, police departments, and the FBI about the evils of marijuana, using the same rhetoric: "Marijuana is the most violence causing drug in the history of mankind." Another of his favorite lies stated, "Marijuana is reducing thousands of boys to criminal insanity." And in those years, Hearst newspapers and others confirmed the rhetoric. *Anslinger is credited with single-handedly causing marijuana to become illegal.*

Scheming for the Marijuana Tax Act of 1937

One of the Treasury Department lawyers asked Anslinger, "Have you lots of cases on this? Horror stories, that's what we want."[14] Not to disappoint this man, Anslinger stated unequivocally that marijuana caused young and old to turn to violence and that it was "criminalistic" (turning people into criminals). The misled public jumped on the bandwagon of the time and did not resist when marijuana was made illegal in 1937.

Anslinger was quoted in the May 1938 issue of *Scientific American.* How would your parents have felt had they read the following article in 1938?

Marijuana is "a more dangerous drug than heroin or cocaine." Authority for this statement is United States Commissioner of Narcotics H. J. Anslinger. Mr. Anslinger's statement was made as part of a report on narcotics appearing in the bulletin of the Federal Bureau of Investigation. *Science Service* quotes Mr. Anslinger:

> I am surprised to learn that certain police officers have been inclined to minimize the effects of the use of marihuana. . . . These officers should review some of the cases that are reported to the Bureau. They would, I am sure, be convinced that the drug is adhering to its Old World tradition of murder, assault, rape, physical demoralization, and mental breakdown. A study of the effects of marihuana shows clearly that it is a dangerous drug, and Bureau records prove that its use is associated with insanity and crime. The user loses the power to resist emotions, and may commit violence which knows no bounds, when disorders of the intellect have reached a point of incoherence. During this dangerous phenomenon, evil instincts are brought to the surface and cause fury to rage within the user.[15]

What study? What records? Anslinger's falsehoods were presented to the FBI as fact and given as sworn testimony before Congress. They were also presented as fact to parent-teacher groups, law enforcement agencies, and the press.

Marijuana was no longer identified with medicine. Now it was, among other frightening charges, "The Assassin of Youth." There was never any proof of such negative claims against marijuana. During those early days of reporting, there were no news reporters calling for a "reality check." There was no *60 Minutes*, which frequently exposes the dishonest intent of anyone causing the public to suffer needlessly, including the federal government. *60 Minutes* has presented shows that demonstrate marijuana's medical benefits.

There are too many other courageous writers and broadcasters, too many worthy publications, to mention them all. A few are ABC's Dean Edell, radio and television physician; Consumers Union, which published *Licit & Illicit Drugs*; Garry Trudeau, creator of the comic strip "Doonesbury"; Jack Herer, author of *The Emperor Wears No Clothes*; Andrew Weil, M.D., and Winifred Rosen, authors of *From Chocolate to Morphine*; *High Times* and *Playboy* magazines; MTV, which does honest drug reporting on television; Lester Grinspoon, M.D., author of *Marijuana, the Forbidden Medicine*; Ernest L. Abel, historian and author of *Marijuana: The First 12,000 Years*; and Dan Baum, author of *Smoke and Mirrors.* Also, check the Internet at http://www.druglibrary.org/. as well as NORML for their list of publications.

Now that criminal laws are already in place against marijuana, it's exceedingly difficult to change them—unless the public en masse demands change from their legislators: "I'm mad as hell and I'm not going to take it anymore!" Perhaps one day we will emerge from beneath the blanket of propaganda that smothers us and embrace those famous words, first uttered by a very angry newscaster in the movie *Network.*

Another part of Anslinger's scheme was authoring the following hysterical story:

> The sprawled body of a young girl lay crushed on the sidewalk the other day after a plunge from the fifth story of a Chicago apartment house. Everyone called it suicide but actually it was murder. The killer was a narcotic known to America as marihuana, and history as hashish. It is a narcotic used in the form of cigarettes, comparatively new to the United States and as dangerous as a coiled rattlesnake.[16]

Such stories were typical of the Bureau of Narcotics' "educational campaign."

On October 16, 1933, Victor Licata used an ax to murder his mother, father, two brothers, and a sister in their Tampa, Florida, home. The following day the police chief of Tampa declared "war on marijuana" after reading the investigating officer's report that marijuana cigarettes had been "indirectly to blame for the wholesale murder of the Michael Licata family."[17]

A psychiatric examination of Victor Licata found that not only was he insane, but also his family had a history of insanity, and many relatives had been committed to mental institutions. The

Tampa police had attempted to have Licata committed a year earlier (six months prior to his using marijuana). But his parents argued that they could better take care of him at home. He remained in their custody.

He was ultimately sentenced to the Florida state mental hospital where he was diagnosed as suffering from permanent psychosis, which was no doubt responsible for his crime. In 1950, he hanged himself.

There was no evidence that Licata killed his family while under the influence of marijuana. Nevertheless, Anslinger perpetuated the fiction that a marijuana user was a demented, knife-wielding, half-crazed maniac running senseless through the streets, slashing at anyone unfortunate enough to cross his path. Lack of evidence that pot caused Licata to kill in no way prevented Anslinger from citing the case during hearings on the Marijuana Tax Act of 1937 as an example of the dangers of marijuana:

> In Florida a 16-year-old boy, under the influence of this drug, killed his parents and his brothers and sister. The evidence showed that he had smoked marihuana.[18]

In Anslinger's book *The Murderers: The Story of the Narcotic Gangs*, he once again used the Licata murders, which he knew were *not* caused by marijuana. Anslinger wrote:

> Much of the most irrational juvenile violence and killing that has written a new chapter of shame and tragedy is traceable directly to this hemp intoxication . . . A sixteen-year-old kills his entire family of five in Florida . . . Every one of these crimes has been preceded by the smoking of one or more marihuana "reefers."[19]

A release from the U.S. Bureau of Narcotics stated, "A young man identified as J. O. confessed he murdered a friend and put his body in a trunk while under the influence of marijuana."[20]

In a 1939 *Journal of the American Medical Association* the facts put forward were quite different: "J. O. was examined in this clinic," Dr. Bromberg reported. "Although he was a psychopathic liar there was no indication in the examination or history of the use of any drug. The investigation by the probation department failed to indicate use of the drug marijuana."[21]

In the April/June 1966 United Nations *Bulletin on Narcotics*, written by a member of the Advisory Committee, U.S. Bureau of Narcotics, there was another example of duplicity. In this new version, J. O. was quoted as saying, "I was fearless after smoking marijuana cigarettes and would not have done this [the murders] without marijuana."[22]

Anslinger's lurid news stories were read by the country's lawmakers, the courts, and police. One of the most emotional uses of false marijuana propaganda was the claim that schoolchildren were being lured into using pot by drug pushers, frequently identified as foreigners—Mexican Americans or African Americans. The supposition obviously was that American children were being debauched by foreigners.

Courtney R. Cooper, author of *Here's to Crime*, conspired with Anslinger. He wrote about "marijuana sex-perversions" and other nonsense:

> Apartments are run by ghoul-minded women; in such apartments high school students gather on the promise that reefer-smoking will put music in their souls and a release from all moral restraint; nothing is said about eventual insanity. Then suddenly a girl wanted to dance. Immediately everyone wanted to dance. The movements were of sensuality. After a time girls began to pull off their clothes. Men weaved naked over them; soon the entire room was of the wildest sexuality. Ordinary intercourse and several forms of perversion were going on at once, girl to girl, man to man, women to women.
>
> This is one of the great reasons why girls who are little more than children are now being placed in whorehouses by members of prostitution syndicates, why young boys of otherwise straight habits suddenly join up with dangerous gangs, why there are constantly more murders committed by youth."[23]

Ignorance has continually compounded marijuana hysteria. Tabloid-type writers joined the stupidity to make a fast buck. Such stories began appearing in books, magazines, and newspapers. Here's an example:

> Marijuana is the murder drug, and it is the marijuana that makes him pick up his knife and start to kill. You can grow enough marijuana in a window-box to drive the whole population of the United States stark, staring, raving mad . . . But when you have once chosen marijuana, you have selected murder and torture and hideous cruelty to be your bosom friends."[24]

My parents, along with millions of other naive parents, and thousands of police, judges, teachers, and students were exposed to such writings. Many still believe them today. Because of deceit, parents were terrified of marijuana. They preferred alcohol, even though countless teenagers died from drinking "contests"—seeing who could drink the most in the shortest time—or fatal auto accidents, or violence from over-indulging in alcohol.

The 1937 Marijuana Tax Act

For two years, between 1935 and 1937, Anslinger held secret meetings with his superiors in the Treasury Department. His department (the Federal Bureau of Narcotics and Dangerous Drugs [FBNDD]) clandestinely led the way to the Marijuana Tax Act of 1937. Under the act, manufacturers, sellers, distributors, and importers had to register with the treasury secretary and pay what was described as an "occupational tax." Marijuana transfers were to be taxed at $1.00 per ounce, or $100 an ounce if the dealer was not registered. The act inflicted a five-year imprisonment term, a $2,000 fine, or both for possession of any amount of marijuana, no matter how small, if the tax was not paid first. The Federal Bureau of Narcotics prepared a standard marijuana bill reinforcing the national proscription against use and possession that the states were hustled into signing. The nonmedical use of marijuana was illegal in all states; consequently, the act set up a form of self-incrimination. It was a "Catch-22."

There is little doubt that the two years of secret Treasury Department meetings were intentionally designed to keep doctors from having enough time to prepare arguments about the proven medical benefits of marijuana. Marijuana had been so demonized that the doctors were no longer able to recognize it as their coveted medicine, cannabis. No researchers or people in favor of marijuana use were called to testify. They learned only two days prior to the hearings that cannabis, which medical doctors had been prescribing to patients in the United States for over 100 years without one fatality, was now being called marijuana. It was being made illegal, and they and the public were being conned.

One medical doctor, Dr. William C. Woodward, also an attorney, testified on behalf of the American Medical Association (AMA). With such short notice, only Dr. Woodward was available to attend the hearings to defend cannabis.[25] The doctor was frustrated by the fact that the marijuana tax bill had been in preparation in secret for two years.

Dr. Woodward and the AMA did not believe the propaganda expounded by Anslinger and his "yes men." After hearing false testimony, he challenged the Treasury Department. (The following excerpts are from the U.S. Congress, House of Representatives, hearings before the committee on Ways and Means, Hearings on H.R. 6385, 75th Congress, 1st Session, 1937). Dr. Woodward stated:

> The danger was only in the minds of the Bureau of Narcotics! There was no evidence suggesting that marijuana posed any danger to the country.

The doctor assumed there must be some basis for all the furor over marijuana in the press. Woodward asked why the facts upon which these statements were founded had not been introduced as firsthand testimony. "Since when did press coverage constitute anything more than hearsay?"[26]

"During the past two years," he told the committee, "I have visited the Bureau of Narcotics probably ten or more times. Unfortunately, I had no knowledge that such a bill as this was proposed until after it had been introduced."

The reason, of course was that the bureau didn't want any opposition. By presenting its case without notification, it forced the opposition to attend virtually unprepared and without their own expert witnesses. After he testified about the benefits of cannabis, Dr. Woodward was curtly excused from the hearings.

The 1937 Marijuana Tax Act was introduced by the Treasury Department's assistant general counsel, Clinton M. Hester, who stated that after a two-year study it was revealed by the Bureau of Narcotics that the drug marijuana was "being used extensively by high school children in cigarettes." Its effect, he told a House committee, "is deadly."[27]

Owing to the two years of secrecy, there was virtually no opposition to the Marijuana Tax Act of 1937. Few professionals or the general public understood that cannabis and marijuana were the same herb.

Estimates of how many Americans were using marijuana were never presented and never discussed. No qualified experts were summoned to support the bureau's claims that children were using marijuana, that marijuana was causing Americans to commit crimes, or that marijuana was "deadly."

What the committee heard were excerpts from newspapers and magazines describing the dangers of marijuana. Hester reported, "The leading newspapers of the United States have recognized the seriousness of the problem and many of them have advocated federal legislation to control the traffic in marijuana."[28] What the committee did not know was that the bureau had supplied many of the untrue, gruesome stories on which the newspapers based their appeal for something to be done.[29] (Appendix I gives more details of the 1937 Marijuana Tax Act hearings.)

The government's "expert medical witness" was Harry S. Anslinger. Commissioner Anslinger was able to unload his own "medical opinion" on the dangers of marijuana. His sworn statements were filled with fabrications.[30] One leading piece of evidence to be introduced on behalf of the Treasury Department was Eugene Stanley's article "Marihuana as a Developer of Criminals."

Another "expert" witness for the government was Dr. James Munch, a pharmacologist who had been giving marijuana to dogs. Asked if the drug altered the personality of dogs, the pharmacologist answered with an unqualified, "Yes, so far as I can tell, not being a dog psychologist."[31]

Dr. Woodward's positive testimony regarding the medical benefits of marijuana appears to have been intentionally misrepresented. As the transcript of the House hearings shows, it was made to appear that a "Dr. William *Wharton*" gave testimony on behalf of the AMA, and that he gave the measure for prohibition his full support![32]

When the Marijuana Tax Act bill was debated in Congress, only one question was asked: Did anyone consult with the AMA and get their permission (to prohibit the sale of marijuana)? Representative Fred M. Vinton answered for the Ways and Means Committee: "Yes, we have a Dr. Wharton, and the AMA is in complete agreement!"[33]

Marijuana was found guilty without a trial and sentenced to death. Beneficiaries were the former Federal Bureau of Narcotics and Dangerous Drugs, now the Drug Enforcement Administration, the underworld, the giant DuPont Corporation, the alcohol and tobacco companies and pharmaceutical interests as well as the fastest growing industry, prisons.

Not one word of any positive marijuana report was used by Anslinger during the Congressional marijuana tax hearings of 1937. The ensuing years produced many different studies that demonstrated marijuana's relative harmlessness. The DEA continues to reject all positive findings.

Just before the bill came to a vote in the House of Representatives, a short exchange took place showing that Congress wasn't aware of what the drug marijuana was, even though they were being asked to outlaw it!

> *Mr. Snell*: What is the bill?
>
> *Mr. Rayburn*: It has something to do with something that is called marijuana. I believe it is a narcotic of some kind.[34]

With befuddled ignorance the House and Senate passed the Marijuana Tax Act in September 1937. The slaughter of marijuana killed more than a drug. It killed a nontoxic medicine.

During the Congressional hearings it was stated: "The purpose of House Resolution 6385 is to employ the Federal taxing power, not only to raise revenue from the marijuana traffic, but also to discourage the current and widespread undesirable use of marijuana by smokers and drug addicts, and thus *drive the traffic into channels where the plant will be put to valuable, industrial, medical, and scientific uses*" [emphasis added]. The bill was to control only the "recreational" use of marijuana.

The legislators, as well as the Federal Bureau of Narcotics and Dangerous Drugs, recognized in 1937, just as the DEA currently knows, that marijuana has medical value. They have deceived themselves by denying it. And poor misunderstood hemp, being in the same family but without the intoxicating or medicinal ingredients, was also found guilty without a trial. The act was confusing to medical doctors and laypersons alike.

Importers of tons of "marijuana" seeds that were sold as bird seed were only familiar with the word "hemp." The new law lumped the two names together. Consequently, no one in the hemp industry had time to present a strong case to keep hemp legal. The industry could not comprehend the reason for the illegality of hemp seed.

State Governments Follow Suit

After federal anti-marijuana legislation, state governments followed the leader. Anslinger next succeeded in driving marijuana out of legitimate medical practice, despite the pro-marijuana stand of the AMA. He convinced Dr. Ernest Fullerton Cook, chairman of the Committee on Revision of the United States Pharmacopoeia (USP) to have marijuana deleted from that official compendium in 1941.[35]

Since 1937, most state laws have specified that marijuana penalties should be the same as those for heroin, so as heroin penalties escalated throughout the years, so did those for marijuana. A few examples of state penalties in force as of January 1, 1970, follow:[36]

- Alabama: One marijuana cigarette, not less than five years. Second offense could be 40 years. Probation prohibited in all cases.[37]
- Colorado: Mandatory minimum for first possession, two years. First sale, ten years. No parole.[38]
- Georgia: Sale of marijuana to a minor, life imprisonment, even for a first offense. Second offense punishable by death.[39]
- Illinois: First offense, not less than ten years and as much as life.[40]

The Marijuana "Steppingstone" Theory

The marijuana "steppingstone" or "gateway" theory that marijuana leads to hard drugs is another story that was contrived to scare parents. It makes as much sense as saying drinking grape juice leads to wine drinking. Or drinking prune juice leads to more dangerous laxatives! Perhaps a more logical statement would be to say drinking beer leads to hard liquor. Yet millions of beer drinkers never touch hard liquor. This type of constant mutilation of truth by Anslinger caused millions of sincere Americans to believe marijuana to be a steppingstone to hard drugs. In 1951 Anslinger again perjured himself before Congress (and provided one more example of the kind of lies that frightened parents): "Over 50 percent of those young addicts started on marijuana smoking. They started there and graduated to heroin; they took the needle when the thrill of marijuana was gone," he testified.[41]

Anslinger was involved with the League of Nations and every other international organization possible, selling every country in the world on the spurious "deadly" effects of marijuana. It's quite probable that marijuana would be legal not only in the United States but also throughout the rest of the world, had it not been for the perjury constantly committed by power-famished Anslinger.

Anslinger Forced to Resign

In 1962 President John F. Kennedy forced Commissioner Harry S. Anslinger to resign after Anslinger tried to censor publications and used such outrageous references as "ginger-colored niggers," on Federal Bureau of Narcotics stationery. Anslinger had convinced Congress that about 50 percent of all violent crime committed in the United States was by "Mexicans, Latin Americans, Filipinos, Negroes, and Greeks and those crimes could be traced directly to marijuana."[42]

Just one more example of the duplicity, hypocrisy, and corruption of the former head of the Federal Bureau of Narcotics and Dangerous Drugs is this bit of chicanery: Anslinger had been supplying morphine illegally for years to his friend Senator Joseph McCarthy. His reason: "So the communists would not be able to blackmail this great American Senator for his drug-dependency weakness."[43]

Conspiracy?

The 1937 Marijuana Tax Act authorized DuPont to supply synthetic fibers for the government and the domestic market—without competition from hemp. The evidence of a conspiracy between the government and corporate America is that DuPont is still the major producer of man-made fibers, while no one in the United States has legally harvested textile-grade hemp in sixty years.

The federal government has ignored all positive evidence regarding the medicinal benefits of marijuana, even from the 48 percent of oncologists who would prescribe marijuana to cancer patients if it were legal.[44] The figure would no doubt be closer to 90 percent if the oncologists were not bombarded by untrue government reports.

Depriving patients of medicine for political reasons is unconscionable. The cruel and dangerous hoax is not from marijuana users but from the government. Lies are a severe addiction of the anti-marijuana cultists. It's time to end the marijuana conspiracy—and the deception of the century.

4

Who Benefits from Marijuana Prohibition?

Alcohol, Tobacco, Pharmaceuticals—and Uncle Sam

The ill and dying are the primary losers when it comes to marijuana prohibition. Very old and terminally ill patients are frequently too lawabiding to seek out marijuana as medicine. Alcohol and tobacco are our country's chosen legal drugs and euphorics. They not only produce billions of dollars in profits for their manufacturers and stockholders, but they also result in billions of tax dollars paid to Uncle Sam. It's in the mutual interest of the government and these businesses to prevent the use of a benign botanical called marijuana.

The same can be said of pharmaceutical companies. They make billions, and Uncle Sam gets his cut. Dozens of profitable pharmaceutical relaxants, such as Valium, are prescribed by doctors. Why would drug companies allow an old-timer like pot, which can produce much the same result as Valium, to cut into their billion-dollar industry?

For more than fifty years tobacco companies had doctors in their pockets. Doctors were even endorsing cigarettes in newspaper and magazine ads and on radio. There were so many doctors endorsing cigarettes that jokes were fabricated. Perhaps you've heard this one: "Yes, two out of three doctors who use Camels say they prefer women!"

The tobacco companies and the government have been taking care of each other. Only recently has the government started to back away from its cigarette chums after the public became enlightened. We finally became outraged when we learned that 340,000 to 425,000 people die each year from nicotine addiction and its deadly side effects. The federal government is still subsidizing tobacco growers. Tobacco farmers could thrive without government subsidies by growing hemp to replace nicotine tobacco.

Synthetics Manufacturers

The DuPont Corporation's slogan was "Better things for better living through chemistry." At one time DuPont was our country's largest munitions supplier. As most people know, Uncle Sam works closely with multinational corporations that can provide products rapidly in time of war.

DuPont patented a process for making plastics from coal and oil and a new way of making paper from wood pulp. The materials necessary for manufacturing rayon, paper, and plastic could have come from the hemp plant, thereby saving our forests and keeping our rivers pristine instead of polluted with toxic chemicals.

Between 1935 and 1937 Congress and the Treasury Department were convinced through secret testimony presented by DuPont directly to Herman Oliphant, general counsel for the Treasury Department, that hemp seed oil could be replaced with the corporation's newly produced synthetic materials. Corporate President Lamont DuPont stated, "Synthetic plastics find application in fabricating a wide variety of articles, many of which in the past were made from *natural* products. The chemist has aided in conserving natural resources by developing *synthetic products* to supplement or wholly *replace natural products*" [emphasis added]. That was in

1937. Was it coincidence marijuana and hemp both became illegal in 1937?[1]

Today the DuPont family is worth approximately $9 billion.[2] Our government protects these giants of industry by keeping pot illegal. Troublemaking marijuana growers who could provide competition are kept in prison longer than many murderers.

Petrochemical products are derived from petroleum or natural gas. The same products could also be produced from nonpolluting hemp. What do giant industries such as DuPont all have in common? Not only are they multi-billion-dollar profit makers, they have an uncle who is their protector.

Prohibition Won't Halt Pot Use

Since the beginning of recorded history, people throughout the world have looked to drugs to find relief from frustrations and tensions. Drugs are also used as entertainment, for a temporary change in reality.

"So let's let 'em have their booze. We'll tax the hell out of it," Uncle Sam seems to say. There is a lot of money in those heavily taxed bottles, and the government has the public's breezy support. (Uncle hasn't lied about alcohol for over sixty years as he has about marijuana.)

In December of 1840 Abraham Lincoln said, "Prohibition . . . goes beyond the bounds of reason in that it attempts to control a man's appetite by legislation and makes crime out of things that are not crimes. . . . A prohibition law strikes a blow at the very principles upon which our government was founded."

Government Prospers from Marijuana Ban

In 1984 federal law gave authorities the right to seize the property and assets of drug dealers without criminal charges, and these seizures proved to be a boon to local and federal law enforcement agencies, adding in some cases millions of dollars to police coffers. The state and federal governments split the take.

Citizens who once enjoyed the presumption of innocence and the protection of the Constitution against illegal search and seizure saw their belongings seized without benefit of judge or jury. Seized and sold property is 100 percent government profit, encouraging more seizures. When police can confiscate property from innocent citizens and force them to fight in civil court to retrieve it, then the government is no longer punishing criminals—it is stealing.

Backyard pot growers fell into the government's trap and could not afford attorneys to fight for them. Their bank accounts, homes, cars, and other valuable possessions were confiscated; 80 to 90 percent of all such seizures were never returned.[3]

Across the country, people carrying large amounts of cash with no apparent drug connection have been stopped in airports or elsewhere and forced to surrender their money to authorities. Even when the accused is a marijuana smoker, the punishment far outweighs the crime. For example, a man in Manton, California, had ten acres, a house, and a barn confiscated because three marijuana plants were growing on his property.[4]

Law enforcement agencies like to explain seizure laws as the government's way of retrieving ill-gotten gains. That's certainly a commendable concept, but no one expected the government to discard the rest of the criminal justice system in the process.

Any property can be seized by the police if they believe it was bought with the profits of illegal activity or used to further a crime. The only justification police need to take property is probable cause, which could be an erroneous tip from an anonymous informant. Attorney fees to regain property can run into the thousands of dollars.

Important parts of the Bill of Rights do not apply in forfeiture proceedings. According to *USA Today*,[5] "Police seize millions of dollars in cash each year because police dogs indicate money smells like drugs even when no drugs are found and no arrests are made." After thirty years of living in Hawaii, I left in 1987. My home on the Hilo side of the Big Island was surrounded by four miles of lava from an ongoing volcanic eruption. Roads were covered with 5 to 20 feet of lava. Squatters hiked in and moved into vacant homes, mine included. At some future time that property will once again be valuable. On September 20, 1994, I received a letter from the DEA:

> Dear Mr. Ford:
>
> Your property located in the Royal Gardens subdivision in the County of Hawaii is being utilized at the present time to cultivate and facilitate the cultivation of marijuana.
>
> Unknown persons have taken residence on the above mentioned property with your knowledge and are believed to be responsible for the cultivation of this marijuana. It is the intention of the Drug Enforcement Administration to seize this property under federal law.
>
> If you have any questions regarding this matter, you should contact your attorney.

I felt relieved they called me *dear* Mr. Ford. The statement that these unknown persons were there with my knowledge was *totally untrue.* If they were unknown, how could I know them? And only an idiot would knowingly allow anyone to grow pot on his property. There are hundreds of vacant acres in that immediate area where pot could be grown. Why would someone plant pot in my backyard with *my* knowledge! I didn't contact my attorney; I don't have an attorney.

I repeatedly tried to contact the resident DEA agent in Honolulu. It seemed he was continually unavailable. I called so many times I suspect I finally made the agency more crazed than it already is. Finally my calls were returned. I made it clear I had no way of knowing who was in my home and that I would take whatever legal action was necessary to thwart any crude takeover of my property by the DEA. They dropped the seizure attempt.

Since 1985 federal seizures of property have increased by 1,500 percent. By January 1997 the total value of property seized was over $4 billion. Financial incentives can cause citizens to be set up, because informants receive cash rewards.

On October 2, 1992, thirty-one people from law enforcement agencies stormed Donald Scott's 200-acre ranch in Malibu, California. Scott's wife screamed when she saw the intruders. When sixty-one-year-old Scott, who no doubt believed thieves were breaking into his home, came out of the bedroom with a gun, he was shot dead. A drug task force was looking for marijuana plants.

Scott had refused earlier to negotiate a sale of his property to the government. DEA agents were ready to seize the ranch. No marijuana was found.[6]

After a five-month investigation, Ventura County District Attorney Michael Bradbury concluded that "the Los Angeles County Sheriff's department was motivated, at least in part, by a desire to seize and forfeit the ranch for the Government." A deputy said that if the DEA could find as few as fourteen marijuana plants, the government could seize the entire property. Scott's death was ruled a "justified shooting."[7]

In New Hampshire, Kevin and Bridget Perry were arrested for growing four marijuana plants behind their home. They pleaded guilty to a misdemeanor and paid a fine. The government seized their twenty-seven-year-old mobile home, worth $22,000, for "facilitating" a drug crime. It took a fifteen-month legal battle to regain their home.[8]

The federal government seizes cars, airplanes, boats, real estate, money, computers, fax machines, and other personal property. Seizures have become a profitable business for the government. Twenty days after seizure, the property is forfeited automatically unless the person has enough money to hire an attorney. The government is immune from a countersuit. Public defenders work for the state. Frequently deals are made, not always to the property owner's advantage. Prosecutors and police defend their atrocious actions of seizing property and incarcerating hundreds of users by claiming that the dangers of marijuana use require that drug users to pay a severe price to deter others from the use of grass.

The Department of Justice knew that its actions were probably unconstitutional, yet it refused to stop. Instead, it started filing even more cases.

In 1994 the U.S. Court of Appeals in San Francisco ruled that prosecuting an accused drug dealer and separately seizing his assets amounts to double jeopardy. That ruling would have led to the release of hundreds, and possibly thousands, of nonviolent marijuana "criminals." Or perhaps the government would have at least been forced to return its illegal booty. In May 1989 Justice Harry

Blackmun stated, "The government may not criminally prosecute a defendant, impose a criminal penalty upon him, and then bring a separate civil action based on the same conduct and receive a judgment that is not rationally related to the goal of making the government whole."[9]

On June 24, 1996, the Supreme Court reversed itself and ruled that it is not "double punishment" for prosecutors to seize a criminal's house and assets after he has been sent to prison. However, the Court may have a tough time convincing people who have gardens of marijuana used as medicine for themselves and their ill friends.

Major Corporations Are Beneficiaries

Campaign contributions from special interest groups and individuals are not called bribes. However, influence seekers have paid hundreds of thousands of dollars to members of Congress in return for boring after-dinner speeches. Are those big bucks paid out for the bad food and the boring speech? Hardly.

When alcohol and tobacco companies can afford to spend up to $6 billion a year on advertising and promotion, that's a drop in the proverbial bucket to prevent the relegalization of marijuana. Pot could prove to be serious competition for such companies.

Pharmaceutical enterprises would lose millions of dollars a year if people could minister to many of their ills free of charge. The far-reaching power of pharmaceutical companies controls much of the FDA.

The government has launched a massive campaign of misinformation and scare tactics to discredit vitamins and nutritional healing. The pharmaceutical industry is worried. One-third of all Americans now visit alternative health care providers such as herbalists, chiropractors, and nutritional healers. An estimated sixty million Americans take vitamins and other dietary supplements daily. The use of self-healing substances like marijuana has become a threat to the pharmaceutical companies.

NORML, *High Times*, and *Omni* (September 1982) indicated that Eli Lilly & Co.; Abbott Labs; Pfizer; Smith, Kline & French; and other pharmaceutical companies would lose hundreds of millions to billions of dollars annually if marijuana were legal in the United States. In 1976 these drug companies, at their own insistence, by lobbying, were able to get the federal government to *prevent all positive research into medical marijuana.*[10]

FDA agents, with guns drawn, have raided health food stores and the offices of alternative physicians. Why? The FDA receives tremendous flat fees from pharmaceutical companies to approve drugs (up to $300 million dollars). Drug companies happily pay. Such approval guarantees them a legal monopoly for their new medications. The FDA (like the DEA) justifies its attack on vitamins by claiming they are dangerous. Their safety record (like marijuana's) proves otherwise. Virtually no one has ever died from nutritional supplements, even when they have been used inappropriately. The FDA's concern is that vitamins and herbs (like pot) are natural substances and cannot be patented. FDA approval does not guarantee that a drug is safe. Far from it. Up to 140,000 people die annually from adverse drug reactions.[11]

How would producers of alcoholic beverages like it if millions of Americans could acquire a free high, without a hangover? How would the tobacco industry react if marijuana, a product that is not physically addictive, were legalized? We must not neglect the pharmaceutical companies, either.

It's thought provoking to note that the *Physicians Desk Reference* (PDR) consists of some 4,000 pages and lists around 50,000 drugs for 25,000 illnesses. Hundreds of these drugs can cause death. Warnings and contraindications are presented that tell of such side effects as liver damage, kidney stones, respiratory failure, and death. We use more drugs than any country in the world. Yet we're not allowed to use marijuana, a nontoxic medicine.

About one-half of the money supporting the 4,000 Families Against Marijuana and other such organizations is contributed by *drug and pharmaceutical companies*! The other half is supplied by Action, a federal agency of VISTA (Volunteers In Service To America), and by *liquor and beer manufacturers*, such as Anheuser-Busch, Coors, and Philip Morris (producer of Miller Beer), as a "public service." Politicians receive "gifts," sometimes hundreds of thousands of dollars, to pass the "right" bills in Congress to keep those purveyors of toxic chemicals in business.[12] Those companies go out of their way to demonize marijuana by including it in the same category with drugs that are highly addictive.

August A. Busch III, chairman of the board and president of Anheuser-Busch Inc., producer of Budweiser, Bud Light, Natural Light, Michelob, Michelob Golden Draft, and Golden Draft Light, in his message to shareholders for the first quarter of 1992, made the following statement:

> Anheuser-Busch Companies' gross sales for the first quarter of 1992 were $3.02 billion, an increase of 3.4% over gross sales of $2.92 billion for the first quarter of 1991. Consider that beer is a legal beverage, produced by a strictly regulated industry which employs hundreds of thousands of Americans and contributes billions of dollars annually to the American economy. *Crack, cocaine, marijuana and heroin are produced by a criminal element which makes no contribution to our society* [emphasis added]. We are not alone in our position. Prominent people outside the alcohol beverage industry agree with us, including religious leaders. During an address last November at the Vatican, Pope John Paul the Second said, and I quote, 'There is certainly a clear difference between resorting to drugs and turning to alcohol. Whereas the moderate use of alcohol as a drink does not, in fact, clash with moral prohibitions and only abuse is to be condemned, taking drugs is, on the contrary, always illicit because it involves an unjustified and irrational renunciation of thinking, willing and acting as free persons."

Busch went on to say:

> Pope John Paul's remarks were entered into the Congressional Record by Congressman Charles Rangel of New York, and we have called them to the attention of the Office of National Drug Control Policy. Further, we have emphasized to lawmakers that when they review policies dealing with alcohol it is important to consider the growing body of scientific evidence which has found that moderate consumption of alcohol beverages produces certain health benefits. There are now indications that public awareness of these studies is growing. According to a Gallup poll taken in January of this year, 58%

> of American adults are aware of research linking moderate drinking to lower rates of heart disease. We will continue to communicate good news of this nature to lawmakers and other key groups across this country."[13]

Moderate alcohol use, particularly red wine with dinner, does appear to lower cholesterol levels. Alcohol *abuse* also can result in death. In spite of lobbyists, the government in 1992 included alcohol in the war on drugs.

If marijuana were legal, it also would be a regulated industry. Medicines that could be produced from marijuana would contribute to the health of people around the world at prices they could afford. Hundreds of thousands of Americans could also be employed in the marijuana and hemp industry.

Who pays for and who does the research linking moderate drinking to lower rates of heart disease? Any one company, such as Anheuser-Busch, which nets hundreds of millions of dollars a year, can afford to get any message it desires out to the public, while NORML has virtually no money to get its message to lawmakers, religious leaders, and others to fight against widely circulated unscientific facts. Recently an advertisement by NORML asked for the donation of a fax machine. NORML is a altruistic educational organization that operates on a shoestring budget.

America's Fastest Growing Enterprise: Prisons

More than one-third of all federal drug prisoners are serving time for marijuana offenses, according to the U.S. Sentencing Commission's 1993 Annual Report. This translates to as many as 20,000 inmates who spend more time in prison than drive-by shooters who kill. It's costing taxpayers around $30,000 a year per inmate. Marijuana offenders occupy valuable prison space that could otherwise be used to imprison violent criminals and sex offenders.

A report released December 3, 1995, by the Department of Justice shows the number of Americans behind bars jumped by nearly 90,000 during the twelve months ending in June. Most criminal justice experts describe the war on drugs as the single most important factor in rising rates of incarceration. In the federal prison system, drug offenders have increased 1,000 percent.[14] The Nixon-inspired War on Drugs cost taxpayers $1.5 billion in 1981 and $15.3 billion will be spent in 1997; in 1998, it will be $16 billion. Are we winning yet?

Prison, Drugs, and Gangs

Some of the dozens of older teens I interviewed have been incarcerated for possessing or selling drugs. It's crucial to understand their rage. "We know we're not getting honest information. We're not stupid."

A former gang member told me, "Sure, we punish by killing sometimes. But so does the state. You bet we're going to get even when we get out. While in prison we're taught how to make bigger drug sales. With drug prohibition, there's big bucks out there. Our government points out the corruption in Mexico and Columbia. Hell, our FBI, CIA, and the DEA are gaining from drugs. It's big business."

Here are some other thoughts the teens shared.

"They take our driver's licenses away for smoking pot, even if we're *not* in the car."

"Alcohol kills thousands of people a month. Pot never killed anyone, and they put us in jail for it!"

"A friend said pot and heroin are in the same category, so when he got busted for pot he switched to heroin. He got some bad stuff and he died. They don't warn you not to mix alcohol with heroin. I think they want you to die. It's free anti-drug publicity."

"My parents make me listen to those 'Partnership for a Drug Free America' TV spots. They lie, and kids know it. Remember the Amtrak train accident in 1987? The commercial said, 'They say pot doesn't kill, but I lost my wife and two kids in a train accident caused by marijuana.' Court records showed no tests for THC were done. The engineer accused of smoking pot was, in fact, drunk. And how about that commercial that showed a sad couple who said they couldn't have kids because the husband used to smoke pot?"

"Kids steal parents' Prozak, Ritalin, Valium, Dalmane, and alcohol. Some die from taking too much. But parents force us to take a drug test for pot!"

5

Are We Being Protected from Evil—or Honesty?

WHAT ARE THE ANTI-MARIJUANA GROUPS and the government trying to protect marijuana users from? Addiction, poison, evil, or honesty?

If it's addiction, marijuana is not any more physically addictive than ice cream, chocolate, television, sex, or the Internet. (I'm sure the Internet is far more addictive!)

If it's poison, as was charged during the *Reefer Madness* days, there is no medical evidence of even long-term marijuana use being poisonous.

If it's death, no one has ever died from a marijuana overdose.

If it's evil, they must explain why marijuana is more evil than legal substances like alcohol or nicotine.

If it's honesty they're protecting us from, they deserve high marks for unjustified fear-mongering.

The drug war is a dismal failure. When something doesn't work, isn't it time to at least *study* alternatives?

Former Surgeon General Dr. Joycelyn Elders favored marijuana as medicine. Strike one against her. Dr. Elders was an example of outspoken courage. She felt we would reduce crime if drugs were legalized. She felt this alternative was worth *studying*. Strike two. For such an "outrageous" suggestion it was demanded that she immediately be fired. During the time Washington was deciding how to expel her, she managed to advance other "outlandish" suggestions. She was attacked for stating that condoms are not the solution to teenage pregnancy, but *if* a youngster is sexually active, condoms should be available. "If we teach kids what to do in the front seat, we should teach them what to do in the back seat as well," she said.

It's imperative that we support courageous people in government, even if we don't approve of every suggestion they make. Should they be fired because, at times, they may have embarrassed those who like the status quo?

At the December 1, 1994, World AIDS conference in New York, the participants searched for a way to stop AIDS. As they were talking about alternative methods of sexual release to prevent the spread of AIDS, Dr. Elders was asked her views on masturbation. She said that it was part of human sexuality and something that *perhaps* should be covered in schools. She wasn't advocating teaching kids how to masturbate. She was telling them that contrary to what they may have heard, masturbation in private does no physical harm. Strike three.

In grade school I recall children whispering to their friends, "Did you hear the latest medical information—that if you masturbate you will go blind? Or hair will grow on the palm of your hand?" When the boys and girls who heard that startling "news" thought no one was looking, they would gingerly turn their palms face up to have a peek, much to the amusement of their friends. There would never have been such jokes if honest sex education had been offered. Without honest and courageous people like Dr. Elders, we are left with those who will not "insult traditional values."

As compensation for her honesty and courage, President Clinton accepted Dr. Elders' resignation on December 10, 1994.

Government Myths about Marijuana

The government has become a slave to the marijuana misinformation it created. It can't let go of the scare tactics. The accusers are caught up in their own conspiracy and hoax.

The government and organized anti-marijuana hate groups defend their policies with these faulty assumptions:

- Myth #1: Marijuana is so dangerous and addictive that the most extreme sanctions our society has must be used to suppress its use.

  Truth: First, marijuana is not physically addictive. Second, making a drug illegal does not make it unavailable. All common illegal drugs are available on the street in neighborhoods of all social and economic strata. Illegal drugs are frequently delivered to homes and even by some prison guards to inmates.

- Myth #2: Any use of marijuana is drug abuse; people cannot use it responsibly.

  Truth: According to the National Academy of Sciences in 1982, "Over the past 40 years, marijuana has been accused of causing an array of anti-social effects, including: in the 1930s, provoking crime and violence; in the early 1950s, leading to heroin addiction; and in the late 1950s, making people passive, lowering motivation and productivity, and *destroying the American work ethic in young people* [emphasis added]. Although belief in these effects persists among many people, they have not been substantiated by scientific evidence."

- Myth #3: Marijuana use causes social problems such as teenage drug addiction and is a threat to public safety.

  Truth: Today there is an increase in alcoholism among children. Alcohol use is much more of a threat to public safety than marijuana ever was. So is the use of crack cocaine and other illegal drugs. Ironically, millions of teenagers hear adults tell them how dangerous marijuana use is, but when they see adults using it at home or thousands using it at outdoor concerts, they note that virtually no one is harmed by it. So they laugh off warnings about alcohol, nicotine, crack, heroin, and other drugs—warnings that might save their lives.

- Myth #4: Marijuana is a steppingstone to hard drugs.

  Truth: The old government story about marijuana being a steppingstone to other drugs is false. Marijuana is more apt to be a substitute for other, more dangerous drugs. Ask yourself, if marijuana were to disappear, would the use of other drugs increase or decrease? (It should be noted that users of drugs such as crack, methamphetamine, cocaine, and many other drugs use marijuana when they want to "mellow out," or come down from the high, so they can go to sleep or, in a few hours, be able to go to work without being "speedy.")

A while ago I was grocery shopping. Passing by the liquor department I noticed a gentlemen in his thirties. I introduced myself and said I was an author completing a book on marijuana. I asked him if he felt marijuana was a steppingstone to other, more harmful drugs. He said, "Well, we used to use it in high school, primarily to tweak Uncle Sam's nose. But I have to admit, I have used other drugs, so I guess I'd have to say it was a steppingstone.

I then asked, "If marijuana didn't exist, what would you have done?"

He smiled and said, "We'd probably gone in for 'huffing.'"

"What would you have inhaled?" I asked.

"Same stuff lots of the kids do today that don't want to get caught smoking pot or have it show up in a urine test. Probably cleaning solvent, airplane glue, whatever was around."

"Thanks," I said. "You answered my question."

- Myth #5: Today marijuana is ten times stronger and more dangerous than in the sixties.

  Truth: In the May 1994 issue of *Normal Report,* John P. Morgan, M.D., with the Department of Pharmacology,

City University of New York Medical School, stated, "Samples of pot from the early '70s came from stale, low-potency Mexican 'Kilobricks' left in police lockers, whose potency had deteriorated to sub-smokable levels of less than 0.5%. These were compared to later samples of decent-quality domestic marijuana, making it appear that potency had skyrocketed. Domestic pot did increase in the '70s, however the range of potencies available has remained virtually unchanged since the last century. Stronger potency is actually healthier for the lungs because it reduces the amount of smoke one needs to inhale."

- Myth #6: Marijuana prohibition improves public safety.

  Truth: States that have decriminalized marijuana have lower overall drug abuse rates.[1] In Alaska, accident rates held constant or declined following the legalization of personal marijuana use.[2] Recent government statistics showed that the highest rates of cocaine abuse in the west were in Nevada and Arizona, the states with the toughest marijuana laws.[3]

- Myth #7: Marijuana is a dangerous drug, and it cannot be used even under a doctor's supervision.

  Truth: Please see Chapter 2, "Marijuana—Medical Miracle Herb" and Chapter 15, "Relegalize Marijuana" for irrefutable evidence to the contrary.

Uninformed Pot Hate Groups Spread Falsehoods

The central assertion of the existing drug policy of the United States is this: certain drugs are so dangerous that their use represents a mortal danger to society and justifies extreme intervention by the state. Opponents of marijuana law reform claim their tactics are legitimate because of the "harmful" effects of marijuana use. Millions of Americans believe marijuana laws are illegitimate because the claims of marijuana's harmful qualities are without scientific foundation.

As in any war, people take sides. Too frequently, there are radicals who twist and bend the truth to justify their uninformed means to an end.

Organized anti-marijuana groups are constantly announcing "new evidence" that marijuana is as dangerous as previously believed. In May 1973 the *Washington Post* reported doctors' claims that marijuana use contributed to the growth of abnormally large breasts on young men. Today, Parents' Resource Institute for Drug Education (PRIDE) warns that marijuana "sometimes leads to deficient puberty in adolescent males." There is little or no empirical or scientific evidence to support this claim. PRIDE says a symptom of this "deficient puberty" is "loss of energy." Before it was discredited by scientific analysis, this accusation had a different name: "amotivation syndrome." This syndrome originated with the racist claim that marijuana use made Mexican Americans or African Americans lazy and dangerous. Single studies are not unassailable proof of scientific fact. Using qualifiers like "may" and "sometimes," as PRIDE does, does not mitigate the misrepresentation of scientific research.

Here's an example: both the Partnership for a Drug Free America (PDFA) and PRIDE charge that marijuana smoke has more cancer-causing chemicals than tobacco and therefore is more likely to cause cancer. But there is no scientific evidence linking marijuana to cancer.

PDFA has been criticized for other falsehoods. A notorious television public service spot, aired in 1987, featured the EEG (electroencephalogram) "brain-wave" readings of a "normal" youth and another youth under the influence of marijuana. The test was actually simulated (the EEG machine was not connected), and the false ad was pulled from television.[4] Common sense suggests another test. Where are the large numbers (or even one instance) of lazy, infertile, large-breasted young men with brain damage and head, neck, and lung cancers that would prove these extremist accusations? It appears that if marijuana is not dangerous, it's the responsibility of law enforcement to make it so.

Marijuana users include ordinary people who are employed—productive taxpayers who use pot for medical reasons or for relaxation in the privacy of their homes, generally on weekends. They are not impaired.

Marijuana Convictions Are Big Business

Prosecutors use unfair sentencing guidelines to increase the severity of marijuana cultivation offenses. Sentencing guidelines assume that every plant will yield five to six times more marijuana than plants actually produce. Those who grow marijuana for personal use are treated by the courts as if they were major traffickers. This treatment makes it easier for police to keep seized property and brag to the press about the "big bust," which soothes the public when they are asked to cough up more tax dollars to catch those nasty marijuana criminals.

The more seized marijuana by weight that can be reported, the more money the DEA receives from the state and federal government for equipment—helicopters, planes, dogs, cars, guns, boats—and personnel. It would be difficult to continue the farce of marijuana interdiction and the smashing in of doors of private homes if the DEA reported that it recovered twenty ounces of marijuana, rather than twenty pounds. By reporting tremendous numbers of "pounds" and "tons" of marijuana seized, the DEA seeks to justify its horrendous costs.

If the DEA were to report that it eliminated four pounds of marijuana in a day and the cost to taxpayers was $60,000, the public wouldn't approve the outlandish costs of eradication. The DEA frequently weighs the plants when they are wet so it can say, "This office seized 100 pounds of marijuana with a street value on the east coast of one million dollars." Too frequently this includes the worthless male plants, the branches of both female and male, the leaves, and the stalk.

If you've ever dried a bunch of flowers, you'll understand that when dry, these flowers are like a feather and weigh a fraction of what they weighed when green. Or, if you prefer another analogy, the dried marijuana is like a floppy disk, but the DEA also weighs the computer, screen, and keyboard. The DEA is aware of its "hallucinatory" deception in reporting the actual salable weight of marijuana. The exaggeration could provide a chuckle if people weren't going to prison or getting killed. It's reminiscent of the Vietnam War body count. The government wasn't honest then and it isn't honest now. At least with the Vietnam War and with alcohol prohibition, our country finally realized we could not win those wars and ended them.

A couple growing marijuana for their own medicinal use might sprout fifty seeds and plant them in the ground, hoping to end up with five mature plants after pulling up the males and losing others to the elements. If they are arrested for growing fifty plants that might be a foot tall, they could be charged with possessing marijuana and cultivating it for sale, a felony. If convicted in federal court, they could lose their home and their children and receive up to a ten-year prison sentence.

Punishing the couple by sending them to prison costs taxpayers at least $40,000 a year for a victimless crime by nonviolent citizens (an average of $20,000 each for state prison). Such costs do not include lost taxes that the couple would have paid as workers. There's also the cost of placing the children in foster homes while the parents are incarcerated. When only the husband goes to prison, some of the mothers and children end up on the street, homeless.

Most plants grow to five to six feet in height at most and will produce three to four ounces of usable "colas," or "buds," the flowering and most potent portion of the female plant.

At Hawaiian luaus I've seen a pound of marijuana used up in a few hours. Everyone would have a great time, eating, laughing, telling jokes, dancing, singing, and playing the ukulele. Some did the hula, while others gazed out over the ocean, meditating. Nevertheless, if the DEA joined the party and grabbed the stash of marijuana used for the entertainment, the grower could be convicted of growing with intent to sell and face years in prison. Had he been arrested twice as a young man for selling a few ounces of pot to his friends, he could wind up subject to federal law—and flung into prison for the rest of his life.

What about selling a little of one's pot to a friend with a migraine headache? (Pot will stop most migraines.) Selling is a felony. Is it better to let your friend go to a dealer who not only sells pot but also at a later date tries to interest your friend in black market painkillers, crack, "acid," or heroin? Work must continue to relegalize marijuana.

Positive and Negative Effects of Marijuana

Some first-time marijuana users feel nothing. On the other hand, some who smoke too much the first time have an overreaction to the feelings of the high, which otherwise would be positive. Spatial perceptions and time appear to slow down. Colors may be distorted and enhanced. Free-flowing thoughts enter one's mind. Many times a revelation can produce a new insight. The mouth becomes dry. The heart beats a bit faster, which generally is not noticed but can cause a few first-time users to push the panic button. A panic attack generally includes one or more of the following: feeling of unreality, fear of losing control, shortness of breath, or nauseous or upset stomach. Such an experience rarely happens if the person is first advised what to expect from the high. Remembering frightening government warnings, such as that marijuana causes violence and insanity, or the threat of ending up in prison can produce a panic attack.

After I graduated from college, I visited a friend in Los Angeles. One day during my visit he had a migraine headache.

I have a bad back that at times goes into muscle spasms. Pot stops the spasms in minutes. My friend had never used marijuana before. I suggested it for his migraine. After a few inhales we heard a siren. He was certain someone had smelled the smoke and had called the police. He tried to hide in his portable cardboard closet. It collapsed. Next, he attempted to crawl under his bed. He didn't fit. I pointed to a fire truck whizzing past. He finally broke up laughing. He had panicked. Even so, his migraine was gone!

Excessive marijuana users may display respiratory irritation. Similar results take place when too much of any smoke is inhaled.

Excessive use of any drug, or even some foods, will create ailments or accidental injuries due to temporary impairment.

A person's memory can also blank out during the high as he listens to new information or becomes aware of new sensations. (Generally, users are having so much fun they are not paying attention to what others are saying). The sensation of temporary memory deprivation can be humorous. Comedian George Carlin said, "One of the problems that marijuana's having being legalized—no one can remember where they left the petitions."

Obviously, the marijuana experience, on the whole, must be good or 35 million Americans would not continue to use marijuana. With marijuana experiences will generally be enhanced. However, if someone wants to fight, he will probably fail. He is more apt to start laughing.

A seasoned paramedic of Evansville, Indiana, reported in the fall 1995 *Freedom @ NORML*:

> I am a paramedic and have been involved with emergency rooms and prehospital care of patients and can honestly say that I have never encountered a hostile person, worked a fatality, or been involved with a domestic dispute where pot was involved. Alcohol—yes! Pot—no! This is in ten years of working the streets.

6

Our Legal "Killer Drugs"

IN THE UNITED STATES MARIJUANA FIRST EMERGED in the 1920s, at a time when the abuse potential of other drugs such as cocaine and morphine was first understood. As a consequence, government propaganda caused marijuana to be regarded as similarly dangerous. It was erroneously classified as a physically addictive drug similar to cocaine, morphine, and heroin. How did the government manage to get the public to believe marijuana was physically addictive and evil?

Frequently, propaganda is subtly presented, sometimes with a government-sponsored motion picture. Leonard Maltin's 1991 *TV Movies & Video Guide* lists 19,000 films that have been produced by the federal government or by contractors under federal grants.[1] One of the most successful propaganda movies ever fabricated was *Reefer Madness*, the movie America believed. Filmed in 1936, it prepared the public for the 1937 prohibition of marijuana.

Reefer Madness displayed teenage girls, after a couple of puffs on a joint, falling into a stupor and allowing men to use them sexually. It showed young people becoming violent and committing murders after smoking one marijuana joint! It showed one marijuana cigarette causing insanity! *Reefer Madness* opened with this warning:

> "Marijuana is a violent narcotic. Its first effect is sudden, violent, uncontrollable laughter. Then come dangerous hallucinations, followed by emotional disturbances, the total inability to direct thoughts, the loss of all power to resist physical emotions, *leading finally to acts of shocking violence . . . ending often in incurable insanity*" [emphasis added].[2]

And that was only the opening of a terror-filled movie that horrified millions.

Parents of the 1930s are still frightened by the lingering memory of that fiction-filled motion picture. Now the government substitutes new twists to get parents to fear marijuana and has still not publicly denounced the falsehoods in *Reefer Madness* or other government-sanctioned, untrustworthy, marijuana horror stories.

Who could blame parents after seeing and hearing such effective propaganda? They forbid their children to experiment with marijuana, yet many look the other way when their teens try alcohol and nicotine—far more dangerous and addictive drugs.

The DEA has no incentive to produce accurate information about marijuana. The government does not pay to hear the positive effects of marijuana, only the negative.

I've been told by publishers and agents that if I would write a book *condemning* marijuana, similar to *Marijuana Alert,* I could look forward to some big money because the public has been conditioned to be more interested in hearing the evils of marijuana—and because the government and anti-marijuana organizations would promote such a book. I prefer to gamble—and possibly make nothing—by reporting the truth. Government researchers who come up with positive marijuana effects find their grants are not renewed.

Zero Deaths from Marijuana

In the thousands of years of use, there has never been a recorded death attributable to marijuana. That's a far better record than over-the-counter drugstore medications and the common foods we eat, such as contaminated meat and chicken, which continue to cause severe illness and death in many. The *Encyclopedia of Drug Abuse* (1995) says this about marijuana:

> A lethal dose has never been established since no deaths directly related to the action of marijuana have been reported. Research with mice indicates that for a human weighing approximately 154 pounds a lethal dose of marijuana containing 1% THC would be 15 pounds smoked or 30 pounds eaten—all at once.[3]

Nicotine: The True "Killer Weed"

During the 1930s when I was in grade school, it was a treat to visit the neighborhood grocery store and purchase penny candy. An eighteen-inch licorice stick was a penny, as were jawbreakers that barely fit into our little mouths.

What generally got our attention in the glass candy counter were the packs of "cigarettes." They were labeled with pictures of the various brands that appeared genuine. Inside were peppermint sticks with red coloring on the end. They were almost the length of a commercial cigarette, just like Dad smoked.

These candy cigarettes enticed us the way "Joe Camel" grabs the attention of children today. We looked forward to the day when we could smoke the real thing, just like Dad. Some of the kids in school were so intrigued by the candy cigarettes that they picked up cigarette butts from the gutter and rolled their own real ones, after paying two cents for a package of rolling papers. Encouraged by the simulated packs, some eighth graders actually bought real packs. "They're for my Dad," they told the storekeeper.

Most of the athletes in high school thought they could quit smoking cigarettes whenever they wanted. Many of them tried to stop, but they had misjudged the addictive power of nicotine. Most of those who began smoking as teens—those who are still alive—are still lighting up. They've tried to quit but can't. Their skin looks gray. Cigarette companies never warn you that you'll become their addict nor that eventually their product will produce death.

Dr. David A. Kessler, FDA commissioner, in the December 24, 1995, issue of *Parade* said, "Nicotine addiction begins when most smokers are teens, so let's call this what it is: a pediatric disease. Three thousand youths become regular smokers each day, and nearly 1,000 of them eventually die from a smoking-related illness."

I was hooked myself for a couple of years during my twenties. After moving to Hawaii in 1957, I volunteered to be the subject at the University of Hawaii in a test of endurance in sensory deprivation. The test was to learn if an adult could remain under water for two days and nights in a 210-pound deep sea diving rig.

It was imperative that I be in top condition. My schedule included running three miles a day, swimming three miles in the ocean, and working out with weights for a hour and a half each day for three months.

I got easily winded. After the first mile of running I was ready to collapse. I could barely swim a quarter mile. I was frightened. I had thought I was in great shape. With a pair of scissors I cut my cigarettes in half. By smoking only half a cigarette at a time, I was able to cut my smoking in half and still get that nicotine "hit" twice an hour. The following week I cut the cigarettes into thirds. The fifth week I tossed the rest of the last pack into the garbage can. Had marijuana been easy to obtain or (better still) legal, I would have been satisfied to smoke a couple of joints a week and would never have become addicted to nicotine.

By the sixth week I had enough stamina to achieve my goal—and even exceed it. As it turned out, I remained under water for seventy-six hours and forty-two minutes, breaking a world record (October 26, 1959). This feat was the subject of a feature story in *MD* magazine and on the news wires, television, and radio. (It made a great story because I nearly died. The generator failed, and by the time they pulled me up, there was thirty seconds of air remaining in the heavy copper helmet.)

When my wife and I moved to Hawaii in 1957, I created Dave Ford Motors—"Home of Hawaii's Finest Cars." I was the only dealer in Hawaii to offer a one-year guarantee on a used car. Business began with only one salesman, Addison Smith. "Ad," fifty years old, was a fine salesman who helped the business grow to seven sales people within one year.

The only disappointing thing about Ad was that he almost always had a cigarette smoldering in an ashtray or dangling from his mouth. "How about quitting, Ad?" I'd ask. Ad's cough worried me. "Come on, Coach," he'd tell me. " Give me a break, I can't quit. I've tried too many times. I'm down to two packs a day."

In late 1959, it was obvious that Ad was losing weight. "Do us both a favor, Ad. Go to the doctor and get checked, okay?" After several weeks of my nagging, Ad finally did see a doctor and was off for several days while undergoing various tests. When he returned, he was frightened. "Uh, Coach, I think I need a little time off. I'm fine. I just need some rest. Okay?"

A week later I learned that Ad was in Queen's Medical Center in Honolulu. I went to visit him "How're you doing, pal?" I asked. "Oh, I'm fine, Coach. Just a little case of lung cancer." I was stunned. Ad smiled and reached under his pillow and removed a pack of Lucky Strikes (a jarring brand name). He flipped one between his lips and lit up.

"You've got to be kidding, Ad. What would your doctor say?" Ad smiled pathetically, tilting his head. "What the doctor doesn't know won't hurt him!" "Ad, that's not funny. You've got to quit now!" Tears welled up in his sad blue eyes. "I can't, Coach."

Three weeks later, Ad was dead.

Ad's death was my first personal experience with someone dying from smoking cigarettes. However, smoking friends of my parents were dying frequently of lung cancer, heart disease, strokes, and other illnesses directly attributed to cigarettes. Tragically, many didn't know at that time what was causing their untimely deaths, but they were all heavy smokers. The Tobacco Institute has never admitted that their billion-dollar product is addictive, let alone that it causes deaths.

While heart disease and cancer may be listed as the nation's leading killers, the biggest underlying cause of death is tobacco use. Nicotine addiction takes the lives of close to 400,000 people each year, more than 1,000 a day, primarily from heart affliction and fatal chronic lung disease.

One to two drops of pure nicotine on the tongue can cause death within minutes.[4] Why is it that nicotine is legal, although a known killer, and marijuana is illegal? Marijuana doesn't contain nicotine and never killed anyone. With their $6 billion a year for ads and promotions, tobacco giants can buy the votes of lawmakers.

The Tobacco Institute donated more than $2 million to the Republican and Democratic parties during the 1992 elections, up from $468,000 during the 1988 campaigns. Ralph Nader's Public Citizen and Advocacy Institute condemned both parties for accepting "blood money." With both the Republicans and the Democrats pushing for a drug-free America, it seems hypocritical for them to be such close buddies of the tobacco interests and recipients of vast amounts of donations (or shall we call them what they are: bribes).One of my best buddies was a professional skater with the Ice Follies. He appeared to be in splendid shape even though he smoked a couple of packs of cigarettes every day. One day in the mid-1960s he was playing handball and dropped dead. The autopsy reported heart disease.

As a pilot I have empathy with other pilots. I was told of a pilot who was in serious condition from lung cancer. I dropped by his home and asked if he would like to join me on a flight. He was sitting on his porch smoking! He was thrilled by the invitation, so I helped him to the car and then into the plane. When we returned home I suggested that he quit smoking. "I can't do it," he told me. "I've tried. I get sick; my fingers even swell up. Those withdrawals stop when I smoke again. I need those two and a half packs a day."

A month or so later when I picked him up, he had a urinator strapped to his leg and was so skinny and weak that I had to carry him into the plane. Two weeks afterward, he was dead.

Movies and Television Glamorize Cigarettes

While attending San Rafael High School during the mid- to late 1940s, I was feature editor of our school paper, *The Red 'n White*; commissioner of assemblies; student body president; as well as host of the radio show *Junior Jamboree.* Those credentials gave me the confidence to interview motion picture stars.

In 1946, when actors Humphrey Bogart and Lauren Bacall were shooting a movie, *Dark Passage,* at San Quentin Prison, located only a few miles from San Rafael, I set up an interview. The editor of our school paper joined me.

A scene was being shot in a small clearing along Paradise Cove Road facing San Quentin Prison and San Francisco Bay. On the ground lay two men, seemingly in great pain. Suddenly a car door slammed, and Lauren Bacall came through the brush attempting her rescue of Bogart and the other injured man. After the scene the director yelled, "Cut. That's a 'take.'"

The editor and I got up and chatted briefly with both stars. They were polite and presented the same naturalness of mannerism and expression that we were so familiar with on screen.

I Went to San Quentin Prison

I wanted a more in-depth interview with Bogart. The following day I got permission to enter the prison. I was directed to Humphrey Bogart's location, and I rode my new Indian motorcycle to a black limousine. There was Bogart in the back seat, resting between scenes, with a gun in his lap. The windows were closed, except for one next to him in the rear seat. It was open about two inches, and cigarette smoke was seeping from the window. I noted that the ashtray was full of cigarette butts.

"Mr. Bogart, I'm Dave Ford again, and I'd appreciate it if I could ask you a few questions for the audience of my radio show, who idolize you."

A cigarette was hanging between his lips. This time "Bogie" treated me to his tough-guy image. With a frown on his face he snarled, "I talked with you yesterday, sonny. If you want more talk, speak to my manager." He then calmly pushed a button and the window closed. I thought, "I won't go see that damn picture." But I did.

Humphrey Bogart died about ten years later of cancer of the esophagus.

A few other entertainment idols who were assassinated by nicotine include Yul Brynner, Nat King Cole, Harry James, Lucille Ball, John Wayne, Zeppo Marx, Bette Davis, Sammy Davis, Jr., Steve McQueen, James Franciscus, Edward R. Murrow, and David Janssen. Janssen, star of the television series *The Fugitive*, died at forty-eight of a heart attack. He reportedly smoked three packs of cigarettes a day.

"I'm here because I lied to you," David Goerlitz, then forty-one, told a packed auditorium at Sonoma Valley High School in 1991. He revealed that he was paid $2,500 a day, and up to $100,000 a year, to encourage kids to start smoking. There were six "Winston Men," and Goerlitz was one of the only two who actually smoked. He said he began smoking when he was thirteen to emulate his heroes.

For over twenty years he smoked three and a half packs a day. He once had to inhale oxygen while filming an ad atop a high mountain. He said he noted that none of the executives who worked for the tobacco company smoked. When he pointed that out to them, they said, "We don't smoke the stuff, we just sell it." (Isn't that what heroin dealers say?)

While doubling in a movie for Harrison Ford, he had a minor stroke. Now the left side of his face and part of his left leg are paralyzed. He pointed out that the beautiful ladies in the Winston ads don't smoke and never have smoked.[5]

Smokeless Tobacco

Smokeless tobacco is popular with those who find smoking inconvenient or in places where smoking is prohibited. Users pack finely ground tobacco snuff, also known as dip, between the lower lip and gum, sometimes using two cans daily. It's used by farm workers and "outdoor types." It has been linked to baseball since the game's beginning in 1839[6]—it's an appalling example for youngsters. Unfortunately, when ballplayers are asked to give it up, at least for the sake of the youths who revere them, many feel it's an invasion of their privacy.

The National Cancer Institute found that 40 percent of professional baseball players dip or chew. Dipping half a tin of snuff daily is equal to inhaling thirty to forty cigarettes. Keeping one dip of chewing tobacco in the mouth for thirty minutes gives the chewer the nicotine of four cigarettes. This form of nicotine is so addictive, snuff has been compared to heroin and is reportedly just as difficult to quit.

As much as 70 percent of high school male athletes chew tobacco. Chewing increases the chance of cancer about fifty times over smoking. Most males who dip began to do so at age ten. Babe Ruth, who chewed tobacco, died of throat cancer when he was fifty-two.

On October 14, 1996, *The Santa Rosa Press Democrat* reported that thirty-year-old Casa Grande High School coach Bob Leslie underwent major reconstructive facial surgery. Leslie said his mouth cancer was caused by chewing tobacco; that the cancer appeared at the same spot where he'd been stuffing pinches of tobacco since he was twelve. The eighteen-hour surgery included the removal of his teeth, gums, and chin. The financial cost: $600,000.

A Beautiful Lady Dies

In late 1985, my friend and prominent Hilo, Hawaii, psychologist Jacqueline Brittain, Ph.D., told me of her close comrade, Lois Thomas. Lois had been a heavy nicotine smoker and was dying of a tumorous cancer in her lungs. She and her husband, Jerry, had just returned from Taiwan where they had been teaching. Jerry brought her to Hawaii to die in the loveliest setting possible.

Lois checked into Hilo Hospital where I visited her. She was a beautiful lady. She had emerald green eyes that tried to smile. She was in endless pain. Demerol and morphine made her nod off and forget who visited her. One day while I was visiting Lois, the nurse came in and asked, "Did you have your bowel movement today, Mrs. Thomas?" Tears welled up in the beautiful eyes of this elegant and proud lady. A hospital is not the place to die.

Lois was suffering more each day. Within a couple of weeks, she was on oxygen. Dr. Brittain offered Lois and Jerry an apartment at her home. Lois was propped up so that she could see the lagoon and the ocean, its waves dancing on the rocky shore, embraced by stately coconut trees.

Hypnosis can reduce considerable pain. In high school and college I studied hypnosis. I was primarily interested in how it could be used medically. I asked Lois if she would care to have me hypnotize her. "Yes. If it could help the pain. I'm more afraid of the pain than I am of dying."

Lois allowed herself to go into a deep trance to my words: "You are now in your very own private, exquisite elevator. You're lying on the deep, soft, rich red carpet of your elevator. We're on the tenth floor. As the elevator moves down from the tenth to the ninth floor, you are more relaxed now, Lois. The morphine is eliminating the pain now. Its effect is as powerful as if you had three times the amount of morphine. As we make the descent to each floor you will sink deeper and deeper into relaxed slumber, feeling no pain now."

The hypnosis session lasted about forty minutes. By the time we reached the "ground floor," Lois had a tranquil smile, and her face was relaxed and at peace. She was almost pain-free for several hours after the sessions. I taught her how to self-hypnotize so that during the night when the pain was frequently unbearable, she could retreat to her "elevator."

Jerry became her nurse and was extraordinary. He was there twenty-four hours a day for her. He cooked and baked Lois's favorite foods. I admired and liked this youthful, bespectacled, white-haired, and bearded man. His sparkling clear blue eyes projected the love for his lady that she deserved and which he didn't withhold.

Jacqueline Brittain spent many hours reading to Lois and visiting with her, even though she had a waiting list of patients. I visited Lois, too, and we entered her "elevator" several times a week.

On Valentine's Day 1986, Jerry told me on the phone, "She's not feeling at all well today, Dave, but she would like to see you." I stopped by the florist and picked up a bouquet of flowers. Unfortunately, I arrived too late. Jerry said, "Lois died about a half-hour ago. She was in her elevator."

Dazed, I ventured into her room. There in the bed was this tiny form, white and fragile. I drove to tranquil Kalapana and spent several hours on that magnificent black-sapphire sand beach, watching perhaps the same waves that Lois had loved and watched. I couldn't refrain from weeping at the loss of a courageous lady. It seemed so wrong for Lois—or anyone—to die from nicotine. She was fifty-two.

On November 16, 1996, Dr. Brittain informed me:

> Lois was diagnosed with cancer in Taiwan where she, ironically, smoked Chinese cigarettes named Long Life! I knew Lois as a patient in Colorado during the early seventies prior to their moving to Taiwan. Over the years Lois smoked marijuana on occasion for relaxation. If marijuana were available or legal in China, Lois would have used pot, rather than poisonous nicotine and would probably be still alive today.
>
> In 30 years of practice, frequently counseling drug users, I can openly say that I have never counseled a patient addicted to marijuana. But I have counseled literally thousands of patients who are addicted to nicotine. Many have died as a result of their nicotine usage, but no one I know or have seen as a patient has died from marijuana. Nor have I ever found marijuana to cause violence or to be a "steppingstone" to hard drugs. On the contrary, it is frequently used by hard drug users as an aid in ridding themselves of the craving for cocaine, heroin, or other physically addictive drugs. However, I have noted when people are arrested for marijuana use and are required to subject themselves to periodic urine testing that some marijuana users have switched to cocaine. They give up marijuana only because cocaine is out of the system in six to ten days.
>
> Inactive marijuana can be detected for up to thirty days, although it is not acting as an intoxicant for more than a few hours after use.

Dr. Brittain is also board certified in the treatment of alcohol and other psychoactive substance use.

On April 14, 1994, the chief executives of the top seven American tobacco companies, which include Philip Morris, raised their right hands and swore to God before a congressional subcommittee that they did not believe cigarettes were addictive.[7]

On June 8, 1995, the *New York Times* released a story regarding 2,000 pages of documents the newspaper obtained that demonstrated Philip Morris studied nicotine for some fifteen years and found it affected the body, brain, and behavior of smokers. It appears that Philip Morris's own documents prove the company deliberately manipulated nicotine, which is physically addictive. On July 13, 1995, the *New York Times* reported that the FDA had concluded for the first time that nicotine is an addictive drug that should be regulated.

The U.S. government, while continuing to preach the sham of marijuana being deadly, continues to shove a truly lethal narcotic, nicotine, down the throats of consumers in South Korea, Taiwan, Japan, the Philippines—all over Asia—and other parts of the world. When we're begging foreign governments to stop the flow of cocaine and heroin, isn't it the height of hypocrisy for the United States to export nicotine?

The alcohol and tobacco industries disingenuously encourage marijuana prohibition, while promoting their own products here in the United States and in other countries. And these industries know cigarettes and alcohol are a hundred times more dangerous than *all* illegal drugs combined. Could Uncle Sam, who is seeking a drug-free America, turn out to be the world's biggest drug pusher?

Alcohol—America's Chosen Drug

I am not demeaning social drinking or smoking a few nicotine cigarettes a day by adults but rather pointing out the hypocrisy of punishing those who prefer a milder illegal substance: marijuana.

The use of alcohol appears to be significantly involved in fires and burns, with heavy drinkers particularly vulnerable to fire. In a study that compared fire deaths with other deaths, it was discovered that alcohol was involved in 52 percent of adult fire deaths. Alcohol lowers oxidation in the cells, increasing an individual's risk of being overcome by smoke inhalation. The incidence of alcohol involvement is nearly three times greater in deaths from cigarette-caused fires than in deaths from fires resulting from other causes.[8] A marijuana cigarette will extinguish itself generally in less than ten seconds, whereas a commercial cigarette will continue to burn. Marijuana could be called firesafe.

Each year nearly 50,000 people die on U.S. highways; over half of those fatalities are alcohol related. Accidents involving alcohol also result in injuries to more than a half-million people a year. They cost more than $1 billion in property damage, insurance costs, and medical services. Forty to 60 percent of all fatal crashes involving young people are alcohol-related.[9]

Billions of dollars and thousands of lives are lost each year in alcohol related accidents. State Farm Insurance statistics reveal that more than half of all traffic deaths involve drunken drivers under the age of thirty. Sixty-four percent of drivers fatally injured in auto crashes between 9 P.M. and 6 A.M. had been drinking. One quarter of your auto insurance premium goes toward drunken-driving claims.[10]

No drug, including marijuana, should be used when driving. Yet it's interesting to consider a study conducted by the California Highway Patrol (CHP) published in 1986 by the California Department of Justice, titled *Marijuana and Alcohol: A Driver Performance Study—A Final Report.* In this study, the CHP tested the correlation between marijuana smoking and a person's ability to competently operate a vehicle. To the CHP's surprise and embarrassment, it discovered that some people actually drive better after smoking marijuana.[11]

One reason for this could be that with time "slowed down" while the marijuana user is driving, the tendency is to drive slower rather than faster. The only time I ever drove under the influence of marijuana I was 18 and returning home from San Francisco over the Golden Gate Bridge. A police motorcycle drove parallel to me. My heart was in my throat as the officer throttled back his motor and yelled, "Sir, there is a minimum speed here of forty miles per hour. You're only going twenty. Move it up, sir!"

In high school, students are able to name more brands of beer than presidents of the United States. The tragic loss of life due to drunk driving is appalling. I can't recall all the fatal auto accidents of students during my high school years, but I'm certain it was over a half dozen.

The reason why there are so many teenage auto fatalities is not that teens are poor drivers but that too many will not admit to intoxication no matter how drunk they actually are. Also most teens think they are indestructible.

Alcohol also causes violence, especially at football games. Our San Rafael High School regularly played its archrival, Tamalpais High School. I remember students drinking in cars or pouring alcohol into soft-drink containers, which they drank from in the bleachers during the games without teachers being the wiser. The consequence was numerous fights with students from the opposing school.

Date rape in those days of my youth was, sadly, far from rare. I knew a young lady at school who was offered a ride home from a school party. She was driven to a secluded spot where six guys, who were drunk, raped her. When a young man drove his date to a secluded area and said, "Put out or walk," it was highly likely that he had been drinking.

Times have changed in many ways but not regarding teen alcohol use. Alcohol is still the drug of choice. It's cheaper and easier to obtain than other substances. Binge drinking is becoming more popular than ever. Most universities throughout the country report treating cases of severe alcohol poisoning. Binge drinking is defined as drinking five or more drinks in a row, and it's not only boys who do it.

One of the saddest of all the factors is that too many parents ignore teen drinking. Some of the adults rationalize and say, "At least they're not on drugs." Parents don't realize that alcohol is one of the most deadly drugs for teens.

While attending San Rafael High School, I was senior Red Cross lifeguard at Stinson Beach in the summer of my junior year. Lifeguards soon learned that many men and some women got into trouble in the water after consuming alcohol. Alcohol appears to depress the swallowing and breathing reflexes, which can turn a normal situation into a dangerous one, especially in the ocean.

Swimmers who have been drinking take more risks. The warming effect of alcohol causes some people to remain in cold water longer than their bodies can tolerate. After drinking, too many swimmers won't heed lifeguard warnings. Some swimmers dive into shallow water and break their necks, becoming permanently paralyzed.

I did not witness such tragic consequences with those who I noted were smoking marijuana prior to swimming. Of course, I am not recommending any drug use while engaged in any sport or when working, driving, flying, using any mechanical equipment, or pursuing activities that demand skillful psychomotor performance. I am simply comparing the effects of using the two drugs.

The Story of Fae

During my senior year I was employed as a lifeguard at a resort located on the banks of the exquisite Russian River, some sixty miles north of where I lived in San Rafael. It was a challenging job. On Saturday nights the resort town of Rio Nido would close off a portion of the main road, detouring cars, and hold a street dance. Large bullhorn-type speakers were placed over a two-block area so that the live music resounded everywhere. Several hundred local residents and as many tourists came to dance. Everyone had a bundle of fun.

I was asked if I would act as master of ceremonies and announce the musical numbers. I would be paid $20 each week for several hours' work, which wasn't work at all. That was exceedingly good money in those days. Clearly I wouldn't do anything to jeopardize that extra job.

One of my good friends and a tremendously talented, featured pianist on my *Junior Jamboree* radio show came to visit me one Saturday night. I was exceptionally happy to see him. He found me backstage announcing musical numbers for the street dance. It was my first night on the job. Fae McNally was just seventeen and yet so skillful he could play "Kitten on the Keys" by rolling two oranges nimbly along the keyboard. In fact, Fae was so good that on the *Junior Jamboree* radio show we offered a complimentary San

Francisco dinner and theater tickets for two if someone could hum the first few bars of a song that Fae couldn't play.

I had never known anyone more polite or respectful to people, especially women. He was a true gentleman. But when his father caught him experimenting with pot once and threatened to turn him over to the police, Fae switched to alcohol, and his personality changed.

He was drunk the night he visited me, and I suggested he "cool it" on the drinking. I told him that I just pulled an almost-drowned man out from under the diving and sunbathing raft. "Tell me about it," said Fae with a smile. "I had heard screams of terror," I said. "By the time I got to the raft there was no one to be seen. I dove deep into the water and miraculously connected with an arm and pulled the man to shore where I performed artificial respiration. When the man was finally revived, he admitted that he had drunk too much, got under the raft, and panicked, forgetting where he was." "Quit scaring me. I'm fine," slurred Fae.

Fae was a local celebrity and a well-recognized, highly respected musician. I had heard that he had been playing with Hoagy Carmichael's Teen Agers on national radio. I asked him if he would mind saying a few words to the audience. "Sure, just bring me on, ol' buddy." said Fae. After a happy rendition of "Roll Out The Barrel," I went out on the stage. "Ladies and gentlemen, it's our pleasure to have you meet one of the country's most outstanding teenage pianists, a young gentlemen whose name is familiar to most of you, Mr. Fae McNally." Fae was greeted with thunderous applause. Many people yelled, "Yaaaa, Fae."

Fae went up to the microphone. He held it firmly with both hands, weaving slightly from side to side. There were some thirty seconds of silence.

All was quiet on the road. Then the voice of Fae: "I . . ." and you could hear the echo "I. . . I . . . I . . ." throughout at least two blocks. He continued, ". . . smell . . ." Again a pause and the echo, "smell . . . smell . . . smell . . ."

I was wondering what in the world he was leading up to. The aroma of hot dogs and barbecued chicken that were being sold on the sidewalks?

A few more seconds of silence passed, and then Fae completed his sentence: "cunt!" The word echoed. I felt heartsick and physically ill, and Fae passed out on stage. As I dragged him off the stage, the employer who had hired me, fired me. I didn't blame him. Fae shouldn't have been introduced while he was inebriated.

The next day Fae came to see me. He was mortified. He swore he had a blackout and didn't remember anything of the past night. From too many experiences with alcoholics in the years since then, I can believe that was true. Fae never did learn to control his drinking. He died in his early forties. (I wonder how many people are in prison for a murder committed during an alcoholic blackout.)

Prohibition Doesn't Work

The current craziness of the war against marijuana, pumped up by misrepresentation and governed by desperation, reminds many observers of alcohol prohibition, which began in 1920. Rather than decreasing the demand for alcohol, prohibition surrounded alcoholic beverages with an air of mystery and adventure that added to their status.

Bootleggers and gangsters took over the alcohol business, creating more criminals and violence than the country had ever witnessed, much like today's war on marijuana. The underworld made billions from prohibition, and the government received no taxes. Public outcry finally pressured the government to end alcohol prohibition in 1933. Law enforcement then needed something else "evil" to go after.

Marijuana prohibition fosters crime and promotes more users. Perhaps the most pathetic result for the citizens is that it's monopolizing law enforcement agencies who could spend their time, and our tax dollars, in more worthwhile pursuits, rather than making a crime out of a benign herb that should never have been illegal in the first place.

Unwilling Outlaws

Thousands of creative people—musicians, songwriters, poets, filmmakers, authors, and artists—demonstrate increased creativity after smoking grass. They have been and continue to be punished for a victimless crime. One of the thousands persecuted was Paul McCartney, formerly with the Beatles rock group. Paul celebrated his fifty-fourth birthday on June 18, 1996, and is worth $750 million dollars from his voice, creativity, savvy investments, and royalties. In 1965 the Beatles were honored by the Queen of England. On December 31, 1996, Paul McCartney was knighted by Queen Elizabeth II.

When asked what inspired the words for "Band on the Run," Paul said, "At the time, bands like us and the Eagles were feeling like, and being treated like, outlaws and desperadoes. I mean people were getting busted for pot, that is. And that's about all they were getting popped for. Never anything serious. And our argument was that we didn't want to be outlaws. We just wanted to be part of the regular scene, you know, and make our music and live in peace. *We didn't see why we should be treated like criminals when all we wanted to do was smoke pot instead of hitting the booze* [emphasis added]. And that's what the song was about; it was my reaction to that whole scene. . . ."[12]

And the county judge
who held a grudge
will search forevermore
for the band on the run

Can Marijuana Replace Alcohol?

Many people believe that increased popularity of marijuana will mean a decline in alcohol use. I've known of people who were able to stop smoking a pack or more of cigarettes a day by slowly switching to around three marijuana joints a week.

There are men and women who, while sitting in their car prior to entering a restaurant, will take a couple of inhales of marijuana. Just enough to feel a slight buzz to increase their appetite and enjoy the full food flavors. At their table, they abandon alcohol.

Professor Alfred R. Lindesmith, an Indiana University sociologist, said, "It is of incidental interest that some pot smokers, both old and young, have developed an aversion to alcohol, regarding it as a debasing and degrading drug, a view which is standard among the Hindus of India where alcohol is strongly taboo for religious reasons. Some of these people were heavy users of alcohol before they tried marijuana and feel that the latter saved them from becoming alcoholics."[13]

A Denver beer distributor said, "Our retailers say they can tell when a big shipment of marijuana hits town. The (beer) sales go down."[14] The manager of a discotheque in Miami, Florida, said, "Marijuana spells disaster to the liquor trade. If they ever legalize it, the liquor business is dead." He added that if his young patrons could buy marijuana legally, many "wouldn't touch liquor."[15]

During the 1930s black and white musicians recorded top pot tunes. There was Louis Armstrong's "Muggles" (marijuana), Cab Calloway's "That Funny Reefer Man," Fats Waller's "Viper's Drag," and Benny Goodman's "Sweet Marihuana Brown." A few others by lesser know musicians: "Viper's Moan," "Texas Tea Party," "Smokin' Reefers," "Mary Jane," and the "Mary Jane Polka." Songs were recorded by Columbia Records, Victor, and others.[16]

Between 1943 and 1948, Harry Anslinger kept "criminal" files on many great entertainers who were suspected of using marijuana, including the NBC Orchestra, Louis Armstrong, Dizzy Gillespie, Count Basie, Jimmy Dorsey, Les Brown, the Jackie Gleason cast, vocalist and super dancer Cab Calloway, symphony conductor Andre Kostelanetz, Milton Berle, and even the Kate Smith cast. (Perhaps that's when she sang "God Bless America" so magnificently.)

Coincidentally, while working for CBS television (KGMB) in Honolulu, I interviewed Cab Calloway, Andre Kostelanetz, and comedian Milton Berle. We didn't discuss Anslinger's neurosis or marijuana. Perhaps it was the relaxed manner those professional displayed that caused Anslinger to suspect they used marijuana.

7

Marijuana Alert Madness

Dozens of anti-marijuana books are available. Most, if not all, are written by people who have never had a marijuana experience yet write for the financial reward. For sixty years, a ready market has been created by the federal government for negative writing on the subject. Writers, such as politicians, tell the readers what they have been educated to wish to hear. Those authors cash in on the financial reward from the sale of their books. One such book, I feel, cost the life of a fine young man whom I knew. He became so frightened from reading *Marijuana Alert* that he tried heroin. After his death I promised myself to read and evaluate this book, which played to the fears of parents and to the positions of the Drug Enforcement Administration.

After reading *Marijuana Alert* by Peggy Mann,[1] I was frustrated and infuriated. Here was a writer who had every opportunity to provide both sides of the marijuana debate. I was incensed with the falsehoods I read. I vowed to expose the many unproven marijuana accusations in *Marijuana Alert.*

Author Peggy Mann was no doubt a loving, sincere, dedicated mother who unraveled when she found her daughter Jennifer smoking marijuana. Over the years, like the rest of us, she had been blitzed with frightening pseudofacts proclaiming the disastrous effects of marijuana.

I can't blame Peggy Mann for being frightened, but I do blame her for not letting the facts shape her opinions once she did her research. And I blame her for setting off a public reaction just as reprehensible and widespread as the reaction to *Reefer Madness*, based on a false understanding of marijuana.

Re-inventing *Reefer Madness*

Mann had access to current scientific studies, including those giving proven therapeutic uses of marijuana for patients suffering from the debilitating nauseous effects of chemotherapy. She read about how marijuana eased the muscle spasms of people in wheelchairs and relieved symptoms of glaucoma, often preventing blindness. Yet she chose to ignore the facts and adopt a totally negative approach. *Marijuana Alert* reproduced *Reefer Madness* with a vengeance.

Just as the public began to realize that marijuana was relatively harmless compared to alcohol and nicotine, Mann drove parents frantic. They were terrified that marijuana would drive their children into shocking behavior and that they would drop out of school and possibly spend part of their lives in mental institutions.

I am not in favor of youngsters using marijuana or any drugs until they are of legal age. However, it only makes sense to tell the truth, offering both sides of the debate. By frightening parents and their children needlessly, we create an atmosphere where young people turn to alcohol and other drugs far more damaging than marijuana.

Marijuana Alert—Fact or Fiction?

From the beginning, *Marijuana Alert* embraces a disproportionate playing field. The book begins on a weak note: In the foreword, former First Lady Nancy Reagan says that *Marijuana Alert* is a true story. It isn't. Rather, it is a one-sided story—more fiction than fact—put together from sources who derive money from the government or from other sources that report the negative "scientific findings" about marijuana. Most of these findings are unreplicated. That's not good science. Or ethical book writing.

Mann worked with documented information or interviewed nationally recognized figures who were presumed to be authorities on marijuana: Dr. Carlton Turner, director of the White House Drug Abuse Policy Office under President Ronald Reagan; Dr. Robert DuPont, former director of the National Institute on Drug Abuse (NIDA);[2] Dr. Gabriel Nahas, a pioneer marijuana researcher; and Peter Besinger, former head of the Drug Enforcement Administration, to name a few.

I contend that these "authorities" all had their own agendas for keeping marijuana illegal and frightening the public. In 1981, Besinger stated, "Marijuana is far and away the country's biggest drug problem."[3] Could it be coincidence that he owns a now-flourishing urine-testing business? Turner was forced to resign as drug czar in 1986 after proclaiming publicly that marijuana caused homosexuality, a breakdown of the immune system, and therefore AIDS.[4] DuPont is now profiting from drug testing.

Nahas continues to spread horror stories about marijuana causing chromosome and testosterone damage (unreplicated despite his countless other research attempts). Yet he is promoted for public speaking engagements in the 1995/96 Catalog of Products and Services offered by PRIDE. It advertises his book, *Keep Off the Grass.* Referring to Nahas's book, PRIDE says, "The latest scientific and medical evidence of the damaging effects of marijuana use is presented in this new edition. Memory loss, inability to perform complex tasks, schizophrenia, immune system impairment, cancer, fetal damage and childhood leukemia after a mother uses marijuana are among the harmful effects the author describes." PRIDE also continues to promote Peggy Mann, "as the world's most prolific writer for the general public on the health hazards of marijuana."

Both Columbia University and the National Institute of Health have publicly denounced Nahas's findings. In 1983, Nahas himself renounced all of his marijuana THC metabolite build-up and unique chromosome petri dish tissue-damage studies, conclusions, and extrapolations.[5]

Dr. DuPont stated that marijuana smoking was even more deleterious than tobacco smoking.[6] Could the doctor be unaware of the hundreds of thousands killed each year by nicotine?

Marijuana Alert can frighten the lightest marijuana user. Author Peggy Mann points out that millions of Americans believe grass is far less harmful than tobacco cigarettes or alcohol.[7] The millions of Americans are correct, but they may find their view challenged by Mann's obvious bias.

Mann's inaccuracies posed as truth for a nation and fooled Nancy Reagan and *Reader's Digest*, which reprinted excerpts from the book and *Reefer Madness*-type articles of Mann's, spreading marijuana panic further. Let's debunk those inaccuracies now and put her book to rest.

Potency Myth

Mann's obsession with marijuana's current higher potency compared to years past consumes nineteen pages. She asserts that the higher potency causes the body organs and brain tremendous devastation. Let's set the record straight: If a particular strain of marijuana is more potent, then the pot smoker uses less of it. If it takes less marijuana to get the same high, then there's less irritation to the throat and lungs because less is smoked. (A person drinking 151 proof rum is going to drink less than if it were 86 proof vodka). Consequently, a higher potency, in fact, is recommended for those using marijuana as medicine.

The respected *Merck Manual of Diagnosis and Therapy* is the most widely used medical text in the world. It consists of some 2,800 pages and is the bible of clinical information to practicing health care professionals. It's the medical doctors' encyclopedia. It provides useful clinical information to practicing physicians and its board of directors consists of ten medical doctors. It explains:

> Cannabis (marijuana) can be used on an episodic but continuous basis without evidence of social or psychic dysfunction . . . There is still little evidence of biologic damage, even in the areas intensely investigated, such as pulmonary, immunologic and reproductive functions . . . Marijuana used in the U.S. has a higher THC content than in the past. Many critics have incorporated this fact into warnings, but the chief opposition to the drug rests on moral and political, and not a toxicologic, foundation.[8]

Marijuana Users Don't Need More and More Pot

Mann stresses the negative effects of tolerance and dependence. The implication is frightening—if we believe her, the marijuana user must constantly have more and more of the drug. We hear that even if marijuana were legalized, the chronic pot smoker would still have to have stronger pot in order to get high.[9]

Tolerance means the gradual adaptation of the body to the effects of a drug so that more and more is needed to achieve the same effect. It might take place when a person constantly smokes day after day, but very few marijuana smokers ever do this. Pot smokers know that waiting two or three days between each session of smoking pot is like starting anew. Marijuana is not physically addictive, and users do not feel compelled to become abusers. Contrast this with nicotine. Cigarette smokers are driven by physical nicotine addiction to inhale their drug approximately every half-hour.

The majority of marijuana smokers are like the majority of alcohol users, who generally have a few drinks a week and do not abuse the drug. They get a pleasant feeling from their drink or two and don't have any need or desire to increase their consumption. Clearly, there are alcoholics who are physically addicted, but 90 percent of alcohol drinkers are not addicted to alcohol.

Likewise, most marijuana smokers use grass several times a week. They generally take about three inhalations and they are high, like people who have a couple of drinks, feel a nice buzz, and let it go at that.

Reverse Tolerance

Rather than needing more marijuana, many users report "reverse tolerance." Experienced pot smokers can smoke less and derive the same high. They have learned what to expect from the drug.

Fetal Alcohol Syndrome (FAS) Charged

Marijuana Alert says that a study demonstrated that grass smoking during pregnancy is more strongly associated with adverse fetal outcome than two or more drinks of alcohol or a pack or more of cigarettes a day. Adverse fetal outcome includes these indications:

1. Small size, according to length of pregnancy;
2. Small eye openings;
3. Microcephaly (small head size);
4. Multiple dysmorphic features, including folds of upper eyelid skin that come down over the eye openings, poorly developed philtrum (groove in upper lip), limitation of joint movement, and/or abnormal ears and nose.[10]

Contrary to Mann's assertions, marijuana is not associated with fetal alcohol syndrome. A 1982 study cited by Mann has been refuted by a study by Dr. Susan J. Astley of the University of Washington. This study found no link between marijuana exposure and the birth defects of fetal alcohol syndrome.[11]

Dependence

Marijuana Alert says there is a certain pride in being an addict.[12] The book is so scary that at times it frightened even me—because of the false alarm it sends up. Usually, though, I found myself laughing at the one-sided, pathetic, and biased information reported by Peggy Mann that just isn't so.

The book uses as an example a youngster whom the neighborhood voted "most likely to be a millionaire before he hit thirty."

However, after two years of smoking pot daily, he cared only about getting stoned. He was sent to eight psychiatrists, all of whom discarded marijuana as the problem. He was sent to psychiatric hospitals. The doctors there prescribed tranquilizers—and he became addicted to *them*! He was found dead in an orange grove. The authorities didn't know if it was a suicide or if he died from taking too many tranquilizers. His parents said he began dying years before when he became addicted to marijuana. (If that's a true story, then I apologize for shaking my head.)

That is a highly questionable scenario for the average American parent dealing with an average child. The type of child who would smoke daily for two straight years is generally predisposed to self-abusive, destructive behavior. He is clearly mentally unbalanced, a child who sees himself as a loser. It's a stretch of credulity to accept that this behavior belongs to a youngster who had been voted by the neighborhood to be a millionaire by age thirty.

There is little question that young people who lack motivation frequently smoke a lot of pot and accomplish little. However, it is doubtful that marijuana caused them to be that way. Heavy pot smoking is far more likely to be a symptom of a lack of motivation rather than a *cause* of it.

Yes, admittedly there are youngsters who abuse marijuana—or who sell heroin or who drink a fifth of liquor a day. These are disturbed young people. But to use such a far-fetched example to show the "devastating effects of marijuana" is ridiculous and irresponsible.

Of Mice and Monkeys

Marijuana Alert goes into frightening detail about the effects of marijuana on "teenage" rhesus monkeys. The testosterone level of a THC-injected male "teenager" dropped to that of a castrated animal.[13] That's enough to scare any father of a teenage son.

Mann gives us several pages on the horrible effects of marijuana on sex and reproduction in male monkeys and mice. For example, THC-impaired "teenage" male mice preferred slinking into a corner to relating to sexy "teenage" female mice. And when they reached adulthood, the males got fat and either refused to mate or started to mate and lost interest.[14] After a hefty list of similar examples, Mann admits that there is controversy among researchers as to whether, in fact, marijuana affects the testosterone level of human males.[15]

Female mice and monkeys have their own "Effects on Sex and Reproduction" chapter. Mann cites a study using rhesus monkeys whose hormones were so inhibited from smoking grass that there was no normal menstruation for three to five months. The inference was that pot affects reproduction.[16]

Yet University of Iowa researchers were unable to find evidence of marijuana use inhibiting or altering male or female hormones, even of regular users. The study measured levels of testosterone, luteinizing hormone, follicle-stimulating hormone, prolactin, and cortisol in men and women who used marijuana regularly and in an equal number of nonusers. Six other studies contradicted the one Mann cited. What they found was that chronic use of marijuana didn't affect concentrations of any of these hormones.[17]

Monkey Business

Marijuana Alert appears to be asking readers to believe that the same results obtained with monkeys could apply to humans. It says that pot-smoking monkeys hit and bite other monkeys and under high stress could wound or even kill a cagemate.[18]

The book also tells of the use of rhesus monkeys to illustrate how brain cells are killed by marijuana. The book reasons that if the findings on monkeys could be extrapolated to humans, exactly the same results would be realized.[19] One can understand why *Marijuana Alert*'s author was convinced her information was correct. Dr. Robert Heath, who headed the "monkey business," was chairman of the Department of Psychiatry and Neurology at Tulane Medical School and chairman of the departments of Psychiatry and Neurology at New Orleans's Charity Hospital. He also worked at a veterans hospital and at two state hospitals. Heath's staff developed an adaptation of an infant's respirator, which forced smoke through a face mask into the monkey's lungs.

Their conclusion: permanent alterations in brain function and structure in monkeys occurred as well as dramatic brain cell damage in the frontal lobes of the brain. They were certain far more damage would occur in humans with their larger frontal brain lobes.[20]

One of the "scientists" pointed out that for adolescents who used pot, the quality of their long-range goals often changed. He used as an example one youngster who planned to attend law school. After smoking grass he decided to become a guitar player in a rock group, even though he played no instrument. Another pot smoker, made aware of his impaired memory, felt he didn't need his memory because he decided he wasn't going to college anyway.[21] The reported injury to the brain and reproductive systems of humans is the result of defective research, generally conducted by excitable government-paid opponents of marijuana.

There was a problem, however, with the "scientific" studies. In 1980, *Playboy* magazine and NORML, after six years of requests, had to sue the government under the Freedom of Information Act. Finally, they received an accurate accounting of the Heath rhesus monkey report that had been used nationally and internationally.

The monkeys had been strapped into a chair and pumped the equivalent of sixty-three Colombian-strength marijuana joints in five minutes of oxygen deprivation. Such oxygen deprivation causes brain damage and the death of brain cells. It would be comparable to connecting a human's nose to the exhaust pipe of a car and running the engine for fifteen minutes.

The Heath monkey experiment was a study of asphyxiation and carbon monoxide poisoning, not marijuana use. Independent researchers agreed that the findings of the Heath experiment regarding marijuana were without value.[22]

False Alarm

Marijuana Alert has frightened many away from marijuana, just as Peggy Mann wanted. Her book changed the way Americans think about marijuana. Our children go through phases of experimenting—it's natural. (Most well-adjusted parents do the same.) We do our best to teach them common sense and a value system that will sustain them through the really risky experimentations—like alcohol, sex, daredevil stunts, driving fast, and so on. If we can see marijuana experimentation as just one more phase, decidedly less risky than other drugs, then we can trust our children to make good decisions. Unfortunately, Peggy Mann frightened parents so much that many now allow their children to drink alcohol, thinking they are choosing the lesser evil.

Savvy news people know that the representations of Mann's "scientific evidence" in *Marijuana Alert* and her articles on the devastating effects of marijuana are not true. Expose this evidence to the light of honest research by impartial medical doctors and scientists who are not paid by the federal government to come up with pseudo-scientific findings about marijuana, and you get a different artillery of facts to use against this marijuana drug war. The facts in her book are one example.

Mann refers to a briefing President Reagan held. There was an array of the top-ranking heads of the federal government, those who are paid to present marijuana propaganda the government wants us to hear. She mentions that the wife of one of the VIPs overheard a reporter say, "I'll be glad when he [President Reagan] stops the BS and I can get out and smoke a joint!"[23]

I have met teenagers who were so frightened by Peggy Mann's book, which their parents demanded that they read, and by her *Reader's Digest* articles that they quit smoking pot. They switched to alcohol, cigarettes, crack, methamphetamine, LSD, cocaine, heroin, glue sniffing, or some combination of these. Mann deluded the very teenagers she purported to help by omitting the fact that marijuana is less harmful than any of these substances. Marijuana is less harmful than nicotine and alcohol, a point she skirts around. Instead of putting out the fire of deception, she re-ignited America with a hysterical panic about marijuana.

Marijuana Alert frightened the public with tales of young people sent to psychiatrists or psychiatric hospitals because of the debilitating effects of marijuana. The hospitals, she claims, reported that their patients were withdrawn and displayed a Pandora's box of psychiatric disorders, including indolence, withdrawal, anxiety and apprehension, depersonalization, derealization, suicidal thinking, fear and agitation flashbacks, narcissism, paranoia, decreasing cognitive and intellectual function, gradual decline of emotional life, increased irritability, panic attacks, racing heart, sweating, palpitations, blackouts, and symptoms of senility. The book mentions that most of these disorders require sedation of the patient.[24] Mann's book also asserts that although a person drinking alcohol eventually sobers up, a young person smoking marijuana twice a week does not get "sober."[25] Mann states that people might drink quite heavily for twenty to thirty years without alterations to the brain, but using moderate or heavy pot, even for a short time, causes brain damage. Such sleazy and untrue information is still reported in magazines, on television, and by the Drug Abuse Resistance Education (DARE) program presented by police departments to young students.

Scary stories, yes, but a false alarm. Such symptoms are a rarity. In the instances of psychiatric disorders, they generally occur during the time of the "high," which lasts only a few hours at most. But some psychiatrists and psychiatric hospitals make their living with scary diagnoses, as do those who write books like *Marijuana Alert.*

There will always be a few pot users who are unstable to begin with, and those pot smokers would have experienced similar problems with alcohol or any drug—often without a drug. Some people experience disorientation during their first use if they have not been briefed on the effects of grass. These effects include the feeling of time slowing down, increased awareness, sensitivity to touch, increased appetite and enjoyment of food, and easy laughter. Some have temporary difficulty concentrating during the time they are smoking because so many ideas flow into the mind. However, the presence of free-flowing ideas can be an asset to a creative person.

I have known hundreds of pot smokers, and less than one percent ever had a problem. And when they did, it was gone as soon as they "came down" from the high. Frightening young people with largely untrue threats of lasting symptoms will only cause distrust when the truth is learned. It's far better to present both the negative and positive sides of any drug.

The Real Problem

The real problem is usually the panic reaction of parents who learn that their child is smoking pot. If their only experience with marijuana comes from reading such books as *Marijuana Alert*, they may overreact with shock and feel that their child should be hospitalized or arrested. That's enough to give the child a panic attack. Anyone who has ever been to a rock concert has no doubt been in the midst of thousands of young people smoking grass. Very rarely do problems occur—and they're minimal compared to those caused by people on alcohol.

There is no question when speaking with victims of cancer, AIDS, multiple sclerosis, and glaucoma that they find marijuana far more beneficial than many prescribed medications. Mann scoffs at the idea that marijuana has any positive use. Her Chapter 13 in *Marijuana Alert*, "Marijuana as *Medicine*?" speaks to her prejudice, aversion, and lack of understanding regarding the proven medical benefits of marijuana. Marijuana is not the problem. *Marijuana Alert* is the problem.

A Tribute to Bobbie

In 1982, I purchased a home in Keakaha, located a few miles out of Hilo on the Big Island of Hawaii. The home was on the ocean. The land was extraordinary: 18,000 square feet, zoned hotel-apartment. There were coconut trees and every tropical flower and plant imaginable from orchids to anthuriums. A blue swimming lagoon and the ocean with its white frothy waves breaking on the black lava rocks lined the grassy shore. Immediately next door was an eight-story condominium apartment building with a swimming pool. I planned to retain this property for five to ten years then build a condo on it, keeping the penthouse.

The view was dazzling. I enjoyed spending time on that property, and I began painting the home while enjoying the ocean panorama. However, the tropical jungle has a way of reclaiming its domain; soon the ocean view was losing out. It was then time to open up the view to see more of the sparkling blue Pacific.

One day in 1986 I stopped to rest after hacking at the ocean-hiding vines with a machete. "How about some help there?" The voice belonged to a young fellow with shaggy blond hair who appeared to be in his mid-twenties. He was dressed in a T-shirt, cut-off Levis, and rubber sandals. "The name's Bobbie. I'm a good worker. I enjoy hard work. I need a job and I'll work cheap."

"What kind of wages are you looking for?" I asked. "Seven dollars an hour. I do painting, too, and also some carpentry. Check me out. If you don't think I'm worth seven dollars an hour by the end of the day, you owe me nothing. Is that fair?" "You bet it is. When would you like to begin?"

He took the machete from my hand. "Right now." Bobbie started full-bore. I stood fascinated, watching him slash his way toward the ocean. He moved several times faster than I did. I envied Bobbie's youthful enthusiasm and energy but felt at that rapid pace he wouldn't make it through the day, like a marathon runner who starts out at the head of the pack but drops out two miles later.

I went back to painting the trim. Bobbie never did slacken his pace! He stopped twice briefly for water and went right back to work.

I'd never seen anyone work more assiduously. At the end of the day Bobbie returned to the house. He had a marijuana joint hanging from his lips.

"Nice work, Bobbie," I said. "Is that joint your reward for a good day's work?"

"Heck, no. I smoke two or three joints a day when I'm working. That keeps me working. I can daydream but the arms keep truckin', and it makes the work fun for me! But I don't work all that much, 'cause I do a lot a fishin', and I don't smoke when I fish. I don't think the fish like the smell of pot." He smiled.

I was amazed. I had read of Africans in the diamond mines smoking grass to keep themselves working at a fast pace, but I had had my doubts. In Hawaii I did witness many people laboring while they smoked but never anyone working as consistently hard as Bobbie. I thought he might be on speed.

"I have to admit, Bobbie," I told him, "after a few hours at that fast pace, I concluded you might be on speed."

"Naw. This is the only drug I do. I'm planning on getting married, and I want a couple of kids. Most of them other drugs aren't good for your body. I'll stick to grass."

The next morning, Bobbie started at seven. By the time I arrived around ten he had already accomplished what appeared to be a day's work. I could already see almost a third more ocean view. There was a joint in Bobbie's hand. "I've been chopping away," he said, "thinking one day before too long I'm getting married, and we're gonna have a handsome son, and him and me are goin' fishing!"

In the next month Bobbie completed the clearing and helped finish the painting. He labored with a carpenter friend of mine as we did remodeling and constructed a new lanai. Bobbie never slacked off his rapid pace, sometimes working till 8 P.M. I never had a better worker, nor one who was so mellow and happy working.

One day when Bobbie arrived for work, for the first time he looked sad. "What's happening, Bobbie?" I asked.

"Damn, I just read a book, I think it's called *Marijuana Alert.* It says grass kills your brain cells and affects a guy's sex hormones, as much as if a guy was castrated! Ya might not have a baby, no matter how much you want one. I'll never smoke grass again."

"Bobbie, you can't believe everything you read." "I do when Nancy Reagan endorses the book. She gotta know!" I didn't know the book at the time, so I didn't say anything more. Bobbie did a good average day's work. But it was as if the Duracell battery was finally giving out. It was strange not to see a joint in his hand. At the end of the day he asked for his check. "I'm going to Kona. My girl moved there, and I'll get some work there. It's been nice working for ya."

We had a beer, chatted for a time, and then Bobbie said, "Aloha. I'll come back and check out the job and see how you did without me!" I knew I would miss Bobbie.

It wasn't a week later that a friend told me Bobbie was dead. Not wanting to smoke pot anymore, he tried heroin. (Of course that was not a bright thing to do, but tragically there are a lot of Bobbies out there.) The friend said, "I heard that the guy with Bobbie showed him how to inject himself. Bobbie injected himself, threw the syringe like a dart, and it stuck in the wall. And Bobbie apparently dropped dead." Bobbie was just twenty-eight when he died in 1986—a year older than my son.

8

Marijuana Is Medicine—and More

AFTER COLLEGE I MOVED TO THE LOS ANGELES AREA where I rented a room in Pasadena for $5.00 a week and went to work as a salesman for Grolier, publishers of *The Book of Knowledge* and the *Encyclopedia Americana.* Within six months I was fortunate to be made top salesman for the eleven western states and was then hired as a sales trainer. (In that position, I found utilizing hypnosis was a tremendous aid in assisting salespeople to learn their presentations in hours, rather than days.)

Soon I was residing in a chic apartment complex in Hollywood. Most of the residents of the tastefully furnished apartments were people working in the motion picture industry.

Artistry

I discovered that a large percentage of the choreographers, set directors, costume designers, actors, screenwriters, songwriters, and musicians who lived in the complex smoked marijuana. They did so while lounging around the swimming pool, rehearsing, designing, or writing for their productions. They said marijuana enhanced their creative abilities.

The jazz musicians I met said they frequently, though not always, got high before going into the recording studio. They said marijuana aided ideas to flow from them and onto the music tracks. With time seemingly slowed down when they used grass, the musicians were able to add notes to their music. I knew dozens of entertainers who used marijuana to help them get into their character roles or into their music. And never did I witness one of them violent or angry when pot was the only drug used.

Sleep

My primary marijuana use was as a sleep aid. My mother was magnificent. The only negative, which she couldn't have known at the time, was that when we as small children were put down for a nap she pulled the window shades and turned off the radio. If people dropped by to visit, she had them whisper. The result was the creation of exceedingly light sleepers. Consequently, my children were intentionally exposed to naps with natural light, the television on, or music playing. They are sound sleepers. When I've had a hard time with street noises and the like, I've taken a few puffs of pot and dissolved into dreamland. When one is tired, pot becomes a sleeping aid. When one is wide awake, it's a euphoric.

On June 6, 1995, newspaper headlines proclaimed, "Scientists Find Sleep Chemical." The findings were published in the journal *Science.* They are expected to lead to better drugs offering *natural* sleep, not analogous to sleep caused by sleeping pills. They will be a boon for forty million Americans who suffer from sleep deprivation. The chemical has been tested on cats and rats, which enjoyed a great sleep. A chemist from the Scripps Research Institute in La Jolla, California, Richard Lerner, stated:

> What's exciting is this is just like ordinary sleep. There is one close cousin to this compound, THC, the active ingredient in marijuana, which is not a substance that occurs naturally in the brain, but definitely has an influence on it.[1]

Muscle Spasms

After three years in the Los Angeles area I moved to Portland, Oregon, where I learned the construction business. A year later, after obtaining my pilot's license and purchasing my first airplane in my early twenties, I began construction work in Alaska. There I noted that marijuana was openly smoked socially and for medication.

One of my carpenters, "Shortie," was a World War II veteran who had been injured in the war. At the end of the first solid day on the job, I saw that he walked with one shoulder several inches lower than the other.

"Oh, my aching back, and I'm not kidding!" Shortie told me after I drove him home. "I've gotta tell ya, I have bad back spasms. What eases them more than anything are a few 'hits' of grass." He opened a small metal container on his coffee table, removed a rolled joint, and lit up, drawing in a few long inhalations. After a few minutes I heard an unwinding moan of relief. His facial muscles relaxed visibly. When he walked me to the door, his shoulders were straight. He sighed, "Now I'll be able to sleep."

Seasickness

After six months of working during the spring and summer in Alaska, I returned to Portland. I decided to travel via steamship to Seattle, by way of the Vancouver Islands. The ship was first class in every way. I was certain it would be a smooth cruise. Not so.

My stateroom window offered a spectacular view of the glaciers, fishing villages, and small, unpolluted towns. During the second night out, it was so rough that few passengers slept. In the morning about 150 queasy, almost seasick people, including me, were gingerly eating soft-boiled eggs, bacon, and prunes. The only breath of sunshine was a man, perhaps in his mid-sixties, with white hair and a handlebar mustache. He was actually solo dancing to the live music from the combo in the corner of the dining room as he smilingly balanced his full breakfast tray. How I envied him, wishing I had taken whatever seasick medication he had fortified himself with.

About halfway through our debatable breakfast, a boy of about twelve years started walking down the marble stairway toward the dining area. He was tenaciously holding the highly polished brass rail, then he began swaying back and forth. And the sounds began. "Aaaa. . . uuhhh . . ." All of us, I'm certain, were praying. "Please, don't get sick, little guy." Suddenly he threw up with such force that the vomit splattered all over the passengers sitting at the front table. Within ten seconds all of us were sick.

The marble floor was so slick from stomachs emptying that the stewards who were trying vainly to mop up the mess also became ill. A lady with blue hair got sick into the grand piano. Then the pianist threw up all over her head.

Attempting to recuperate, after a shower and change of clothes, I gingerly hobbled up to the promenade deck and slumped into a deck chair. There was only one other person taking in the breathtaking beauty of the glaciers and azure-blue ocean. It was the old gentlemen, the only one not ill in the dining room earlier. A blanket was pulled snugly to his chin. He was nine chairs to the stern of me. Out of his mouth protruded a long cigarette holder, reminding me of President Franklin Roosevelt. What caught my attention was the pungent sweet aroma of marijuana!

As casually as possible I moved to within two seats of him and introduced myself. "Nice to meet *you*, son," said the old man. "The name's Ronson." What amazed me is that he never attempted to stop smoking the grass. I couldn't keep this thought to myself. "I can't help but recognize the fragrance of good marijuana. Aren't you concerned that someone might report you to the captain?" He smiled and looked at me with his twinkling red eyes. (Grass dilates blood vessels.) "The only other person out here is you, son. Are you going to report me?" I felt foolish. "Of course not."

"Mr. Ronson, would you share with me how you refrained from being seasick?" I asked.

"Actually, the medication was prescribed by a doctor," he said. "I'm a retired structural engineer. There were times I was out on a scaffold ten or twelve stories above the street. I was concerned that the muscle spasms in my legs would make me fall.

"That condition led to depression, which encouraged my early retirement. Finally had to walk with a cane. Doctors prescribed medications that gave me vertigo, which assured a fall sooner than later. And their medicine didn't agree with my stomach.

"An old college buddy of mine from Stanford who is in internal medicine suggested I smoke marijuana. Hell, I hadn't smoked grass since we were buddies in school." Mr. Ronson took a deep inhalation, held his breath for about ten seconds, and exhaled in my direction. I really didn't mind that second-hand smoke.

"Nevertheless I remembered that it provided relaxation and a good night's sleep, with some damn sweet dreams," said Ronson as he continued his monologue. "My doc friend said that at the first tinge of muscle spasms, or of queasiness aboard ship, take a few puffs of pot. What it does to settle a stomach is a mystery he said, but it almost always does the trick. Ol' doc added, "'There's little question that it will take care of your depression, and those muscle spasms.'"

The old guy took his cigarette holder out of his mouth and looked lovingly at the joint, which was now a roach. He shook his windblown shaggy white hair as he admired the sun glistening on the blue glacier as we slowly plowed through the ocean swells.

"My leg spasms and depression were gone the second day. Now I just smoke a couple of times a week. Do you smoke grass, son?" "I do now and then," I offered. "I found that a glass or two of wine was relaxing, but frequently I ended up with a headache about midnight. With the grass I've never had a headache or hangover."

Mr. Ronson reached into his vest pocket and produced a nicely rolled joint. He smiled and handed it to me along with his lighter. I put it to my nose. It had that sweet aroma of fresh marijuana. I lit up and inhaled. After the second drag the stress and nausea began melting away. I felt more relaxed than I had in days. Ronson nodded approvingly, and said, "If they'd legalize the stuff, some of our stressed-out legislators would relax—without a hangover."

Nervousness

While residing at the new King Tower apartment building in Portland, I met a lovely lady who worked in the office of that building. She was beautiful in every way. We were married in June of 1952 in her home town of Lebanon, Oregon. We were both 24. We elected to leave Oregon and settled in Hayward, California. In addition to continuing construction work, I was doing advertising for a Hayward automobile dealer. One frosty February morning in 1957, a car drove in with five young Hawaiians. I asked how the weather was in Hawaii. One of them laughed, "In Hawaii, it's summer—all the time!" I went home for lunch and asked my wife if she would like to live in Hawaii. "Let's go, Dave!" was her answer. Two weeks later we were on a ship headed for the islands.

It wasn't long before I was working full time in television. I wrote and performed television commercials and interviewed dozens of celebrities. Among them were ballerina Dame Margot Fonteyn, the Reverend Billy Graham, Charlton Heston, Richard Widmark, and Bing Crosby.

In 1966 I had the pleasure of interviewing vocalist/actor/musician, and entertainer *extraordinaire*, Wayne Newton. In addition to his singing talents, Wayne plays seven instruments, yet I found him to be a humble person. I went to Las Vegas to film an interview with him and the world-famous trumpeter and band leader Harry James. After the interview, Wayne said, "If there's anything I can ever do for you, Dave, just let me know."

The following year, 1967, I was asked to produce and be master of ceremonies for an extravaganza benefit for the Disabled American Veterans to be presented at the exquisite Waikiki Shell under the stars and across the street from the warm, gentle Pacific Ocean.

Stress

There were 10,000 people in the audience. Hawaii's finest local stars as well as nationally recognized entertainers generously performed without pay. Even professionals become nervous prior to performing. One of them vomited. Someone passed a joint around, and a few of the more nervous took a couple of puffs. I empathized with them (so much so that I took a couple myself). Pot often works better than the Valium or alcohol that some entertainers use to relax prior to facing thousands of people. The strained expressions dissolved. Then those relaxed, mellow people went out on stage confident and professional—and performed their numbers beautifully.

One of the stage crew had also taken a couple of inhales of pot. A few minutes later he came over to me and told me that the smoke had caused him to remember that he had seen Wayne Newton checking into a Waikiki hotel. (Wayne was scheduled to do his own show at Honolulu's International Center Arena in a couple of days.) I recalled what Wayne had said in Las Vegas during our filmed interview. "If there's anything I can ever do for you."

"Please track down Wayne," I said. "Tell him our show is in progress, and mention in a joking way that he told me if he could ever do a favor—this would be the favor!"

Less than a half-hour later there was a smiling Wayne shaking my hand backstage. "We've been up all night traveling, Dave. But just tell me what I can do."

"If you would just sing one number that would be great, Wayne," I said.

"Glad to, Dave."

Wayne Newton went out on stage as though this was his big opportunity. He contributed three snappy numbers: "Bill Bailey, Won't You Please Come Home," "Bye Bye Blackbird," and "Red Roses for a Blue Lady." Wayne proved what a true trouper he is, going on unrehearsed with our big band. The audience screamed for more. "My momma always said when you're with nice people, never overstay your welcome," he said with a smile. Wayne is an example of the stars who generously offer their talents for a worthwhile cause. He was not present when the joint was passed around, nor was he aware that it was put to use.

Other Benefits of Marijuana

After 15 years living on Oahu, our family, now with two youngsters, moved to the majestic Big Island of Hawaii in 1973.

While on the Big Island, I produced *The Voice of Hawaii*, a weekly half-hour talk television show, through a CBS affiliate. The show featured interviews with judges, politicians, visiting celebrities, and even former prison inmates. One ex-prisoner said he was able to kick his heroin habit, which he got in prison, by switching to nonaddictive marijuana. During the 1970s, pot was as close as it could be to being legal in Hawaii. People smoked in parks, on the beaches, and in theaters.

I interviewed the well-known attorney Hyman Greenstein when he was running for governor of Hawaii. At that time, in addition to his law practice, he was representing NORML for Hawaii. A few years later he contacted me and suggested a novel way to get the audience's attention and demonstrate that pot users can speak, think, and behave quite rationally and normally. He suggested that we smoke a joint on live television! We did. We discussed marijuana's medical benefits, and by our example, viewers saw that those using it could act completely normal. The interview was a success, as scores of positive letters attested. Afterward, a police officer who was outside the studio exclaimed, "Great show!" We never heard anything else from the police.

I constantly met people who were helped by marijuana as medicine. For two years I participated in the Jerry Lewis Telethon for the State of Hawaii. I learned that the majority of people in wheelchairs suffer from muscle spasms. Many of them use marijuana to ease those spasms.

The medical use of marijuana was intriguing. Off camera I interviewed literally hundreds of people who used marijuana. Many smoked it to neutralize the agonizing effects of chemotherapy.

Depression and Alcoholism

Much of our savings during thirty years in Hawaii was invested in land on the Big Island. In February of 1983, volcanic eruptions began on the east flank of the island and have not ceased as of this writing. Prime properties, including most of mine, were devoured by the lava eruption, said by Hawaiians to be caused by Pele, the ravenous "goddess of fire."

At the time my parents, who lived in the wine country of picturesque Sonoma, California, were in need of some TLC. Mom, at eighty-five, had contracted dreaded Alzheimer's disease. Dad was ninety-five, still healthy, driving his car capably, and taking care of Mom. I felt it was time to be with them. Having been widowed, remarried, and divorced, I was free to go. In mid-1987, I completed business activities in Hawaii and left for Sonoma to move in with Mom and Dad and to *be there* for them.

It wasn't like the old times when Mom would cook her marvelous meals, always with a smile and love of cooking. She did insist on making me toast. But instead of placing the bread in the toaster she inserted two napkins. Dad had been coping and never phoned or wrote telling just how bad Mom had become. He was bathing and dressing her. Often during the night she would leave silently and wander around town till we found her. We resolved that she should be in a convalescent home that offered twenty-four-hour medical attention.

During fourteen months of living with Dad, we became closer friends than ever. I took him on picnics, and we enjoyed long conversations about projects and adventures we'd both had over the years. During that time I drew the floor plans for a home that would back up to the exquisite Sebastiani vineyard.

For the first time, I noted despair in Dad. He was depressed over Mom's mental incompetence. I briefly thought of obtaining some grass and having him smoke a little but decided against it. He trusted me implicitly, but I couldn't help remembering his negative feelings about marijuana when I had mentioned it as a youngster. However, I was convinced that had he not been brainwashed by government horror reports, he would have been a good candidate and experienced far less depression over Mom's sad condition. He did have his couple of drinks of Scotch before dinner. I elected to leave it at that.

Marijuana as a Reducer of Alcohol and Other Drugs

When dear Mom was confined to the convalescent home with Alzheimer's disease, our family was heartbroken, especially Dad. He never stopped loving that gallant lady who was his best friend for so many years. She was also her children's best friend and a beloved friend of everyone who knew her. Dad would say, "You'll be home soon, Mom," and I'd see a tear drop from his anxious ninety-six-year-old face. He knew better. The convalescent home, we all understood, was Mom's last stop.

A "convalescent" home is a pathetic place. The odor of urine floods visitors' nostrils. Patients are tied into their wheelchairs, suffering muscle spasms and claustrophobia. They are fed like babies. They grit their teeth, real and false, against the indignity, and the food dribbles out of their mouths.

One day when Mom was coherent, she said, "Son, many of the people here, thought to be senile because they slur their words and act depressed and have memory loss, are alcoholics. Some told me how they would fall down when they were drinking. I've seen them with their hidden bottles their friends bring them. And most of them have been drinking for years."

For the older population, the first drug of choice is alcohol. The second is Valium. When the two are ingested to numb the pain in an already depressed person, the body responds with increased depression. An older, depressed alcoholic runs the highest risk of committing suicide. A 1988 Mayo Clinic study reported that 41 percent of persons age sixty-five and older enrolled in the clinic's alcoholism treatment program first showed symptoms of alcoholism after age sixty. Could marijuana come to the rescue? I dream of the day when marijuana will be as acceptable to the public as aspirin.

Can you think of a botanical that might overcome depression, increase appetite and well-being, and produce a daily smiling, mellow senior citizen? Imagine how those "caged" convalescent patients would act about an hour after their doctor-approved brownies were passed out. Valium, tranquilizers, sleeping pills, alcohol, and a lot of other medications would be in jeopardy, and these drugs are very big business, especially with senior citizens. Pot does not cause violence or self-destruction. Have you ever heard of spousal or family violence when the only drug used was marijuana? Have you ever heard of anyone smoking marijuana and then holding up a bank? (They'd probably start laughing on the way to the heist and decide to have a snack instead.) Have you ever heard of anyone lying in the gutter with just a joint in his hand? Or have you heard of anyone smoking marijuana and then committing suicide?

Marijuana Psychotherapy?

There may well be a day when violent, sullen, and hostile prisoners are given marijuana during their sessions with the prison psychiatrist. (They wouldn't be driving home after the therapy session.) Marijuana is a bit of a truth serum. It makes it easier to express oneself and gives one a desire to communicate. It makes the smoker relax. Hostility would melt like snow on a beach in Waikiki. I personally witnessed that phenomenon when I rode a motorcycle during my younger and wilder years. There are bikers who not only love to ride but also to fight. I've seen brutal fights stopped when someone called "time out"—and handed the fighters a joint. Soon they were mellow and—surprising to me—frequently put their arms around each other or shook hands.

A prisoner given marijuana would then be open to psychotherapy. As conditions are today, most prisoners receive no therapy and are more hostile, resentful, and violent than ever when they are released into society. To prevent recidivism, it is critical that when the prisoners return to society, they feel they were helped to make long-lasting behavioral and attitudinal changes in prison.

Recidivism is costing taxpayers billions of dollars because prisoners frequently leave their cells hardened, more anti-social, and determined to get even with society for locking them up. Prison only locks up the problem. It doesn't cure it.

The system must be changed so that instead of receiving punishment, prisoners receive treatment for the problems that caused them to be in prison.

My Hope for the Future

I hope to see marijuana-geriatric research. I predict that under a doctor's supervision, hundreds of thousands of older people could be treated with marijuana and weaned away from alcohol and nicotine. The alcohol hangover demonstrates all too painfully that one's body is attempting to reject the poison of alcohol.

Marijuana would be appropriate in controlled settings as part of a doctor's therapy for certain patients who find it difficult to express themselves. For this to become reality we'll need a campaign of truth about marijuana. It is my most earnest hope that the government will allow research into the medicinal properties of marijuana.

There are no "Marijuana 101" classes in medical school, and most medical doctors know very little about the drug's therapeutic powers. When these powers are truly understood by doctors and by lawmakers, marijuana will be close to positive legislation.

Without grass, people who can't keep food down because of extreme nausea are dying in needless agony. I hope the administration in Washington will be persuaded to see the truth about the medical benefits of marijuana, study it, face the reasons why it is illegal, and change its status to legal. Marijuana must be legalized in all states for the millions of patients who currently are subjected to toxic medications that weaken their immune system, rather than strengthen it.

Washington ought to recognize that current prescribed medications subject innumerable patients to severe side effects. It is unconscionable that for the millions of physically ill marijuana is illegal and that, further, these patients are the targets of constant false fear-mongering.

Marijuana prohibition is causing unnecessary deaths as former users switch to lethal drugs. It is the *unavailability* of marijuana that causes pot users to use far more dangerous drugs. The country must be educated that marijuana is not dangerous. The public and the government have opened their minds to accept the fact that nicotine kills hundreds of thousands each year. Now they must open their minds to the fact that marijuana has never killed one person and that it offers amazing medical benefits.

On June 20, 1995, on a Discovery Channel special, "The Cronkite Report: The Drug Dilemma," former CBS news anchorman Walter Cronkite—regarded internationally as one of the most trusted figures in America—called the drug war a failure. He called for a bipartisan commission to study alternatives to prohibition. He concluded by saying, "We cannot go into tomorrow with the same formulas that are failing today."

There will never be a drug-free America. We can aspire to that end but that's not the world we live in. Political leaders must have courage and admit that reality and vote for a proven way to reduce human suffering.

Nothing is perfect, but marijuana thus far is the safest drug nature has created.

9

Hemp Is Not Marijuana!

ARCHAEOLOGISTS HAVE FOUND EVIDENCE OF HEMP being used in China more than 10,000 years ago. When twisted strands were found to be far stronger than individual strands, the Chinese began spinning and weaving fibers into fabric, which took the place of animal skins. In China hemp was used for making shoes and clothes.

The Chinese cherished the mulberry plant because it was the food most eaten by silkworms. However, silk was only for the rich, whereas hemp was for everyone. Hemp was so respected, along with the mulberry plant, that the Chinese called their country "the land of mulberry and hemp."[1]

Hemp Was as American as Hot Dogs, and Just as Safe

By 1630 half of the winter clothing worn by Americans, and all of their summer clothing, contained hemp fiber. During the Revolutionary War, demand for the plant skyrocketed. In 1850 it was confirmed that hemp was being grown on 8,327 plantations and was America's third largest crop. It was exceeded only by cotton and tobacco.[2]

Hemp and marijuana must be separated if either or both are to be relegalized. They are frequently confused, even by experts. An entire book could easily be written about the thousands of uses of hemp and why it should never have been included with the prohibition of marijuana. Following is a brief look at amazing hemp.

Hemp contains a minimal 0.3 percent THC.[3] It does not intoxicate, and with almost no THC content, it is not medicine. Hemp is a valuable source of food for birds and humans and of fiber for strong, durable cloth or paper that can last hundreds of years.

Just as it was wrong to make marijuana illegal, it was dishonest to declare hemp illegal. They're in the same family, but hemp's THC content is negligible. Hemp might be compared to a cherry tree that doesn't produce cherries. The tree is valuable for its wood, but not for its fruit.

The argument against hemp production does not hold up to scrutiny: hemp is worthless as the drug marijuana. It is questionable whether eating the seeds or smoking hemp would even register in a sensitive blood or urine test, and it surely would not get a user high.

The problem is that the impotent hemp plant resembles the marijuana plant and is therefore *possibly* confusing to government authorities. Nevertheless, they realize that hemp is competition to petrochemical companies (fuel for cars), the cotton and timber industry, and producers of synthetic fabrics.

Hemp's Economic History

Hemp may have been the first crop cultivated by humans, as early as 8000 B.C. in the Middle East. Hemp textile industries were introduced at about the same time in human development as pottery. Hemp provided the sails and rigging for ships that engaged in worldwide commerce and made Columbus's trip to the New World possible. Other fibers would have decayed somewhere in the mid-Atlantic.

Hemp replaced papyrus as the source of the paper that eventually fostered the spread of written knowledge. Hemp was the largest cash crop in the world until the late nineteenth century, when the products of new technology replaced it, causing it to be thought of as obsolete, which it is not.

Hemp seed was also widely respected and used as food for humans and for birds. The hemp seed increased the health of birds and produced higher quality feathers.

Hemp was used for centuries for clothing, sails for ships, and the canvas used on the covered wagons going west. The clothing for the Continental Army was made from hemp fibers. In fact, clothing for all countries was made from hemp fiber until the early 1900s. George Washington grew hemp on his farm in 1765.

In the formerly lush Himalayan regions of Bangladesh, Tibet, and Nepal, there is now only a light moss covering barren lands as flash floods continue to wash millions of tons of topsoil away. Hemp seeds put down a ten-to-twelve inch root in just thirty days. This compares to the one-inch root put down by rye or barley grass subsidized by the U.S. government. The hemp seeds would prevent flooding—and starvation.

Hemp was the major cash crop in the United States, including most of the areas now suffering from family farm foreclosures, until just before the Great Depression in the late twenties and early thirties. It is still a viable cash crop and could be grown on marginal lands, between crop seasons, or on fallow land to enrich the soil. Hemp is the best energy biomass crop identified to date, and it could produce the raw materials to provide renewed economic growth in rural and "rust belt" communities.

With some 50,000 commercial uses, hemp is the most versatile, renewable, natural resource on the planet. Hemp alone will provide billions of dollars in annual revenue if it is again allowed to be used for textiles, food, fuel, cordage, paper, and thousands of other uses.

The Many Uses of Hemp

Hemp as Fuel

Biomass is the term used to describe all biologically produced matter. Hemp is the only biomass resource capable of making America energy independent. About 6 percent of contiguous United States land area put into cultivation for biomass could supply all current demands for oil and gas. The foundation upon which this may be achieved is the emerging concept of "energy farming," wherein farmers grow and harvest crops for biomass conversion to fuels.[4]

Pyrolysis is the technique of applying high heat to organic matter. Methanol-powered automobiles and reduced emissions from coal-fired power plants can be accomplished by biomass conversion to fuel utilizing pyrolysis technology. This could save the American family farm while turning the American heartland once again into a prosperous source of clean energy production. Biomass conversion by pyrolysis has many environmental and economic advantages over coal and oil.

Pyrolysis facilities could run three shifts a day. Some 68 percent of the energy of the raw biomass could be contained in the charcoal and fuel oils made at the facilities. This charcoal has nearly the same heating value in British thermal units (BTU) as coal, with virtually no sulfur. When countries use charcoal instead of coal, the problems of acid rain will begin to disappear.

Hemp is the number one biomass product: ten tons per acre can be produced in approximately four months. It is a woody plant containing 77 percent cellulose. (Trees produce 60 percent cellulose.) This energy crop can be harvested with equipment readily available. Hemp is drought resistant, making it an ideal crop in the dry western regions of the country.

At the rate we're going, by the year 2000 the American government will have to take a good look at our petroleum reserves. Will we then go to war with the Arabs for the privilege of driving our cars? Will we strip our land for coal and poison our air so we can drive our automobiles an extra 100 years? Will we destroy our forests for our energy needs? Hemp is nonpolluting.

It is time the government once again respond to our economic emergency, as it did in World War II, to permit our farmers to grow American hemp so we can once again become energy independent and pollution free.[5]

Hemp for Clothing

Fabrics manufactured from hemp are more insulating, softer, stronger, more water absorbent, and longer lasting than cotton fabrics. Hemp fiber holds its shape as well as polyester, but it "breathes" and is biodegradable because it is completely organic. It has been valued for its durability since before recorded history. It can be woven to be as coarse as burlap, as smooth as silk, or as intricate as lace. The canvas sails on generations of ships and the original Levi jeans were all made of hemp. The quality of this natural fiber has yet to be surpassed.

Hemp for Paper

Paper made from hemp lasts many times longer than paper made of wood pulp, without yellowing, cracking, or otherwise deteriorating. Hemp pulp does not require as much of the acids needed to break it down as wood, does not cause dioxin pollution, and has been called the "archivist's perfect paper." Paper made from wood fiber lasts only twenty-five to eighty years because of its acid content, while paper made from hemp fibers lasts for hundreds of years. The Declaration of Independence and the U.S. Constitution were both originally drafted on hemp. Restriction of hemp has led to the destruction of about 70 percent of American forests since 1937.[6]

Hemp: "New Billion Dollar Crop"

When I was ten, my favorite magazine was *Popular Mechanics*. In February 1938, *Popular Mechanics* came out with a story that caused my attention to be directed toward hemp. It was the first time I had understood the word "billion," referring to money. I had no idea of the tremendous versatility of hemp or how much it could help the American economy. The title of the story was "New Billion Dollar Crop." At today's dollars, the title would read "New Eleven Billion Dollar Crop."

The story said American farmers were promised a new cash crop with an annual value of several hundred million dollars. "It is hemp," the article said, "a crop that will not compete with other American products. Instead, it will displace imports of raw material and manufactured products." The story went into detail from the farmers' point of view, explaining that "Hemp is an easy crop to grow and will yield from three to six tons per acre on any land that will grow corn, wheat, or oats. It has a short growing season, so that it can be planted after other crops are in. It can be grown in any state of the union. The long roots penetrate and break the soil to leave it in perfect condition for the next year's crop."

As the years passed, I continued to learn of more uses of the extraordinary hemp plant than I ever dreamed possible.

In 1942, during World War II, our country desperately needed hemp for our military. It was *mandatory* for farmers to attend the showing of the film, made by the U.S. government, *Hemp for Victory* (Department of Agriculture, 1942). Hemp harvesting machinery suddenly became available at little or no cost to the farmers. Some 300,000 acres of hemp were to be harvested by 1943. Farmers and their sons were exempt from serving time in the military if they grew hemp. (Now they'd serve time in a penitentiary.)

Here is an excerpt from the sound track of *Hemp for Victory*:

> In 1942, patriotic farmers at the government's request planted 36,000 acres of seed hemp, an increase of several thousand percent. The goal for 1943 is 50,000 acres of seed hemp . . . Now with the Philippine and East Indian sources of hemp in the hands of the Japanese and shipment of jute from India curtailed, American hemp must meet the needs of our Army and Navy as well as our industry . . . [Here we see workers] spinning American hemp into rope yarn or twine in the old Kentucky River mill at Frankfort, Kentucky. All such plants will presently be turning out products spun from American-grown hemp: twine of various kinds for tying and upholsters

> work; rope for marine rigging and towing; for hay forks, derricks, and heavy duty tackle; light duty fire hose; thread for shoes for millions of American soldiers; and parachute webbing for our paratroopers. As for the United States Navy, every battleship requires 34,000 feet of rope . . . American hemp will go on duty again: hemp for mooring ships; hemp for tow lines; hemp for tackle and gear; hemp for countless naval uses both on ship and shore. Just as in the days when Old Ironsides sailed the seas victorious with her hempen shrouds and hempen sails. Hemp for victory!

The above motion picture script produced by our Department of Agriculture might have added that the U.S.S. Constitution (Old Ironsides) could not have sailed without hemp. In addition to her sails, her log books, maps and flags, even the Bibles were made from the fiber of hemp.

The Current Status of Hemp

In history class we condemned other countries for burning books or hiding historical facts from their citizens. In the United States, however, hemp history has been eradicated! Have you ever read any history books about hemp grown for "victory" during World War II? Or even the history of marijuana or hemp? This dereliction of integrity is a smear on history.

Hemp cultivation is legal in many eastern European countries. In February 1993, England legalized hemp cultivation. British Home Office Minister Michael Jace, in an official press release announcing the change, noted that "these plants have been grown on the continent for more than 20 years without any problems—this decision will allow United Kingdom farmers to gain a share of the market currently occupied by European Community partners."[7]

The Drug Enforcement Administration stubbornly refuses to recognize the distinction between marijuana and hemp. Soon, the United States may hold the dubious distinction of being the only major economic power to prohibit cultivation of a crop that provides the best hope for halting the destruction of the world's forests—as well as eliminating starvation throughout third world countries at practically no cost.

10

Pot/Drug War Atrocities

THIS CHAPTER CONTAINS A FEW TESTIMONIALS and stories of persecution, examples of the thousands injured, imprisoned, wrongfully punished, or killed because of the war on drugs.

Atrocities Occur Everywhere

Even if they were nowhere near their cars when they used pot, millions of Americans could lose their driver's licenses for at least six months if convicted of marijuana use. A state can lose a percentage of highway funds unless it participates in this latest federal law supported by California's Governor Pete Wilson. California itself stands to lose $100 million in highway aid.

As of October 1994, federal laws require *three-month* license suspensions for convictions of *driving* under the influence of alcohol. Consider how unfair it is for a person with AIDS, cancer, or some other illness, or just smoking grass in the privacy of home for relaxation, *not even in a car*, to be punished for twice as long as a drunk driver.

On September 15, 1995, NORML's California state coordinator, Dale Gieringer, Ph.D., felt he had convinced the legislature to reject the discriminatory "Smoke a Joint, Lose Your License" law. However, on February 20, 1997, the California Assembly voted to continue taking away people's driver's licenses if they were convicted of possessing marijuana, even if they weren't in their cars. Then on March 10, 1997, the state senate staged a mutiny against the federal mandate and voted to snuff out this unfair law.[1]

On March 20, 1997, I asked Dr. Gieringer about the two bills being presented to the governor and his opinion as to whether Governor Pete Wilson would continue the dismal law. "Absolutely. He's made it quite clear. The question is whether he's willing to modify it." Gieringer added, "Polls show that a solid majority of Californians support medical marijuana and oppose 'Smoke a Joint, Lose Your License.' Governor Wilson should stop defending bankrupt federal marijuana laws that are needlessly clogging our courts and creating crime."[2]

The U.S. Department of Transportation's National Highway Traffic Safety Administration (NHTSA) had this to say:

> The incidence and role of drugs in fatally injured drivers (Terhune et al., 1992) indicate that marijuana—if not consumed in combination with alcohol or other drugs—is not a major road-safety hazard. Alcohol is."[3]

In the state of Washington, no advertised rewards are offered to encourage citizens to turn in murderers, rapists, robbers, child molesters, or criminals who prey on the vulnerable. Even hard-drug dealers have no advertised bounty on their heads. However, there is a well-publicized $5,000 reward for informants who will report marijuana gardens.[4]

Consider this story of a kidney patient using marijuana as medicine:

> I'm an end-stage renal patient on kidney dialysis three days a week. I was growing and using marijuana as medicine. I was arrested and charged with felony cultivation. When the police entered my trailer they found one plant. They brought so many police some had to wait outside. Several weapons, flak

jackets, ski masks and an assortment of vehicles were present. My neighbors thought I had killed someone. They were appalled that the police did this to me for one plant, plus the tremendous cost to taxpayers.

I was taken to jail in handcuffs. They said I would have to pay for my urine test. I told them, "I don't pee! I'm on a dialysis machine. My kidneys don't work." Not wanting to pay to bring someone into the jail to administer dialysis three times a week, I was released with a fine.

J. Largo, Florida[5]

Possessing wild hemp meant life in prison for this person:

I am an inmate in a Alabama prison, serving a life sentence without parole for possession of 10.9 pounds of the hemp that grows wild in Missouri, Kansas, Nebraska, Iowa, and several other states. This all started out as a joke because this stuff looked like marijuana. I brought some of it back from Missouri. It will *not* make you high no matter how much of it you smoke.

The Alabama crime lab said it was marijuana, and the trial judge denied us permission to obtain a sample and have our own testing done to see if it had any drug in it. I feel like the only reason I am here is because I am a poor person and had to have an Alabama court-appointed attorney. He only talked to me two times for less than five minutes at a time before I went to trial.

Vernon McEhay, Springville, Alabama

P.S.: There are several people in the Alabama Department of Corrections, serving life and life without parole sentences for marijuana. One man here got life for one joint.[6]

A Bayview, Idaho, teenager faces a possible life prison term for selling a fellow student $40 worth of marijuana. Kootenai County Magistrate Paul McCabe ruled that the fifteen-year-old boy will be tried as an adult under the state's tough Drug-Free School Zone law, which carries a minimum sentence of five years and a maximum life term for conviction of selling drugs near a school facility.[7]

On November 11, 1994, the Associated Press reported the story of Bill Best, a sixteen-year-old Norwell, Massachusetts, boy who couldn't tolerate the pain and nausea of his weekly chemotherapy treatments. "I feel the medicine is killing me instead of helping me," he said. Bill packed his duffel bag, sold his few precious possessions, and ran away. The tragedy here is that Bill could have been spared that pain and the vomiting caused by chemotherapy had his doctor been able to prescribe a few inhalations of marijuana prior to his chemotherapy. Parents and most doctors are terrified of marijuana because of its illegality and the untrue "facts" relating to this herb.

Sod farmer Donald Clark, resident of Myakka City, Florida, in the early eighties, grew some marijuana in a swamp. So did a lot of his farmer neighbors. Clark was arrested in 1985, did a little time, and ended up on probation. A few years later federal authorities decided that Clark's case had been a "conspiracy" (they should know what *that* is) and charged Clark again. The courts said it wasn't double jeopardy. Clark gave pot plants to other farmers and came up with improved growing methods. So the authorities said he was the ringleader.

His twenty-seven codefendants made a deal and pleaded guilty. Clark would not. He turned down an offer to plead guilty in exchange for six-and-a-half years in prison. He asked for a trial, was convicted, and got the only sentence possible under our tough new laws: life in prison. This fifty-year-old ex-sod farmer was shipped off for life. (In federal prison there is no time off for good behavior.) Even the judge said she thought the law was too harsh.[8]

Here's another horror story, this time from south of the border:

> I was arrested in my rented apartment in San Miguel de Allende, Guanajuato, by Mexican federal agents on October 14, 1990, for the "horrendous crime" of bringing 15 marijuana seeds into Mexico and growing my own—50 three inch high clones in a three-by-three foot box. This was strictly for personal use—I do not traffic or sell drugs.
>
> I have reason to believe the D.E.A. had a hand in my arrest—I bought my indoor equipment with credit cards and had it shipped via UPS. Now for the shocker. My sentence for

this "crime," handed down in August 1991 was an incredible 11 years!

If you are a foreigner (read American) there are no benefits, no good time, no work time, etc. An American will do 70% to 80% of his sentence. A Mexican national will do approximately 40%. I am a 45-year-old American citizen with a valid U.S. passport traveling in Mexico on a visa. My reason for being here is business. I buy folk art in Mexico and sell it in the Los Angeles area where I grew up, and where my family and I live. If this (Mexican) prison is any reflection, the War on Drugs is a dismal failure perpetrated by politicians on both sides of the border, but the pressure mainly comes from the U.S. government. Of a population of some 350 people in this prison, seven are Americans.

Sincerely yours,
Jason De Mayo
Salgedo 31
Guanajuato, Gto. 36000,
Mexico[9]

This Colorado resident couldn't believe the sentence he could receive for growing three marijuana plants:

On September 20, the local police department executed a search warrant on my home while I was away in the mountains. My nosy and ungracious neighbor had called them to report suspicious activities concerning gardening activities in my backyard. Yes, you guessed it. I was growing the "evil weed" in my backyard for personal use. I grew 3 plants, of which one had flowered and I had harvested four days earlier.

First they wanted to set our bond at $50,000 each (for my wife and me), though it ended up $5,000 each. I find this to be way out of line for growing marijuana for personal use. Second, since they weighed everything I grew, mostly leaves from the two plants still growing, they claim it was 4 pounds and therefore I was intending to sell it. We were charged with cultivation and possession with intent. The judge told us we would get 4 to 12 years in prison for these crimes, double if aggravating circumstances are found! Is this for real? These punishments are way out of line for the crimes committed. I knew growing pot was illegal but I never thought it was this illegal!

R. & C. H.
Loveland, Colorado[10]

A Georgia man is serving seventeen-and-a-half years in prison for what crime?

I suspect it's going to take considerably more than this letter to awaken Americans to the horrific effects of our "drug war," but I must try. Technically, I suppose, I'm guilty of conspiracy to import marijuana. I don't feel guilty. My lawyer says I haven't a chance of beating the conviction on appeal.

I agreed to sell my fishing boat to a group of people who intended (I later discovered) to smuggle pot. The fact that I backed out of the deal, took my boat back, and saw to it that they couldn't use my boat to smuggle, didn't stop me from being arrested, tried, convicted, and sentenced to 17.5 years in prison, simply for knowing about a plot to smuggle marijuana (conspiracy).

I'm 48 years old. I've now lost everything I spent my life working hard to earn. Family, friends, home, business, everything—gone! Be advised, folks, there's no more of this "do a couple of years and you're out" stuff. In the federal system, maximum good time is 54 days per year, with no parole. The earliest I can be released is June 27, 2006.

To the people of America I say "*beware!*" The last world leader to successfully turn a country's people against each other was Adolf Hitler. Wake up! Wake up I say! The dreadful record of history is stuck in a devastating groove.

Sincerely yours,
James P. Calhoun
Jesup, Georgia[11]

And now, here's a story of entrapment:

I was a college graduate hoping to attend medical school—Now I'm sitting in a federal prison for the next five

> years. Police ensnared a friend and pressured him to set me up; with a very low price for buying pot.
>
> S. K.
> Tallahassee, Florida[12]

For eighteen years the DEA has had an ongoing, unwritten payment policy designed to "encourage" package openings at Seattle-Tacoma Airport. Those "rewards" vary between $500 and $1,000. If money or drugs are found, airline employees are instructed to call the DEA. Thus the government successfully vilifies all Fourth Amendment protections against unreasonable search and seizure. Surprisingly, airlines in Seattle allow their employees to open packages they deem "suspicious," security threat or not.[13]

A California man lost his home for having just three marijuana plants:

> Hello! Would you please send me information on forfeiture? I had ten acres and a beautiful house and barn that I built myself. The Feds confiscated it because I had three pot plants growing on the property. That's pretty ridiculous, unjust and unconstitutional.
>
> Jeffrey
> Manton, California[14]

This disabled war veteran was abused by the DEA, an agency of the government he once proudly served:

> My home was raided on September 27, 1991. It was a "no-knock" search for marijuana cultivation. I have no left leg and my hips have been replaced, along with my knees, left shoulder and elbow. I have had a kidney transplant also, and I smoke marijuana for nausea.
>
> These animals put me on the floor and tore my home apart. They found a bong (pot pipe). They gave me a citation and walked out. They left my home with no doors on it, and me on the floor. It took me about 40 minutes to find a way to get off the floor.

> I spent ten years in the service so that people could live free in this country, but I guess things don't work out that way in America.
>
> Guy
> Nebraska[15]

In my early twenties, I had a friend my age who was a writer for an advertising agency. Bert told me that many of his colleagues during "think tank" sessions used grass to brainstorm creative ideas. He joined in and reported there was no doubt that creative ideas flowed much faster with the absence of the usual stress. He said he was complimented on the quality of his work. He told how drinking alcohol used to be fun to break the ice at social gatherings. However, he said now and then a mean streak surfaced with alcohol and he took it out on his wife, sometimes physically. "With pot I'm always relaxed and mellow and now I'm a pussycat with my wife. At cocktail parties I just have a glass of sparkling water and no one knows the difference."

Bert went to a dry cleaners to retrieve some clothes. He waited longer than usual for the clerk to locate them. Sirens were heard as several police cars pulled up to the curb. Bert thought, "Boy, what luck. I'm going to see some action!" He did. Four police officers stormed into the cleaners with guns drawn. Suddenly Bert was terrified as he realized he was the "action." Panic overtook him and he dived through a plate glass window and began running, recalling that he had a marijuana cigarette in the pocket of his sport jacket. He ended up with severe lacerations on his face and body.

For resisting arrest and possession of the marijuana joint, he was sentenced to two years in prison. The sentence was later reduced to one year. He was repeatedly raped in jail. Overcome by shame and the loss of his job, within a year of his release he committed suicide.

Tom Cahill of Fort Bragg, California, is a photographer and journalist. In years past, Tom was a victim of prison rape.

Since 1984, he has directed People Organized To Stop Rape of Imprisoned Persons. He estimated prison rapes in the United States at 43,000 per day, a 1993 estimate.

I spoke with Mr. Cahill on July 14, 1994. He related that he was so badly injured during his prison rapes that he is on a government pension. He emphasized that upon his release from prison, marijuana coupled with psychotherapy helped him cope with the trauma and humiliation in the early years after his ordeal. He said, "It's frightening to contemplate the additional thousands of rapes that will now take place with the "Three Strikes and You're Out" law.[16]

Judge Charles W. Hallect of the District of Columbia Court of General Sessions, in testimony before the House of Representatives Special Subcommittee on Alcoholism and Narcotics on September 18, 1969, explained why he no longer gives jail sentences to youthful marijuana smokers:

> If I send a marijuana offender to jail even for 30 days, Senator, he is going to be a victim of the most brutal type of homosexual, unnatural, perverted assaults and attacks that you can imagine, and anybody who tells you it doesn't happen in that jail day in and day out is simply not telling you the truth. How in God's name, Senator, can I send anybody to that jail knowing that? How can I send some poor young kid who gets caught by some zealous policeman who wants to make his record on a narcotics arrest? How can I send that kid to that jail?
>
> I can't do it. So I put him on probation or I suspend the sentence and everybody says the judge doesn't care. The judge doesn't care about drugs, lets them all go. You just simply can't treat these kinds of people like that.[17]

Dr. David E. Smith of the Haight Ashbury Free Medical Clinic in San Francisco reported in June 1971 that among the psychiatric patients served by his clinic were twenty-five young men with serious psychoses—all of whom were imprisoned for possession of marijuana and all of whom suffered psychiatric breakdowns following homosexual rape while they were incarcerated.[18]

Another death caused by a "no-knock" drug raid occurred in Garland, Texas, in 1991: Wearing ski masks and dressed in black, police burst into a mobile home. They were waving guns as they thundered in. They kicked down the door of a bedroom that Kenneth Baulch shared with his seventeen-month-old son. Baulch was seen holding something. A police officer shot and killed him. The object was an ashtray. Police said Baulch was advancing on them. A lawsuit contends he was shot in the back.[19]

An additional "no-knock" drug raid also occurred in Titusville, Florida, in 1989: The home of a fifty-eight-year-old painter, Charles DiGristine, was raided during a "no-knock" night intrusion. Police discharged a concussion grenade as they smashed through DiGristine's front door wearing dark clothing and black masks. His wife screamed. DiGristine ran into their bedroom to get a pistol. An officer crashed into the bedroom. Gunfire was exchanged and the officer was killed. The only drug found was a small amount of pot owned by DiGristine's sixteen-year-old son. DiGristine was charged with first degree murder. A jury acquitted him.[20]

An innocent man was handcuffed and kicked by DEA agents in Guthrie, Oklahoma, in 1991: An ax was used by the agents to break down the door of an innocent man's home. He was handcuffed and kicked in front of his wife and daughters before agents realized they were at the wrong address. They departed without so much as an apology.[21]

An innocent mother was shot in the neck and killed by a SWAT team in 1992 in Everett, Washington: A police SWAT team killed Robin Pratt in a "no-knock" raid while serving out an arrest warrant on her husband. The husband was released after the allegations on which the arrest warrant was based turned out to be false. The *Seattle Times* summarized the raid this way:

> SWAT members threw a fifty-pound battering ram through a sliding-glass door that landed near Pratt's six-year-old daughter and five-year old niece. As deputy Anthony Aston rounded a corner to the Pratts' bedroom, he encountered Robin Pratt. SWAT members were yelling, "Get down," and she

> started to crouch to her knees. She looked up at Aston and said, "Please don't hurt my children." Aston had his gun pointed at her and fired, shooting her in the neck. According to attorney John Muenster, she was alive another one to two minutes but could not speak because her throat had been destroyed by the bullet. She was then handcuffed, lying face down.[22]

This is only a handful of the thousands of stories that occur daily.

The Clinton Administration's View of Marijuana

President Clinton's appointed director of the Drug Enforcement Administration, Thomas Constantine, has with bias undertaken the task of waging war against illicit drug consumers. The primary casualty of any war is truth. In a May 28, 1994, *Washington Times* interview, Constantine stated:

> Many times people talk about the nonviolent drug offender. That is a rare species. There is not some sterile drug type not involved in violence—there is no drug user who is contributing some good to the community—They are contributing nothing but evil.[23]

Perhaps you would like to keep in mind, Mr. Constantine, that President Kennedy smoked marijuana. Former Vice President Dan Quayle smoked marijuana. Vice President Al Gore smoked marijuana. Newt Gingrich smoked marijuana. Supreme Court Justice Clarence Thomas smoked marijuana.

Those are but a few among hundreds of our lawmakers who have smoked marijuana. And many no doubt continue to do so.

It's tragic that politicians who are discovered to have smoked marijuana, such as Representative Susan Molinari, Bob Dole's choice to give the keynote address at the GOP's 1996 convention, all announce how bad they were to have smoked pot. Molanari said, "It was the wrong thing to do. If I knew then what I know now, I wouldn't have done it." What she knew then, and what she knows now, is that it's illegal.

If only Molinari, Clarence Thomas, and other political pot users had said something like, "Pot helped me relax and sleep before those final exams. Pot is far less harmful than other illegal drugs and most legal ones. But it is illegal, and that made it wrong. Perhaps we should work to change the law." Wouldn't it be refreshing to hear some courage like that, rather than "I was just experimenting." Does that mean they smoked pot in a laboratory? Or lavatory?

In late 1994, President Clinton spoke to students at Framingham (Massachusetts) High School about marijuana. He said, "Every single scientific study that has been done in the last several years shows alarming increases in the toxicity and the danger of using marijuana."[24]

The president should have mentioned that those studies are the result of the anti-marijuana establishment, many members of which are financially supported by the federal government. Had President Clinton understood marijuana, he would have inhaled.

On September 15, 1994, the *Boston Globe* printed the results of a reader call-in survey that asked, "Do you favor legalizing marijuana for medicinal use?" An astonishing 97 percent of the callers said "Yes."[25]

On March 5, 1995, one of America's leading medical marijuana authorities, Lester Grinspoon, M.D., was in London. He took part in a live debate on BBC television. The topic was "Should marijuana be legalized?" In less than half an hour, over 137,000 phone calls came in. Ninety percent were in the affirmative.

No Federal Assistance for Pot Users

Students planning to attend college take notice: Drug offenders are ineligible for federal assistance, which includes student loans and scholarships. A person found guilty as a child molester or rapist can obtain a student loan, but a person convicted of possessing a few grams of marijuana, even though it may have been used as medicine, cannot. Nor can a convicted person obtain a small business loan or a scientific, artistic, or academic research grant.

Use of National Guard Avoids Fourth Amendment Protection

Americans are protected against abuse by their own military. Federal troops cannot enter private property or dwellings and cannot detain or search civilians. That protection was enacted in 1879 and called the Posse Comitatus Act.

The challenge was how to get around such protection so that the most sinister drug war in the history of the United States could follow. And the answer came. The National Guard could do all the things our own military couldn't legally do. The federal government would pay the guard with our tax dollars to prowl around our constitutional rights.

At the 1991 National Guard Association Conference, Lieutenant General John B. Conaway, chief, National Guard Bureau, put it this way:

> Our commander in chief has declared war on drugs. Our mission as America's National Guard in this war is clear: make America drug-free in as short a time as possible using any means necessary no matter what the cost.[26]

Adding insult to injury, Army Chief of Staff General Gordon R. Sullivan at the 1991 National Guard convention, clarified it even further:

> You (the National Guard) represent us in uniform in ways that the active forces cannot unless certain laws are changed. You are part of a Total Army dedicated to protecting our values and our way of life.[27]

Do the values and way of life of the National Guardsmen include entering private property without a search warrant? Smashing down doors? Pulling people out of cars? Unjust search and seizure followed by arrest—ending frequently with years in prison—for marijuana?

A guardsman on active duty for special work can search anything or detain anybody on his commanding officer's authority alone.[28] Is this what our forefathers had in mind when they created our Bill of Rights to protect us from exactly that type of gestapo tactics?

The National Guard Almanac reports that 90 percent of the 7,000 guard members across the country serving on active duty for drug interdiction were in civilian law enforcement prior to their active guard drug duty. As of August 1992, 19,495 guard-assisted arrests had been made—three times as many as throughout 1991.[29] (Figures don't delineate how many of those arrested were using marijuana as medicine, how many were cancer, glaucoma, or AIDS patients, and how many were in wheelchairs.)

Guardsmen searched 120,000 cars in 1992 and entered 1,230 privately owned buildings, as opposed to 436 buildings in 1991. According to the Defense Department, by October of 1992, guardsmen had made 6,537 uninvited intrusions. Almost all of their time and our money was for marijuana interdiction. In 1989 their budget was $40 million. For 1993 it was estimated to be around $420 million.[30]

The role of America's military in the war on drugs will continue to escalate until we, as voters, say "Get out of our homes. We've had enough already."

Recent Rulings

On June 20, 1996, the California State Supreme Court ruled that judges do have the same discretion as district attorneys in three strikes cases, allowing them to set aside prior convictions in these cases if they believe the sentence is too harsh.

If judges are not allowed such an option we might as well eliminate judges, convince ourselves we're saving some money rather than lives, and sentence people by computer. It would be wise to keep in mind that we are on the road to bankrupting our states by warehousing nonviolent offenders at a cost of $20,000 to $40,000 a year each.

On July 10, 1996, the GOP-controlled Assembly voted to reverse the California State Supreme Court's June 20 ruling. Three strikes are alive, and sick, in California. Anyone convicted of two prior violent or serious felonies and convicted of any felony on a third offense—regardless of whether it's serious or violent—

receives twenty-five years to life, or three times the sentence for the third crime, whichever is greater.

Consider this scenario: Maybe you were in college and got arrested for selling pot to a seventeen year old; that's one felony. Then you stole a car several years later; that's another conviction. Now you're thirty. You sold a little pot to a friend, and you'll spend the rest of your life in prison.[31]

Joseph McNamara, former police chief, San Jose, California, and a Hoover Institution Fellow, summed this inequitable situation up best: "The drug war cannot stand the light of day. It will collapse as quickly as the Vietnam War, as soon as people find out what's really going on."

McNamara surveyed nearly 500 police chiefs, district attorneys, lawyers, police officers, public defenders, judges, and college students regarding their opinions about the "war on drugs." Those surveyed said treatment and increased prevention could control drugs more effectively than the hard line that puts users in prison. Ninety-eight percent thought illegal drug use was not primarily a police issue. More than 30 percent said that legalization or decriminalization would cause a decrease in drug use or else not affect it at all. A majority surveyed felt the answer was not more military intervention, police, prisons, or prosecutors. However, McNamara noted, "Elected officials think it's political suicide to be 'soft on drugs.'"[32]

11

Drug Testing

> *The right of the people to be secure in their persons . . . against unreasonable searches and seizures, shall not be violated, and no Warrants shall issue, but upon probable cause.*
>
> The Fourth Amendment to the United States Constitution

DRUG TESTING IS A FORM OF SURVEILLANCE. It reports on a person's off-duty recreational activities just as surely as if someone had been present and watching. When I had cancer, my greatest fear, other than dying, was being tested for drugs and arrested for using marijuana medically.

Drug testing is touted as a panacea for many workplace problems. The millions of Americans who are subjected to these intrusive, degrading tests know better than anyone that drug testing not only doesn't work but also is making a mockery of the United States Constitution. Workers are treated as guilty until proven innocent.

Drug Testing Does Not Measure Impairment

The marijuana high, and any associated impairment, dissipates within a couple of hours, very similar to the effects from a couple of drinks of alcohol. Even though the pot user is free of any drug effect, the person will test positive for marijuana for as long as six weeks after the last inhale. Urine tests *do not* detect the psychoactive ingredient of marijuana, THC, but rather other, *nonactive* metabolites. The tests in no way measure impairment; nevertheless, this fact is ignored by employers in today's anti-drug hysteria. To make matters worse, only eighty-five of the estimated twelve hundred laboratories in the United States meet federal standards for accuracy.[1]

Drug tests do not detect alcohol, our nation's leading drug of abuse. Tests that do detect alcohol are separate, rarely administered, and only detect current impairment. Drug tests do not detect fatigue or stress, the cause of one-third of all workplace accidents.[2]

Drug testing assesses nothing more than how the employee lives his or her private life. Most studies find no correlation between test results and job performance.[3]

With such unfair testing, exemplary employees who were "surprise" tested have lost their jobs or were arrested and sent to jail. Marijuana users are "set up" with drug tests that do not measure impairment. To avoid such discrimination some social marijuana smokers have switched to cocaine, LSD, alcohol, or heroin because those drugs are out of a person's system far more rapidly than marijuana. The firing of people who test positive because they had smoked a joint two weeks ago is yet another government-sanctioned injustice.

Our Bill of Rights Set Aside

On December 16, 1991, the U.S. Supreme Court allowed a U.S. Court of Appeals ruling to stand: that the government's interest in screening out possible drug users outweighed the applicant's constitutional right to privacy. Prior to this decision, only federal employees in occupations related to public safety (e.g., truck and bus drivers) could be tested without cause. This ruling has opened the door to across-the-board drug testing for millions of businesses and is a boon to the drug-testing industry, which is already worth hundreds of millions of dollars. The policy is based upon desperation, power, and money, rather than clear thinking.

Impairment Testing Makes Sense

Impairment testing for those people who are responsible for public safety is understandable. But to cause a person to fail to obtain a job or to lose employment for smoking a joint two weeks ago is wrong. I used to be proud of standing to pledge allegiance to the flag, but now when those words "with liberty and justice for all" are voiced, I find only my lips moving.

A young man applied at a store in Oregon to sell teddy bears at minimum wage. The first demand was for a hair follicle sample as part of a two-year drug background check. He was handed the following form to fill out and was informed that the job depended upon the results of the hair follicle test and the questionnaire:

The following are portions of an actual drug questionnaire for job applicants:

> "SUBSTANCE ABUSE, Informed consent and release of liability/medical authorization. I, ____________________ do hereby voluntarily agree to provide a hair specimen for the purpose of screening for the presence of drugs. I understand the laboratory testing for drugs, Psychemedics Corporation, will perform appropriate tests on this specimen and will use scientifically acceptable protocols to run these tests. If I am a JOB APPLICANT, and the tests indicate the presence of illegal drugs, I understand that I will be denied employment. Further, I also understand that failure to sign this consent and release will terminate my consideration for employment and that I do authorize the release of results of the test to the designated Company Human Resources representative.
>
> I do hereby release Psychemedics Corporation or any testing laboratory designated by the Company, and its employees, its agents and representatives, from any and all liability arising from the authorized release or use of the information derived from or contained in my test results, and any employment decision made based on the results of

this test. I am taking or have taken the following medications within the past ninety (90) days (optional):

Name of medication and dosage

____.

Name of doctor ______________________ issuing prescription (if applicable).

Approximate date medication was taken ___________________.
Include nonprescription drugs also.

I further certify that the hair specimen collected from me will be mine and not adulterated or altered in any manner. My signature below acknowledges that I did read, understand, and agree with all statements and conditions outlined in this informed Consent and Release of liability/medical Authorization.

Applicant/Employee Signature _________________Date______

Witness Signature___________________________ Date______

Store # __________ Location ___________________________

(Author's note: Applicants are asked if they have taken prescription or over-the-counter drugs. One of the most commonly used testing methods, known as EMIT (enzyme-multiplied immunoassay technique), can at times return false positive results for marijuana cannabinoids if the person has recently taken ibuprofen, which is in Advil, Nuprin, Motrin, and Midol[4]—over-the-counter tablets for pain, arthritis, menstrual cramps, fever, PMS, and other common conditions.)

Regarding hair testing, the National Institute on Drug Abuse (NIDA) announced recently that it will fund research on the accuracy and reliability of testing hair samples for traces of abused drugs. The purpose of the funded studies would be to "provide the scientific basis to enable the routine use of such testing in workplace situations," said the NIDA announcement.[5]

The standard method of testing for drugs is urinalysis, but urine samples can be tampered with, and there is a limited window in which drug use can be detected. Proponents of hair-testing claim that hair samples contain up to many months' worth of drug evidence. Psychemedics, the hair-testing company, claims that over 170 companies are already using their drug-testing procedure. The use of hair samples continues, despite the consensus report of the Society of Forensic Toxicologists (SOFT) at its May 1990 national conference, which stated:

> The use of hair analysis for employees and pre-employment drug testing is premature and cannot be supported by the current information on hair analysis for drugs of abuse. Too many critical questions remain to be answered before the results can be accurately interpreted.[6]

NIDA itself has confirmed the findings of SOFT and recommends that hair testing not be used until further research is conducted. Given that hair tests are classified as medical devices and have not been approved, it is amazing that Psychemedics has 170 corporate clients.[7] Thousands of employees are being subjected to a test that can result in loss of employment, and the test is not proven or approved.

In addition to having to supply a hair sample, if the young man wanted to be considered for the job of selling teddy bears, he also had to complete a seven-page "opinion" survey that elicits incriminating answers.

The multiple-choice questions in the survey are arranged in subtle fashion. Some are innocuous and straightforward, such as number 90: "I like sales goals because they give me something to push for." But others are loaded. Take, for example, number 22: "Tom is an excellent employee. One day, away from work, he and a friend smoke a marijuana cigarette. He returns to work only a little high, but able to perform his job satisfactorily. He should be fired." The respondent is asked to agree, on a scale of 1 to 5, or disagree, on a scale of 6 to 10.

Here are other questions concerned with drugs:

30. An organization has no right to inquire about an employee's use of social drugs, as long as it doesn't affect his job.
38. I have experimented with drugs, but it has never affected my job.
44. Smoking a marijuana cigarette is the same as having a drink.
45. I don't believe an individual who smokes marijuana once a week has a drug problem.
52. These days almost everyone experiments with marijuana.

Simple arithmetic demonstrates that the number of people involved in the illegal drug market, estimated at $150 billion annually, vastly exceeds the population of visible "addicts." This group must, therefore, consist predominantly of ordinary people who are typically employed, productive, responsible, and not impaired as they lead conventional lives—just as the immense majority of alcohol users are not alcoholics.

After answering ninety-three questions, the applicant then gets to answer many questions under the category of "Admissions." (They are part of the company's demand for clarification of the answers on the questionnaire prepared by Psychemedics.) For example, if an applicant answers question 38 with "I have experimented with drugs," then company guidelines require that "this applicant not be recommended for employment until a thorough post-survey interview has been completed discussing the applicant's responses, which have resulted in: (Some of the following) High risk in drug attitudes. Drug admissions. Marginal risk in both correlative and drug attitudes."

If the applicant had smoked marijuana two weeks prior, would he have gotten the job selling teddy bears? Would he have obtained the position if he had answered questions 30, 38, 44, 45, or 52 with honesty? Not likely.

The young applicant does occasionally smoke grass. He elected not to play their game and contribute his hair and urine to further the insanity of drug testing in order to qualify. Instead he became a student at the University of Oregon where he is an A scholar.

According to a report to Congress from the secretary, Department of Health and Human Services (RP0785, page 136), titled "Marijuana and the Cannabinoids: Detection of Marijuana Use":

> There is still great controversy regarding constitutional rights of individuals required to have their biological fluids analyzed for the presence of abused substances. However, many private companies as well as government agencies remain committed to drug testing. There are two major reasons for these tests: to determine merely whether an individual has used an illegal drug and to determine whether drug use could have caused mental and physical impairment leading to injury or to other dire consequences.

Consequences like perhaps dropping a teddy bear? It's thought provoking to note that some of the people responsible for holding the public up to such high standards, such as Robert DuPont, own drug-testing laboratories!

Impairment Testing Should Replace Urine Testing

Then-Representative Barbara Boxer's transportation subcommittee held hearings in early 1992 on the subject of impairment testing, sometimes referred to as "performance testing." Impairment tests consist of evaluating a worker's competence through a hand-eye coordination test similar to a video game. The tests are less expensive than urine or hair testing. Impairment tests screen out all persons not fit for duty on a given day, not just individuals who might be under the influence of drugs. Thus both the interests of public safety and individual privacy are better served.[8]

A *Washington Post* editorial on January 24, 1992, commented, "performance testing appears to be more effective than the standard urinalysis now used in the industry both after accidents and on a random basis." The editorial said that 97 percent of railroad accidents are caused by fatigue, illness, stress and other factors not associated with drug or alcohol use. "On an annual basis, the test is less expensive than periodic urinalysis, and it's far less intrusive."

The *Physicians Desk Reference* lists all the negative effects associated with thousands of drugs prescribed by doctors. It has this to say regarding Marinol, as per the manufacturer of that drug (page 2130 of the 1995 PDR edition):

> Patients receiving treatment with Marinol should be specifically warned not to drive, operate machinery, or engage in hazardous activity *until* it is established that they are able to tolerate the drug and perform such tasks safely.

This author does not condone marijuana or any recreational drug use on the job. Yet it's interesting to note that Marinol users are acceptable workers as long as they can demonstrate ability to perform their job—another reason for impairment or performance testing. (Marinol mimics the same psychoactive effects as natural marijuana.)

Urine testing is inherently misleading. Such tests are most likely to indicate marijuana use for medicine or recreational, after-work or weekend marijuana smoking by adult workers. They completely ignore the most common drug problem, alcoholism. An alcohol hangover can affect performance. Hence, impairment testing would make far more sense.

The *Merck Manual of Diagnosis & Therapy*, the medical doctor's bible of factual information, stated in the sixteenth edition, 1992, page 1562 (referring to urine testing for marijuana):

> The testing that identifies an inactive carboxylic acid metabolite only identifies use. It has no correlation with dysfunction, and the smoker may be free of effect by the time his urine is positive.

Citizens must gather the strength to refuse to take bogus, degrading, frivolous, and frequently inaccurate drug tests. Until we resist and voice the Fourth Amendment to the United States Constitution, we will remain the "sheep" of the federal government.

Albert Einstein said it best: "The strength of the Constitution lies entirely in the determination of each citizen to defend it. Only if every single citizen feels duty bound to do his share in this defense are constitutional rights secure."

12

Marijuana in Hawaii and on the Mainland

ARE CALIFORNIA COMMUNITIES GOING TO POT? California continues to spend $1.2 million annually on the interdiction of local marijuana. When pot can easily be purchased on the street, local governments wonder if interdiction is the best use of such high expenditures. An ever-increasing number of residents, including conservatives, are having their doubts.

Most local residents have come to know mom-and-pop growers who don't bother anyone and who deliver millions of dollars to the local economy. Some local merchants may be conservative Republicans; however, they recognize that the country's largest cash crop is good for business. Other states ponder the same rationale.

War on Hawaiian Pot Increases Prices

The Reagan and Bush administrations exerted heavy federal pressure to eradicate marijuana throughout all fifty states. Hawaii's "Green Harvest" began in earnest. Helicopters flew only fifty feet over Big Island homes and landed in yards so DEA agents could pull up pot plants. Frightened children, parents, and animals didn't deter the DEA from continuing its residential terror and its destruction of those herbs. The federally created violence against the botanical and those who used it was escalating at a frightening rate. Having been a resident of Hawaii for thirty years, I can offer concrete examples of what the war on marijuana has accomplished.

"Police-state" power became visible. Large numbers of local populations that had been carefree and open in smoking marijuana retreated to the "closet." The same things were occurring on the mainland—namely, fear and a switch to more dangerous drugs.

During the 1970s and early 1980s, a pound of Hawaiian marijuana could be purchased on the street for $2,000 or less. By the late 1980s, the price of a pound had skyrocketed to as much as $10,000. The federal government rationalizes that if you price all drug users out of the market, people will quit using. You can think about that the next time your home is burglarized by someone hoping to keep his own out-of-pocket dope cost lower.

Hawaii is the quality marijuana capital of the world. Hawaii's pot is world renowned for its consistent quality and potency. This consistency is a tremendous aid to ill patients who want to accurately regulate their medication.

It is imperative to understand that pot is not what we have been told it is by the government: that it causes violence, criminal acts, brain damage, and more. In addition to being medicine, marijuana is a mild euphoric, similar in effect to a couple of martinis (but without the possible hangover) or a Valium (with a smile added).

Marijuana also releases the child in us regardless of our age. It encourages honest communication, potent insight, creativity, humor, and relaxation. It's sometimes referred to as "happy grass" or "sleepy-time pot."

If marijuana were discovered today in some distant rain forest, it would be hailed as a miracle drug. With its dozens of applications, it is almost magical, which is why it has been used universally in various religions for centuries. One can meditate or medicate with ease. Pot encourages peace, not violence. Many pot users look down on alcohol users as violent.

During 1970s, Hawaii's Honesty Made Pot Almost Legal

In 1972, our family settled in the regal Kalapana area, where I had semi-retired. We had the first home constructed in the Royal Gardens subdivision. At 400 feet above sea level, the ocean view was so wide and spectacular that the curvature of the earth could be observed.

Before stop signs were installed, I was able to land our Cessna Cardinal on the road in front of our home. It was paradise. We kept an additional car in the plane's hangar in Hilo. Rather than drive forty-five minutes, we could fly in eleven, providing more time to enjoy the Kalapana beauty.

In 1975 my wife acted on a desire to go into real estate. We already had our sales licenses, and we studied under the coconut trees of the magnificent Kalapana black sand beach to obtain our broker's licenses. We opened our own real estate firm on the Hilo side of the Big Island. We invested heavily in the Kalapana area, including thirty-four oceanfront acres where we planned to develop a "Hawaiian village." It would have had 100 grass-thatched cottages, a swimming lagoon, and shops offering handicrafts that only the talented Hawaiians can create. It would have included a professional recording studio to entice world-famous bands to record there—and write off their trips.

My wife and I were aware that some of the workers on our project would no doubt smoke an occasional joint while working on the resort. We elected not to prohibit such use so long as it didn't jeopardize their job performance. We preferred to see an adult worker smoke a joint rather than drinking alcohol (other than an intermittent beer). We had never noted anyone fighting when pot was the only drug used. Most pot smokers do not use alcohol.

In the mid- to late 1970s, Hawaii's residents smoked grass in theaters, at parks, and often on the job, with no questions asked or urine samples demanded. People behaved themselves on grass. Pot was accepted, and for all intents and purposes it might as well have been legal. Local businesses flourished and eagerly looked forward to each harvest. Thousands of adults in Hawaii of every race and religion used grass. Many of them never touched alcohol. They didn't like the taste, the hangover, or the violence that at times it instills.

Thousands of residents grew enough grass for themselves and their guests. Some grew and used pot only for medical or religious reasons. In Hawaii it is frequently referred to as "the sacred herb" when smoked for religious or medical use.

I can't recall one real estate firm that didn't intentionally or unintentionally, sell property to pot growers. Ours was no exception. Several growers established that their clients were solely cancer patients who sought Hawaiian marijuana because of its consistent quality. Most growers took pride in developing the finest strain possible with consistent THC. With that type of quality control, patients could count on their medicine being pure and doing the job that nature intended.

Here's an example of the openness of pot in Hawaii during the mid- to late 1970s. One of our top real estate salesman ran an ad in *High Times* magazine. Terry Shoneberg was well aware of the medical value of pot and its export to mainland patients. That was a potent market in itself. This was Terry's ad:

> The Gold Rush is on. Yes, Hawaii's gold rush is not only in its "smoke" but in the value of the land on the Big Island (Hawaii) which has become internationally known for its sacred herb. Fantastic land values are still available, but for how long? For as low as $750 down and $50 a month, you can own two or three acres in beautiful Puna, Hawaii. This land has soil and trees and beautiful climate. No credit needed. Owner will finance with no questions asked. Excellent way to start your credit. Hawaii is America's last paradise, and an investment that can't lose. Think what land prices can do if legalization occurs. I am a licensed real estate salesman, and promise honest competent service, and total confidentiality on your purchase. So whether you have $1,000, or $100,000 to buy, I want to be your man in Hawaii. [There was a perforated line where you could tear off the bottom of the ad to send in to Terry.] Yes, Terry, I am very interested in an investment in

> paradise. Please send me more information on specific properties now on the market. I have $_____ to invest, and can handle $_____ a month. Terry Schoneberg, salesman, Dave Ford Real Estate, Star Rt. Box 26-a, Keaau, Hawaii.

The ad response was good. (Today, Terry is a successful, conservative, middle-aged real estate broker in Hilo.)

Marijuana Legalization Proposed in Hawaii

Yes, during the 1970s Hawaii was relaxed. Although most politicians shied away from anything controversial, one politician with courage initiated what was overdue. On February 9, 1973, one of Hawaii's two major newspapers, *The Honolulu Advertiser*, ran a story about a bill that was being considered for introduction in the House to legalize marijuana.

State Representative John S. Carroll (R-12th District) said, "We have a situation now that I see as extremely hypocritical." He was referring to fans who smoked grass at rock concerts, a practice condoned by police. "That's de facto legalization of it," he said. Carroll added that the reports and scientific studies he had read indicated that marijuana should be decriminalized. He said that two years previously he had introduced a bill proposing a $25 fine for possession of marijuana by an adult and a minimum two-year jail sentence for anyone trafficking with a minor. The bill died in committee.

"I've had numerous people talk to me about marijuana and I've always had a hard view on drug abuse," Carroll continued. "But the more I read and understand, the less inclined I am to take such a hard stand." He said he still advocated a hard line on drugs and narcotics such as amphetamines, barbiturates, cocaine, and heroin. But he felt that any imprisonment for possession of marijuana was too punitive. "Just to even go to jail for one day is not right."[1]

John Carroll was honest and straightforward. The reason police have condoned marijuana smoking at rock concerts and "looked the other way" is they know that it is relatively harmless and that pot encourages relaxation rather than stress and violence.

By late 1981 I was deeply concerned about Hawaii residents switching from marijuana to more dangerous drugs because of the hard line the Drug Enforcement Administration was taking in eradicating the herb. I wrote to our United States Congressman, Cecil Heftel, in Washington. In a speech the congressman had mentioned marijuana and his thoughts on its legalization. On October 19, 1981, I received this reply.

> Dear Dave:
>
> Thank you for your kind words about my remarks on legalizing marijuana. I appreciate your taking the time to express and share with me your concerns and frustrations over this issue. Certainly, I would prefer to see the drug totally eradicated, but unfortunately, there are no indications that this is happening. Thus, at least controlling the substance by legalizing it is worth discussing as an option that would perhaps be more satisfactory than the present situation.
>
> Please stay in touch, Dave, and let me know whenever I can be of assistance to you. Thanks again, and in the meantime, my best wishes and Aloha.
>
> Sincerely,
> Cec Heftel, member of Congress

Woodstock: An Example of Peaceful Pot

The events of August 15–17, 1969, will be remembered forever by those who attended Woodstock. From 300,000 to 500,000 "flower children" of the sixties gathered in that New York farm community for a rock concert.

It has been estimated that 99 percent of the crowd smoked marijuana as they listened to the music and songs of such legends as Janis Joplin; Joan Baez; Jimi Hendrix; Johnny Winter; Santana; The Grateful Dead; Crosby, Stills, Nash and Young; Blood, Sweat and Tears; Richi Havens; and Joe Cocker. More than anything it proved that hundreds of thousands of young people not only could survive wallowing in mud created by a cold rain but also could find and share kindness.

The press was hostile toward those young people because they were against the Vietnam War and were not supporting our government's sending soldiers to die for a cause that didn't make sense to them. Anarchy was a word frequently used in describing these teenagers who sought a pollution-free earth, peace on earth, and good will toward others. Must such thoughts be discouraged? Should a substance that encourages such thoughts be illegal?

What amazed millions who read the story of Woodstock was that although the weather was mean, the young people shared their food and even their meager shelter. Only one fight was reported. One of the musicians jumped from the stage and put a lit joint into the mouth of each angry young man involved. After a couple of inhales, rather than continuing to fight, they began hugging each other!

Woodstock was a perfect example of peaceful marijuana. Imagine what would have happened if you'd had a crowd that size with everyone drinking liquor. There is little doubt that the police are very much aware of the use of pot at rock concerts and prefer it for crowd control, rather than dealing with hundreds of thousands consuming alcohol.

The government was not amused by the lack of conformity of those youngsters—not only at Woodstock but also throughout the country—who were smoking pot and refusing to fall in line with authority and obediently march off to Vietnam. They challenged the government. Is that not the American way? Should they have been punished?

The Controlled Substance Act

One must wonder if it was coincidence that in 1970 Congress approved the Controlled Substance Act, which classifies marijuana along with heroin and LSD as a Schedule One drug, meaning a drug with a high potential for abuse and addiction and no known medical use. Was this the government's way of punishing free-thinking young adults? Could it be that the government was afraid of an addiction to peace and love, rather than war and violence? Possibly the greatest danger from marijuana is that it is a gateway to such deviant perceptions as ecological, rational, "one world—one people" empathy. Could that be the "danger?" To whom?

Marijuana became scarce in 1970. LSD was still easy to obtain. LSD sales zoomed.

The New War on Marijuana

Most older adults who smoked grass didn't indulge in alcohol or other drugs until marijuana again became the "evil drug" in the early eighties. Propaganda stories began telling of the "new dangers" of marijuana. The war on marijuana went into high gear with an avalanche of police, DEA, and National Guard intervention. Suddenly, peace-promoting pot users were afraid everywhere in Hawaii and on the mainland. Citizens were afraid to mention grass openly. Many began using nicotine, alcohol, heroin, cocaine, amphetamines, LSD, methaqualone (the generic name for Quaaludes), or whatever drugs were available. Grass became more expensive than gold.

Hawaii's attorney general knew pot prohibition would create worse drug problems:

> Obviously, an all-out eradication attack against the marijuana crops funded by an unlimited supply of money could wipe out marijuana production in Hawaii. The destruction of the industry by this means, however, would create yet another problem: there would simply be a shift to other competitively priced drugs, and as the supply of locally produced marijuana decreased, methamphetamines, cocaine, and imported marijuana would begin flowing in to answer the local demand.[2]

Marijuana began to be imported into Hawaii (and it still is) and arrived from the mainland, from Mexico, and from places as far away as Palau, a U.S. trust territory in the Pacific.

Importers typically repackage the foreign marijuana and peddle it as genuine Hawaiian grass. They double their money in the process. Tourists are often the target for the sale of these alien buds. One joint on Lahaina's Front Street on Maui these days runs $5 to $9.

In the eighties, other drugs, such as crystal methamphetamine, were spreading on Oahu. Soon drug importers realized that the crushing Hawaii marijuana interdiction program, Green Harvest, was an opening to bring more hard drugs to Hawaii. A briefcase can contain a quarter million dollars' worth of cocaine or heroine, whereas pot takes up an enormous space.

Crime stories began making the front pages of newspapers and the evening television news. Most of the violence was caused by drug turf wars and police interdiction efforts, which contributed to the very crime in America they were designed to prevent.

The passive, generally clean-living young men and women who grew marijuana in Hawaii and sold it began to panic when the DEA, National Guardsmen, and local police descended on their crops and homes with military force and vehicles, seizing property and banishing to prison the parents of small children. A few of the growers I knew didn't even smoke pot nor did they drink alcohol or use other drugs. If they had any addiction, it was to health foods—many of them were vegetarians.

Various "happy grass" growers were approached by mainland marijuana wholesale buyers who encouraged them to get rid of their marijuana as soon as possible because of the terror inflicted on them by both the federal and state governments. Those mainland professional pot buyers, who were no doubt connected to organized crime, offered a solution. "Before the police can locate and eradicate your harvest of marijuana, we can help you."

Wholesale buyers offered growers the "opportunity" to trade their stock of marijuana for cocaine or heroin as security. "It's really tough to hide pounds of marijuana. However, you can easily hide our cocaine and heroin." Young, naive growers were told that when the wholesale buyers had sold the marijuana on the mainland, they would return and buy back the cocaine and heroin. Months went by. Those buyers must have forgotten to return.

Before long, some of the growers, who previously were a mellow community, began trying cocaine and heroin. Soon they found themselves in the pitiful situation of becoming addicted to hard drugs. In order to satisfy their habit they began selling cocaine and heroin, which no doubt was the intent of the mainland wholesale buyers. Some also began drinking alcohol. This combination caused a few of the "laid-back" growers to become hostile in protecting their crops. A once agreeable people displayed unpredictable flashes of anger. They reminded me of Native Americans who were traded alcohol and guns for their animals and handicrafts.

The crack epidemic, with its accompanying disorder, was only one result of marijuana suppression. History notes a similar trend when President Nixon proclaimed his anti-pot crusade, Operation Intercept. In 1969, Nixon's narcotic agents were so successful in scaling off the flow of Mexican pot that marijuana-starved youngsters turned to LSD, hashish, alcohol, glue sniffing, sedatives, stimulants, opiates, cocaine, and other strong hallucinogens.[3]

History repeats itself. *Reader's Digest* continues to use *Reefer Madness*-type false claims such as "Marijuana is a gateway drug." In a February 1996 article, the *Digest* pushed for more dishonest television ads such as "the egg in the frying pan." Such ads continue to scare rather than to use proven facts. Regarding hemp the article stated, "It's obvious that hemp is a facade to give marijuana a better name." It also proclaimed, "Teenage marijuana use is linked to criminal behavior." Believing such *Reefer Madness*-type distorted articles, federal agents go after marijuana users with ill will, to put it mildly. However, most agents are only following policy guidelines and superiors' orders. Rather than displaying hostility against the DEA and other government agencies, we must devote our energy toward changing discriminatory laws.

Teachers Can't Present True Information about Marijuana

Teachers could help correct marijuana propaganda if they were permitted to tell the truth. Because of the war on drugs, teachers are afraid of saying anything positive about marijuana because they might face the loss of their jobs.

Imagine if they felt comfortable about reporting the truth about marijuana and could say something like this: "You have the right to know that marijuana is less harmful than alcohol, nicotine, and most other drugs—legal and illegal. You also have the right to know that marijuana is not physically addictive. It is nature's tranquilizer. However, it is *not* for those in school, including students in college. It will relax you to the extent that you cannot intelligently do your schoolwork. If you want to be stupid and use alcohol, marijuana, or other drugs when you are in school and under legal age, I prefer that you quit class right now. I don't want kids in my classes who can't concentrate on their schoolwork."

Sort of scary, gutsy stuff, isn't it? Could it be that we're not conditioned to hear the truth about marijuana? More than anything, this book is about honesty.

13

What is NORML?

Among the hundreds of patients I've met over the years who have had illnesses relieved by marijuana, few were aware of what NORML is or what it stands for. No doubt there are millions of Americans who are equally unaware of this organization's courageous, never-ending fight for truth. NORML informs the public on both the negative and positive aspects of marijuana use. Most media follow government propaganda, frequently not comparing the government's opinions with NORML's and presenting only the negative side of marijuana.

When I had cancer I encouraged people to join NORML, whether they used marijuana or not, out of compassion to help the ill obtain nontoxic, nonaddictive medication.

NORML is the National Organization for the Reform of Marijuana Laws. It is the leading national voice in America calling for the legalization of marijuana. NORML has been educating the public since 1970 by providing honest facts about marijuana and voicing opposition to the extreme measures taken to enforce counterproductive marijuana laws. NORML and this author, and millions of other citizens, have learned over the years that the positive benefits of marijuana far outweigh the negative effects.

NORML's Accomplishments

NORML is a nonprofit organization primarily supported by membership fees and donations from the public. The amount of money NORML has to reach the public with the latest news on marijuana is minuscule compared to the money wielded by multinational corporations fighting the relegalization of marijuana. I estimate the NORML budget to be one dollar for every million dollars spent by the tobacco, alcohol, chemical, and pharmaceutical companies and by special interest groups opposing marijuana legalization. This does not include the millions that government agencies spend to protect big business by constantly fabricating new lies and enforcing stiffer penalties against marijuana users.

Distinguished Board of Directors

NORML, with its constant demand for honesty in reporting marijuana facts, attracts board members with courage, integrity, and in-depth background knowledge on this sensitive subject. The distinguished board as of January 1997 included John P. Morgan, M.D., professor of pharmacology at the City University of New York; Lester Grinspoon, M.D., of Harvard Medical School; and Louis Lasagna, M.D., professor of psychiatry (clinical pharmacology) and dean of the Sackler School of Graduate Biomedical Sciences, Tufts University, Medford, Massachusetts.

Dr. Grinspoon is the author of *Marihuana Reconsidered*, as well as *Marihuana, the Forbidden Medicine* and an abundance of other books and articles. Dr. Grinspoon has stated, "It is ignorant and cruel for the government to arrest sick people who find relief only through their use of cannabis."

Dr. Morgan is the author of the section "Drugs and Abuse" in the medical encyclopedia *Merck Manual*, as well as other scholarly works. Dr. Morgan believes "The government's purpose in regulating medicine is to protect patients from toxicity. Marijuana has no overdose level."

Another brilliant board member is Ann Druyan, author or co-author of several books, including *Shadows of Forgotten Ancestors* and *Comet*, which was on the *New York Times* best seller list. Druyan has also written many magazine articles, was an author of the internationally acclaimed television series *Cosmos*, and is secretary of the Federation of American Scientists.

Other distinguished board members are Kary Mullis, Ph.D., 1993 recipient of the Nobel Prize in Physiology and Medicine; Barbara Ehrenreich, Ph.D., feminist scholar and author; Richard Evans, attorney, Northampton, Massachusetts; and Dale Gieringer, Ph.D., California NORML coordinator, San Francisco. Dr. Gieringer is the author of numerous articles on subjects including marijuana and driving safety, drug testing, and DEA "drug enforcement abuse." Dr. Gieringer is also a co-founder of the California Drug Policy Reform Coalition and of Californians for Compassionate Use. Board member Ansley Hamid, Ph.D., is associate professor of anthropology, John Jay College of Criminal Justice, New York City. Rick Doblin is currently in the Ph.D. program in Public Policy at Harvard's Kennedy School of Government where he obtained his Masters in Public Policy. His thesis focused on the attitudes and experiences of oncologists concerning the medical use of marijuana. The board also includes Dan Viets, attorney, Missouri NORML coordinator, Columbia, Missouri; Lynn Zimmer, Ph.D., associate professor of sociology, Queens College, New York City; and David Boaz, executive vice president of the Cato Institute, Washington, D.C.

In 1992 Allen F. St. Pierre became Deputy National Director of NORML. He received his B.A. in legal studies in 1989 from the University of Massachusetts, Amherst. St. Pierre has appeared on numerous local and national televisions shows. With dignified grace he has presented NORML's views on denying medical access to marijuana and related issues of interest to the country.

Hats Off to a Gallant American—Keith Stroup

By 1969 anyone with even mild curiosity noted that police were arresting hundreds of thousands of people who smoked pot or ate marijuana brownies. The charge was simple possession of the drug. The government propaganda was emphatic: marijuana leads to more dangerous drugs.

The voters did not challenge the government. No one did—except a brilliant young attorney named Keith Stroup. He was aware the government would continue its fabrications that marijuana had no medical value, that it created violence, and that it was responsible for whatever other undesirable effects the government could dream up. Stroup foresaw what has come to pass: millions of nonviolent Americans being arrested, imprisoned, killed, or maimed by "friendly" fire. To counteract the propaganda, he started NORML in 1970 and masterminded the organization through 1979.

Stroup then practiced criminal law for several years, returning to public-interest law and representing family farmers and artists. Stroup was executive director of the National Association of Criminal Defense Lawyers, Washington, D.C., from 1989 to 1995. He currently divides his time between NORML, where he is now Executive Director, and another criminal justice organization. In 1992 the Drug Policy Foundation gave Stroup the Richard J. Dennis Drugpeace Award for Outstanding Achievement in the Field of Drug Policy Reform.

Without Keith Stroup and the creation of NORML, marijuana would not, once again, be recognized and accepted as medicine. Marijuana would not have been legalized by California and Arizona on November 5, 1996, had there been no Keith Stroup.

On November 6, 1996, Stroup said, "These votes demonstrate that the public are ahead of the politicians when it comes to reforming our drug policies, specifically medical access to marijuana. Americans do not believe that denying medicine to the sick and dying should ever be a part of the drug war."

Because of Stroup, one day marijuana will be legalized as medicine not only in every state but also perhaps throughout the world. It will also be understood by the majority of American voters that marijuana should never have been made illegal. And it will be relegalized, for adults, both as medicine and as a euphoric.

Every person who cherishes freedom and honesty is indebted to Keith Stroup.

Honest Marijuana Facts

NORML, with a miniature budget, is educating the public on these points:

1. Marijuana use is not dangerous to an individual.
2. Marijuana use is not dangerous to society.
3. The extreme measures taken to enforce marijuana prohibition are not justified.

NORML's national office functions as a clearinghouse for information on these and related issues, such as urinalysis testing, the popularity of hemp, and the medical uses of marijuana.

NORML serves the public by providing information on marijuana, marijuana laws, and the effect they have on our country. Such material is made available to researchers, government officials, legislators, the news media, other opinion leaders, and individual members of the public.

Perhaps one of the most important of all of NORML's activities is its ongoing effort to record the stories of Americans whose lives have been damaged by marijuana prohibition. The pain of a jail sentence, a false urinalysis, and the inability to obtain marijuana for its medical properties are instances of the profound effect marijuana prohibition has had on American society.

NORML correctly believes the policy of jailing people for marijuana use is based on the premise that marijuana is a dangerous drug, which it is not. Every truthful national or international study has consistently refuted that notion.

Since 1965, over ten million Americans have been arrested for marijuana "crimes." Without public education, our government bases its policies on discredited information. Without public education, social leaders disseminate inaccurate and distorted information. Without public education, failed policies continue.

Many people consider NORML pro-drug. NORML does not advocate the use of any drug, not even marijuana. At the same time,

NORML supports a system under which marijuana may be legally obtained. NORML believes consistency is a true mark of integrity. Unlike many commonly used substances sold over the counter without prescription—such as aspirin, which can cause internal bleeding and death, and rubbing alcohol, which if swallowed can cause death—marijuana is virtually harmless.

NORML's Contributions to Freedom

When people started to question the logic of criminalizing marijuana in 1970, NORML persuaded most of the public to agree that adults should not go to jail for marijuana use. In 1972, when research confirmed that marijuana possessed medical value, NORML filed a lawsuit to compel the government to recognize marijuana's therapeutic uses. NORML helped convince thirty-six states to adopt laws allowing marijuana's medical use. On September 6, 1988, the DEA's own administrative law judge, Francis L. Young, decided the suit in NORML's favor and recommended making marijuana medically available. The federal government ignored its own judge's ruling.

When it became clear that mistruths about the health effects of marijuana were being told, such as the case of its reputed ill effects on the immune system reported in the mid-1970s, NORML reacted by gathering facts, analysis, and research from eminent experts to refute this typical scare story. When the government advocated spraying paraquat on marijuana plants in the United States, NORML led the public outcry that halted the program.

The following federal government's illusory charges are calmly countered by NORML: "Marijuana is more dangerous than heroin or cocaine. Causes death. Causes insanity. Turns people into criminals. Causes genetic deformities. Is physically addictive. Is a 'gateway' to heroin and other hard drugs. Is poison. Causes rape. Is ten times stronger and therefore more dangerous and addictive than in the 1960s. Kills brain cells. Causes fetal alcohol syndrome. Causes cancer. Causes homosexuality. Reduces a male's sperm count as much as if he were castrated. Causes children to join gangs. Encourages gun possession. And has no medical benefit."

Many employers have jumped on the marijuana drug war bandwagon and would just as soon have Dr. Kevorkian, the "suicide doctor," on their payroll as someone convicted of possessing a couple of grams of marijuana. It's hard enough to find secure employment without a drug conviction. NORML points out such deceit in today's pot hysteria.

If you live in a state that has a "three strikes and you're out" law, a felony conviction for marijuana can be the first strike. If you continue to use marijuana after that first conviction, you will continue to place yourself at risk. This is the case among many cancer and AIDS patients. Individuals are currently serving life terms for marijuana offenses that resulted in their third convictions.

NORML Attorney Norman Kent Speaks Out

What follows is a portion of the provocative speech delivered at NORML's 1992 annual national conference by Norman Kent, a lawyer in Fort Lauderdale, Florida. Kent is an expert in medical necessity defenses. He has been a valuable member of NORML and its legal committee for years.

> THAT'S WHY I BOTHER
>
> Just as Magic Johnson defies the stereotype of an AIDS victim, I defy the stereotype of a pot smoker. I am not lethargic, amotivational or a college dropout. I am an individual with a baccalaureate and a doctor of law degree, an individual who has counseled in drug programs and taught in colleges. I am neither a thief, nor a dealer, nor a decadent. I am a practicing attorney who has fought in the courts for the civil, humane and constitutional rights of my clients.
>
> I wake up every day at 4:30 a.m. I swim laps in my pool and I host a three-hour live radio talk show. I practice law from 10 a.m. to 6 p.m. or longer if necessary. I own two other businesses and I work my tail off. God damn it, if at the end of the day I feel like smoking a joint I want to be able to.
>
> I bother because in Florida at least, pot smokers still go to jail, still lose their cars, still pay huge fines—up to $5,000 for misdemeanor possession. They are booked, they are stripped, they are searched, they are handcuffed, they are held, they are

bonded, and they are told to face the wrath of some judge who is universally unsympathetic to my client's plight, worried, as the judges are, about their own unbridled alcoholism, cheating wives and gay sons.

I bother to fight today because the war on drugs has become a ruse. A ruse through which individual rights, freedoms and liberties are being systematically stripped away. Add to the endangered species list the Bill of Rights. Under the Crime Control Act of 1984, the government no longer needs the pretense of drugs to seize your property and forfeit it to the state. The government need only hold a hearing in which they show by a preponderance of the evidence that this may be a drug-tainted asset, and they can keep that property. I have a client in Fort Lauderdale. One marijuana joint was found on his boat after he rented it to another party. It took six months for him to get the boat back. Over $100 million in cash and property has been seized from Florida citizens since 1987.

When you check into an airport, bus or train terminal in 1991 it's as if you were checking into Hamburg in 1941. Instead of SS soldiers with machine guns and [German] shepherds asking "Where are your papers?" there are sheriff's deputies with their friendly beagles sniffing your luggage. It actually took a court decision to tell deputies that they did not have a right to search a man's crotch. That's why I bother.

Our highways are full of deputies looking for individuals who fit profiles, and we permit roadblocks and random searches in the name of this drug war. We find that going to work means not only punching a clock, but pissing in a cup. We are rated and regulated not by the content of our character, the quality of our work, but instead by the quantity of marijuana waste in our urine. Without probable cause or articulated suspicion the bags on our shoulders, the fluids in our bodies and even the trash on our sidewalk can be searched. That's why I bother.

The eighth amendment prohibits cruel and unusual punishment, but the Supreme Court of 1991 upheld a Michigan law that mandated a life sentence for first-time offenders who had in their possession a certain amount of drugs. George Bush now wants all first-time offenders to do jail time. Under this theory, Clarence Thomas's "experimentation" with pot would have earned a ticket to the federal pen instead of the "high" court. I always get a kick out of politicians and guys like Judge Thomas admitting they experimented with pot. Experiment my ass! What did they use? A Bunsen burner?

The issue of medical marijuana is what brings me here today. There are thousands with glaucoma whose traditional treatments have failed and who face the loss of sight, thousands with cancer who face chemotherapy that strips them bald and wracks their strength; the only salvation and response to nausea and vomiting is often the toke of a joint. All good and decent individuals. That's why I bother.

The number of AIDS patients using marijuana grows every day. Some of them will be arrested and prosecuted for their self-medication. One day, a judge will bar the defense of medical necessity because he will say the behavior of two careless and irresponsible men caused their predicament.

Those who are gay have been vilified for their sexual preference. They have been further ostracized for their high prevalence of HIV infection, and have been blamed for the AIDS epidemic. Now they face exile when forced to go to other countries to get experimental new drugs. Now the courts will say that gays are criminals and outcasts for smoking pot to retard the nausea and vomiting caused by AIDS treatments. It is time to fight AIDS, not people with AIDS. There is no magic cure. But there is hope for some relief and at least an opportunity to pass their last days in dignity, rather than retching in a bowl.

For too long, pot smokers have been blamed for social ills our government fails to address. The George Bush school of thought says a toke today makes you a crack user tomorrow. Nixon said that pot smokers become heroin addicts. In Reefer Madness days, you became a mad rapist and leaped out of windows. Anyone who has ever experimented with pot is a victim in the war on drugs. We have been made the scapegoat of modern America.

There is still a battle to be fought. It must be fought by our apathetic friends and peers who take for granted that NORML has run it course, that the battle is over, and marijuana law reform a footnote in history. The government continues to arrest almost 400,000 individuals a year for marijuana. Eventually, if given time, they will get almost all of us. So every time someone I know lights up I hand them a NORML application. If you can afford to buy pot, you can afford to join NORML. If you don't, the next arrest statistic could be you. That's why I bother.

Why You Should Join NORML

To protect our rights under the constitution, join NORML now. If each person who uses marijuana for medicine, religious purposes, meditation, creativity, or relaxation were to join NORML, there is little doubt that this amazing medicine called marijuana would be legal now. It's sad that there are only some 6,000 NORML members, considering there are 35 million Americans currently using pot. NORML should have at least 6 million members from this group alone. Then NORML could afford more than one lobbyist to aid in changing marijuana to a legal substance, at least for the ill and dying.

Regular membership is only $25 a year. The low-income rate is $15. Each member receives a one-year subscription to *Freedom @ NORML*, NORML's quarterly newspaper, which informs members about the issues, medical marijuana, and honest facts.

The address is NORML, 1001 Connecticut Avenue, N.W., Suite 1010, Washington, D.C. 20036 (norml@natlnorml.org).

When you write your will—or purchase life insurance—think NORML! A portion of the proceeds from the sale of this book will be contributed to NORML.

14

Users Share Their Marijuana Experiences

IN THE COURSE OF WRITING THIS BOOK, I INTERVIEWED over 300 people. I asked them to articulate their thoughts, pro and con, about marijuana. And I asked them, too, to try to reduce those thoughts to just a few lines. (Most repetitious statements were not used.)

It is significant to note that among those interviewed, only *two* related negative side effects, which disappeared as the drug wore off after an hour or two. A panic attack generally occurs when a first-time pot user believes the fallacious propaganda that marijuana will cause the user to become violent or go insane.

- "The wonderful thing about pot, it's not physically addicting, like when I smoked cigarettes it took thirty years to quit. I can smoke grass two or three times a week for a month and quit for a month without the craving.

• "With the chemotherapy, all I needed was to smell food and I'd retch. Now that I smoke grass, the nausea is gone, my appetite is back, and I've gained thirty-four pounds."

• "I was an alcoholic. I switched to grass. A much brighter way to go—and without the hangover and dying liver!"

• "The benefits of marijuana in my life have included the reduction of aggression."

• "I use marijuana for religious purposes. One can meditate far easier. You are so relaxed you are open to new teachings of the creator. You are 'tuned-in,' in a way that you cannot otherwise be. I have learned why marijuana has been used in various religions for thousands of years."

• "Being more analytical in all things."

• "I find that after an hour of a karate workout, I get a bit bored. After a hit or two, I get a real second wind with creative new ideas."

• "I read that marijuana suppresses the coughing mechanism. I couldn't believe it. After three days and nights of coughing from a bad cold, I tried pot. Two inhales stopped the tickling. That was the end of my cough!"

• "After my husband and I separated, I just wanted to punch people out till I began smoking happy grass. Then I became introspective. I saw our problem had been a lack of communication. We're back together. I love him more now than ever before."

• "I find it extremely useful for editing purposes, allowing me to immediately evaluate my work from a new perspective and to hear the color and flow of the chosen combination of words."

• "Using marijuana has provided me with a screen against too much reality, which has tended to be quite tragic in my family."

• "Looking back at the adversity in my life I can honestly say that marijuana has kept me young."

• "My epilepsy was helped with pot. It is important, however, to check with your doctor. Some types are helped. Others are not."

• "Sure is neat to get a little high now and then. And not have that alcohol hangover!"

• "I now enjoy life with a properly matured degree of balance."

• "Life may not be any better where I come from, but when I smoke, it seems better, and I can smile!"

• "I was so tired of being urine tested for about every job I applied for, I decided to go on welfare. I could at least smoke a joint once and awhile and feel like a free person."

• "I thought I'd be hooked on heroin for the rest of my life. With the help of grass I was able to quit heroin, and I've quit grass for months at a time with no withdrawals at all."

• "When I can't sleep from the back pain, I take a few hits of smoke and fall into a peaceful painless sleep."

• "When I'm stoned and make love for a half-hour, what could be finer than feeling like it was several hours! And oh, those orgasms seem to last so long!"

• "After the surgery the pain was so intense I couldn't relax. The morphine wasn't doing its job. A friend turned me on to grass. I was finally able to relax, and with the relaxation, the pain greatly eased."

• "For the first time in my life I find that when I smoke a little grass, I can actually carry on a good conversation with my friends. I used to just sit there and listen, 'cause I thought I sounded stupid. I know that sometimes when I smoke I get to laughing and say some silly things, but I'm having fun, and no one's getting hurt, and I'm able to better express my inner feelings."

• "Being in a wheelchair all day, the muscle spasms made me wish God would take me, until a friend in his wheelchair turned me on to grass. My new quality of life is precious and fulfilling."

• Chemotherapy was causing our four year old to vomit for hours. I made some cookies and put marijuana in them. I give him one an hour before his chemo. He doesn't throw up anymore."

• "How could something so fun, so filled with contentment and mellowness, be illegal?"

• "My other friends with AIDS agree that without marijuana they wouldn't have any appetite, and would have given up and died long ago. It stops the nausea and vomiting from AZT. It gives you a reason to keep fighting, and feel more comfortable about the inevitable death."

• "I couldn't swallow a Marinol pill to stop my nausea and improve my appetite. They made me vomit. When I did get one down it took about forty-five minutes to work, and cost $13,000 for a year's supply. Pot works in seconds and only costs pennies."

• "The labor pains were horrific. I couldn't relax, until my friend put a joint to my lips."

• "It's God's gift of medicine and could be *free* if we were allowed to grow it."

• "Pot sure beats the sleeping pills that I was addicted to!"

• "I no longer need Valium to relax my muscle spasms."

• "When we desperately need creative ideas, we smoke a joint. Many of our 'think tanks' would be on 'empty' if it were not for pot."

• "Forget the over-the-counter stuff for PMS or menstrual cramps. Giggle-weed beats it all by far."

• "It's a little like a truth serum. I can tell my husband what I really feel. I can't do that straight or if I have a drink or two. I think marijuana saved our marriage."

• "Listening to music takes on an entirely new dimension. You can hear notes and sounds never before experienced."

• "I've never felt so close to my wife as when we sit by the ocean and watch a sunset."

• "I used to not interact when we had people over to the house, or for that matter even talking with my wife. When I smoke grass I find myself talking, and I'm happy with myself."

• I panicked the first time I smoked. From hearing government stuff, I had a fear of losing control. I had not been advised of the true expected feelings of the high. The next time was super. I was told what the high would provide."

• "We live in a sketchy neighborhood, but when we smoke everything is mellow."

• "Hell, when I smoke I think I'm white. Maybe I'll vote this year!"

• "Once before I went to confession I had a few 'hits,' and did I ever unload!"

• "Making love is a whole new experience of feeling, touch, understanding. A marvelous melting together."

• "When I used to drink, I was a bad drunk. I'd get mean. Never happens on pot."

• "Man, grass makes ya a superman lover. My erections last twice as long and with enormous orgasms!"

• "Jean and I got so hungry smoking *the kind* (pot) one night, there was no food in the house except a gallon can of beans. Damn, we ate it all—and it was delicious. The night was a gas!"

• "Without the help of grass, I don't think I could have got off heroin."

• "I have inspired insight when I write my sermons."

• "I have to admit it certainly relaxes me when I smoke grass. I feel a bit guilty when I am forced by ignorant laws to sentence someone for marijuana."

• "I have some of the best dope in the world. Guess it helps that I fly for the National Guard."

• "I smoke half a marijuana cigarette before my chemotherapy. Before, my doctor (off the record) suggested I try marijuana. I'd previously been puking at home for several hours till nothing came out, and just kept having the dry heaves. Now I don't even get sick, and no vomiting!"

• "Being in a wheelchair all day caused terrible muscle spasms, till I tried pot. Now the spasms are gone in a few minutes."

• "I experience important insights. When I meditate it's truly a religious experience."

• "Writing music takes on new dimensions."

• "There are times when I'm suffering to tears from painful menstrual cramping I take several hits from a joint and fall into painless relaxation. How cruel they won't legalize it."

• "My motorcycle buddy cracked up. His leg was smashed. He was screaming in agony. I put a joint to his mouth. In minutes his body relaxed and the pain eased."

• "My depression worried me. There were times I wanted to end it all, till a friend turned me on to marijuana. It was a godsend. I can now see the light at the end of the tunnel."

• "Saturday nights I used to get drunk and too often ended up in fights. I quit drinking. Now on Saturday nights my wife and I smoke a joint and make love!"

• "A friend was in horrific fourteen-hour labor. The baby didn't want to exit. I finally put a joint of grass to her lips. She relaxed in minutes and a beautiful baby girl emerged."

• "Glaucoma was making me blind. Marijuana saved my sight."

• "Boy, is food delicious!"

• "Marijuana prohibition for the ill and dying is the cruelest injustice since the crucifixion of Christ."

• "Pot being illegal for the sick would be a joke, if it wasn't causing pain and even death to many who are ill. The government is as absurd as the politician who tried to create a bill to make vibrators illegal."

• "With pot, I'm able to get into whatever I'm into! My mind goes into that goal, whether it's my painting hobby, making love, praying, watching a sunset, writing a speech, or just relaxing and chatting with friends."

• "For stress, compared to Valium, alcohol, or any other drug, pot is superior."

Some of the longer comments were these:

• "As you know I have cancer. I was ready to pull the plug, end my life. I've been in pain for so long. I decided to have one last party with my closest friends. A friend offered me a marijuana cigarette. I had never smoked one of those things before. I thought 'those things can kill you.' Then I smiled inwardly. What the heck, I'm going to die anyway. After smoking, I discovered I was laughing for the first time in two years. Now I smoke almost every other night before I go to sleep, when the pain is really bad. It makes me relax, which reduces the pain, and I can mellow out. If marijuana were discovered recently it would probably be called the world's superlative miracle drug, which it is."

• "I find love-making far better when I'm high on marijuana. When I'm straight, there's too much distraction. If I wanted to kiss a lady while straight, there's too much happening in my mind. With grass I can really feel the kiss, the energy of the mouth, and that's all my mind and body are concentrating on. It's like the energies are blending more into body feelings instead of thinking, 'Am I doing this right, is this good for her, will I enjoy it?"

• "Conversation, especially with close friends, becomes more meaningful than the frivolous chitchat of everyday communication. You get beneath the surface and appearances, and penetrate to a clearer vision of reality."

• "Getting high on marijuana allows you to appreciate reality in much more of its complexity than you normally would. Music becomes unquestionably clearer when you are high, even complex music, from Bach to electronic productions. This perception is not lost after the high."

• "As you know, I'm now terminal with cancer. They've given me five pills to take, in addition to the morphine. They are for nausea, appetite, depression, stomach cramps, and sleep. I've been afraid to use marijuana due to its illegality. A friend insisted I try some with a little water pipe, so it wouldn't be harsh. It was good quality pot. Two inhales accomplished everything those five pills with their toxic side effects did!"

• "You can feel what the other person is feeling, like in her body. Your body is telling you when she is close to orgasm, and then you feel it. It's like there is a merging of feelings, body senses. Every touch, every movement is magnified like a hundred times. Touch on the hand or even the toes becomes lovingly intense. Nothing exists except this precious moment. There's a sense of timelessness."

• "Love-making on grass is especially beautiful and tender. Marijuana is not an aphrodisiac in the way alcohol might be considered. It doesn't cause you to want to pounce on the person you are with. However, if you are with the person you love, and you're both high and wish to make love (and I must repeat that marijuana does not break down barriers you don't want broken down), making love on pot is a beautiful experi-

> ence. Every sensual reaction is enlarged and prolonged, including of course the climax. You may say that this sounds like a floodgate of sensuality, but I point out pot does not reinforce sensuality to the detriment of the mind. If you desire it to be an enrichment of a physical and intellectual experience, it will be."

When I wrote television commercials, it frequently would take at least a half-day to write a commercial. I awoke one morning at 2 A.M., went into my den, and took two inhales of pot. In two hours I wrote six commercials that were as professional as any I had ever written. I've found that being refreshed after sleep, creative ideas flow almost faster than I can write them down. Partially due to unique television commercials, my show, Hollywood's Greatest Movies pulled 79 percent of the total Hawaii viewing audience during that time period [per the National Nielsen Rating System].

15

Relegalize Marijuana

Anti-Marijuana Crusaders: Deceiving or Deceived?

How tragic that a benign botanical—one that has a history of more than 10,000 years of general use and more than 5,000 years of medical use and that has never caused one overdose death—is kept from suffering patients who could receive immediate nontoxic benefits. The terror of arrest no doubt causes thousands of patients to die in needless agony.

My bout with cancer brought home a revelation I hadn't previously considered. Many of the anti-marijuana war crusaders—including police officers, judges, legislators, and many in the media—may honestly conclude that marijuana *is* the evil they have been brainwashed for sixty years into believing. Few people could be that heartless intentionally. I now think the federal government has been a part of a conspiracy that has taken on a life of its own. "Marijuana is evil and more dangerous than previously thought," the government proclaims, over and over again.

Our police and legislators generally have the good of the people in mind. However, they believe the government as I once did. The Department of Justice, on the other hand, knows full well that marijuana is relatively harmless.

Tod Mikuriya, M.D., Displays Courage

Dr. Tod Mikuriya headed marijuana research for the National Institute of Mental Health (NIMH) in the late 1960s. Researchers paid by the administration are apt to go along with the government's propaganda. If they don't, some find a prewritten resignation letter on their desk. During 1967-68 pressure was intense for government researchers to come up with only negative "scientific proof" that marijuana was evil, caused violence and insanity, and so forth. Dr. Mikuriya described the atmosphere:

> None of the DHEW (Department of Health, Education, and Welfare) employees wanted to offend any of the Bureau of Narcotics police. One also had to worry about antediluvian congressional types that had it in their power to smite us mightily where it hurt—right in our appropriation. The result was a sectional review committee, which are ostensibly selected for their professional positions and pedigrees, but are really picked for their low risk liability for offending others. Understandably, the research approved and funded by their recommendation could not help but reflect this ethic of inoffensiveness. For the fiscal years 1968 and 1969, NIMH grantees in the area of marijuana research included nine animal studies, twenty-eight social voyeuristic designs, ten chemical experiments, four pharmacological studies and *only two clinical human studies* [emphasis added].

On May 8, 1996, Dr. Mikuriya informed this author that the federal government knew marijuana contained medical properties. The information was declassified in 1971 and has been suppressed. Dr. Mikuriya researched dozens of books written by medical doctors, spanning 133 years. His book, *Marijuana Medical Papers—1839-1972*, contains more than 400 pages of marijuana's medical history. Dr. Mikuriya is a medical marijuana historian and scholar. He says marijuana works in three ways with prescribed medications:

1. As a substitute for a more harmful drug altogether or in part.
2. To decrease the use of another drug to minimize undesirable effects.
3. To suppress the side effects of another drug to permit its use.

Time for Honest Drug Education

The war on drugs has been the most expensive and longest-running unsuccessful war in U.S. history. The emphasis should be on honest drug education. The more something is hidden, whether it's sex education or drug education the more it is sought out. We've accomplished deception. Isn't it time to try honesty?

On August 16, 1996, while visiting San Francisco, U.S. drug czar and retired army general Barry McCaffrey followed in the footsteps of former drug czar Harry Anslinger when he said, "There is not a shred of scientific evidence that shows that smoked marijuana is useful or needed. This is not science. This is not medicine. This is a cruel hoax and sounds more like something out of a Cheech and Chong show."[1] Read up, General, and look in the mirror to see who is perpetuating a cruel hoax on the ill and dying.

In 1982, the prestigious National Academy of Sciences reported that the therapeutic use of marijuana includes positive effects on appetite, nausea, vomiting, epilepsy, muscle spasticity, anxiety, depression, pain, glaucoma, asthma, and the symptoms of withdrawal from alcohol and narcotics. The academy still stands by these findings.

At present, marijuana "education" is a thinly veiled attempt to shock young people away from unapproved marijuana by greatly exaggerating its hazards. Responsible parents, teachers, and police agencies should interest young people in alternatives to drugs. They should also provide honest information that would enable the kids to use drugs nonabusively if they were so inclined. Such education cannot be carried out as long as the government continues to refer to those who use unapproved drugs as drug abusers and criminals.

The federal government needs to turn over a new leaf and deliver education and honesty to itself and to the American public. It's time to take a new approach, particularly when the old way is not working.

As a people, we are all connected; we are all one. Care and honesty should prevail, rather than false hysterical press releases. Anti-marijuana crusaders, including legislators, must be challenged to report the facts honestly. So, too, must some of the media. Chances are these people would open their minds to the medical magic of marijuana if a family member was suffering from AIDS or cancer.

Police organizations such as DARE must be reeducated with an emphasis on truth about the drug, and then they must display their integrity by reporting to students the pros and cons about marijuana. Or discontinue all drug education.

On the one-hour CBS television show "Day & Date," viewers were asked the question, Should marijuana be legalized? On June 4, 1996, the answer was announced: 91 percent said yes; 9 percent said no. (The public has learned on its own that marijuana is virtually harmless.)

Marijuana Research Supports Legalization

Millions of peaceful marijuana users have cried "foul" and implored the federal government to legalize marijuana. Since 1937 the government has insisted that there hasn't been enough time to study the drug's long-term effects.

That is a falsehood. For more than 100 years, no drug in or out of the United States has been more thoroughly researched and investigated than marijuana. The tragedy is that the federal government is aware of the studies listed below and many others, that indicate marijuana is not the problem. The anti-marijuana laws are the problem. What do these studies say about marijuana?

- The Indian Hemp Drugs Commission. In 1894 the commission produced a seven-volume investigative report of 3,281 pages. In India, millions of people for centuries have used marijuana, rather than alcohol, for religious purposes, meditation, and medicine and to produce euphoria. The Indian government was interested in the long-term effects of marijuana. It obtained testimony on every aspect of marijuana use from nearly 15,000 individuals. The conclusion was that marijuana has minimal harmful effects. Suppression would cause people to turn to more harmful drugs.[2]

- The Panama Canal Zone military investigations, 1916 to 1929. A series of military boards inquired into marijuana smoking by American military personnel stationed in the Canal Zone. The boards published a report that concluded in 1929 there was no evidence marijuana was harmful to health or habit-forming and that delinquencies resulting from the use of marijuana were negligible.[3] Recommendation: No criminal penalties for marijuana use.
- The LaGuardia Committee Report, 1938 to 1944. The New York Academy of Medicine established a committee consisting of eight physicians, a psychiatrist, and four New York City health officials. After five years of study they concluded that the medical harm, along with psychological and social problems attributed to marijuana use, had been greatly exaggerated. They said that, at worst, marijuana was a relatively harmless intoxicant and the smoking of it did not lead to an increase in violent crimes, use of other drugs, or other antisocial acts. The report included insight into the 500 "tea-pads" that operated in New York during the 1920s and early 1930s. It said the tea-pad took on the atmosphere of a very congenial social club. When the desired effect from smoking pot had been obtained, the tea-pads that had rooftops found that patrons emerged into the open and engaged in the discussion of their admiration of the stars and beauties of nature.[4] Recommendation: No criminal penalties for marijuana use.
- The Baroness Wooton Report of 1968, United Kingdom. This report cited Great Britain's most eminent drug authorities. The report showed marijuana to be a relatively harmless drug

that did not lead to crime, dependency, or anti-social behavior.[5] Recommendation: No criminal penalties for marijuana use.

- The National Commission on Marijuana and Drug Abuse. The "Schafer Commission" was created by Congress and President Nixon in 1972–73. The blue ribbon panel was headed by Raymond P. Schafer, former governor of Pennsylvania. After months of study, it concluded that marijuana does not cause violent, aggressive behavior; does not lead to the use of harder drugs; does not constitute a major public health problem; does not lead to chromosomal or brain damage; and does not lead to physical dependency.[6] Recommendation: Decriminalization of marijuana.

The final report of the commission was titled *Marihuana—A Signal of Misunderstanding*, a phrase specifically chosen to point out the confusion, misinformation, mythology, inadequate data, and conflicting territorial disputes that the commission had encountered. Decriminalization was recommended so that users would not be outlaws. Personal possession in private would no longer be an offense.

President Nixon, for blatant political reasons, turned down his own commission's recommendation.

- The Jamaican Study, 1970. This study was carried out by the National Institute of Mental Health on Jamaicans who smoked a type of marijuana that is much stronger than that in the United States. The study concluded that marijuana did not cause amotivational syndrome or mental illness and that there were no significant physical abnormalities in individuals who were heavy marijuana smokers compared to a control group with similar social and economic backgrounds. Many marijuana smokers were the children and grandchildren of people who also smoked marijuana. Many of these individuals were probably exposed to marijuana before birth, as well as during their whole adult life, but neither chromosomal abnormalities nor evidence of increased incidence of birth defects was found. The study said marijuana was a relatively harmless intoxicant.[7] Recommendation: No criminal penalties for marijuana use.

- Le Dain Commission of the Canadian Government, 1970. The commission's interim report was perhaps the most expansive of all studies to date. This comprehensive account was written after members of the panel had traveled more than 17,000 miles. They held hearings and interviewed young people who were avid marijuana users after guaranteeing them immunity from prosecution. In all, the commission estimated 12,000 Canadians attended those hearings. A member of the panel was Dr. Heinz E. Lehmann, clinical director of the Doulas Hospital in Montreal, an internationally recognized authority on drugs.

It was an international inquiry. Members of the panel received information from the United States. They traveled to European countries and interviewed hundreds of young people in the drug scene, as well as doctors and hospital staffs. Adult marijuana users were also interviewed: teachers, journalists, business executives, pilots, scientists, politicians, lawyers, and bankers, among others.[8]

Young people frequently contrasted the effects of marijuana with those of alcohol and described marijuana as a drug of peace, "a drug that reduces tendencies to aggression while suggesting that alcohol produces hostile, aggressive behavior."[9]

This commission concluded:[10]

- Marijuana is not an addicting drug. Physical dependence on marijuana has not been demonstrated.
- Users do not develop tolerance in the classical sense—the kind of tolerance that leads to increases in the dosage.
- If users stay high for several days in a row the drug experience loses much of its freshness and clarity and, consequently, they prefer intermittent use.
- In some cases it was reported that psychological dependence was present. This kind of dependency occurs regularly with

respect to such things as television, music, books, religion, sex, money, favorite foods, and hobbies. (Today the commission would no doubt include the Internet.)

- Sleep is the usual consequence of overdose.

No deaths due directly to smoking or eating marijuana have been documented.

- The steppingstone theory that marijuana use leads to heroin use is stated but given little credence. Alcohol and barbiturates rather than marijuana have most frequently preceded heroin use.
- No evidence exists that marijuana smoking leads to lung cancer.
- David E. Smith M.D., of the Haight-Ashbury Free Clinic in San Francisco reported he had not observed any cases of "cannabis psychosis" among the 35,000 marijuana users attending that clinic.

The commission summed it all up by saying that it is a grave error to indulge in deliberate distortion or exaggeration concerning the alleged dangers of a particular drug or to base a program of drug education upon a strategy of fear.[11] The Le Dain Commission recommended, as the overwhelming majority of honest scientific investigative boards have, that serious consideration should be given to legalizing marijuana.[12]

By the late 1970s, with the help of NORML's public education, the majority of Americans favored marijuana decriminalization. Decriminalization was a position taken by notable organizations such as the American Medical Association, the American Bar Association, the National Council of Churches, and B'nai B'rith—and by notable people such as Ann Landers, William F. Buckley, Jr., and Art Linkletter. In a 1996 interview with the *San Francisco Examiner*, referring to the raid of the San Francisco Cannabis Buyer's Club, which had offered marijuana as medicine, Dr. David E. Smith said, "They invaded and hurt something that was working in order to try and discredit the whole issue."

During his 1976 bid for the presidency, Jimmy Carter gave his support for marijuana decriminalization. When he was president, he asked Congress to change the federal law. His request was rejected.

Pot "Information" Is Out of Control

A 1993 example of creating fear appeared in a publication called *Substance Abuse & the Family: A Child's Nightmare.* It was officially sponsored by the Deputy Sheriffs' Association of Santa Clara County, California. The sheriffs no doubt meant well, but they provided the same kind of anti-marijuana propaganda that was in the book *Marijuana Alert.*

On the inside back cover is a full-page photo ad contributed by Barq's Root Beer. It reads, "Some Kids Think Drugs Will Make Them Cool and Laid-Back. They're Right." The photo is of a young boy dead in a coffin.

What fueled the marijuana scare stories? Remember that marijuana first gained notice and emerged in the United States in the 1920s when the abuse potential of other drugs such as cocaine, morphine, and heroin was first understood. The public was misled into believing that marijuana was equally dangerous and addictive. The federal government then erroneously, or perhaps purposely, classified marijuana as a narcotic and made it illegal in 1937, under highly questionable circumstances.

Even if the federal government were found innocent of a conspiracy to protect multinational corporations and to expand its own agenda and job security, it would have to be found guilty today of a conspiracy of silence—of keeping silent about its knowledge of marijuana being not a dangerous drug but being a valuable medicine.

Former Los Angeles Chief of Police Daryl Gates, who resigned in June 1992, testified before the Senate Judiciary Committee on September 5, 1990, that "pot smokers should be taken out and shot." With such a misunderstanding of marijuana, is it any wonder that over 400,000 people are arrested each year for possession?[13]

Tragically, there are probably hundreds of thousands, perhaps millions, of people who think the way former Chief Gates does. They honestly believe that marijuana is evil, poisonous, and physically addictive. None of those things are true of marijuana, although they are for nicotine cigarettes and alcohol.

Such unrealistic views are a reminder of the way many people react when they see an unfamiliar-looking spider or snake. Sadly, they kill it because they don't understand it. They're frightened. And those who have been "educated" by the *Reefer Madness*-type of propaganda are frightened of marijuana, still thinking it causes violence. They want it to disappear from the face of the earth.

Equally disturbing and tragic were statements made by Representative Charles B. Rangel (D-NY), chairman of the House Select Committee on Narcotics Abuse and Control. I listened intently to Rangel. I thought that he *must* be an authority on his subject or surely he wouldn't hold such a responsible position on drug abuse. My mouth dropped open when he said, "If our nation had listened to Peggy Mann [author of *Marijuana Alert*] when she first started writing about this subject (marijuana), we would not be in the fearful drug-ridden state we are in today."[14]

In 1987 and 1988, the debate over marijuana legalization started again. The April 4, 1989, issue of the *American Spectator* reported that the *New York Times* took the position that decriminalization of marijuana would make it easier to fight other drugs. Rangel again gave reckless statistics on why marijuana should never be legalized. He concluded by saying that the *Times* should be ashamed of itself for advocating decriminalization.[15]

Rangel again displayed his lack of marijuana education when he offered his answer to the question asked on the front page of *Parade* Magazine, June 12, 1994: "Should marijuana be legal?" Rangel said, "I will fight with all the vigor God has given me, any step that would expand the opportunities for people to self-destruct."[16] Another offensive example of ignorance (or perhaps of telling people what he thinks they want to hear) was put forward by House Speaker Newt Gingrich on July 15, 1995, when he belittled suggestions from the Food and Drug Administration that tobacco be regulated as a drug. Gingrich said that rather than fighting tobacco companies, the government should focus on drugs such as cocaine and marijuana.[17] (Isn't that a bit hypocritical, Newt, for one who has smoked marijuana and knows better?)

Such a lack of marijuana knowledge, or honesty, cannot be tolerated. Such uninformed thinking is producing ever tougher laws against the world's safest drug. Such uneducated reasoning is causing hundreds of thousands of citizens to be unfairly sent to prison (some to be killed or raped there) or to be killed or maimed by police.

The killings blamed on drugs are not done by people crazed by marijuana. Rather they occur in the war over drug profits at the street level. Until the profit is taken out of illegal drugs, there will be drug dealers and violence.

How about the anti-marijuana crusader organizations that we are constantly exposed to and that we trusted? They may mean well, but they also have been brainwashed. The federal government welcomed them aboard and helps them spread propaganda—with our tax dollars.

California Governor Pete Wilson, who is against medical marijuana, stated in his veto message on October 16, 1995, "The Federal Food and Drug Administration has considered the value of marijuana for medical use. The FDA concluded that marijuana has no recognized medical use."

The fact is that marijuana has *never* been submitted for review by the FDA.

The Shame of PRIDE

In 1976, after their daughter's teenage birthday party, two well-meaning parents panicked when they found marijuana roaches on the lawn. They grouped together other frightened parents who reacted to the hysteria created by propaganda. Soon there arose PRIDE (Parents' Resource Institute for Drug Education) and similar groups, which are now backed by top officials of NIDA and the DEA.

In the mid-1980s, PRIDE published a major drug policy recommendation that favored placing all drug users under quarantine until they could be "cured." The paper warned of an expected a 50 percent cure rate. It did not comment on the lifetime imprisonment of the 50 percent who remain "uncured."[18]

With authoritative leadership, some people become believers of whatever is told to them. PRIDE and other anti-marijuana throngs are good examples of people being brought together by what they believe is the truth.

PRIDE is active with hundreds of thousands of parents and students, and its programs are used in homes and schools throughout the United States as well as in other nations. PRIDE holds an annual World Drug Conference with every state and country represented. Its twentieth annual world conference was held March 5–8, 1997, in Atlanta, Georgia.

Sadly, PRIDE, with the backing of the DEA, which knows better, still professes that marijuana causes damage to the brain and reproductive system.[19] Tragically, some in the media accept reports from organizations such as PRIDE as accurate, and this perpetuates the misinformation.

Such erroneous reports have been continually refuted by scientific evidence. Remember the *Merck Manual of Diagnosis and Therapy*: "The chief opposition to the drug (marijuana) rests on a moral and political, and *not* a toxicologic foundation."

It's public knowledge that Dr. Gabriel Nahas's anti-marijuana studies have never been replicated in countless other research attempts. In December of 1983, to avoid a funding cutoff from the National Institute of Drug Abuse and mockery from his peers, Nahas renounced all his old THC metabolite build-up and unique chromosome petri dish tissue damage studies, conclusions, and extrapolations.[20] Still, PRIDE continues to promote him with these words: "Internationally known pharmacologist and educator, Dr. Nahas is in demand worldwide as a speaker and seminar leader on the subject of addictive drugs . . ."

Partnership for a Drug Free America Equally Guilty of Fabrication

The PDFA attempts to convince the public of marijuana's evil effects by offering the media public service ads free of charge. For example, the frying pan containing the sizzling egg, captioned, "This is drugs. This is your brain on drugs. *Any questions*?" PDFA members apparently felt that fiction was a justifiable means to an end. Hardly scientific, or true. Dr. Donald Blum of the UCLA Neurological Studies Center told KABC news that in another ad, a photo showing the effects of marijuana in fact show the brain waves of someone in a deep sleep—or in a coma. It took weeks before the PDFA removed the dishonest television spot. There was never an apology.[21] Yet such propaganda continues to terrify parents and brings more money to these organizations and to the DEA. *Any questions*?

The deceit must be replaced with honest scientific facts. "Pot-phobia" must end. The public needs to know the truth about drugs, legal and illegal—how they can be used, abused, or misused. When young people are taught that drugs cause addiction and horrible suffering and then they find that marijuana is relatively harmless and fun, it causes distrust of all such warnings. The sensational rhetoric is a lure that encourages many to try the drug.

On February 20, 1996, the Associated Press released a study by The Partnership for a Drug Free America. In this study, 9,341 teenagers, preteens, and parents were queried. In 1993, 74 percent saw a great risk of marijuana addiction; in 1995, only 64 percent had the same view. In 1993, 73 percent believed marijuana led to hard drugs; by 1995, only 67 percent believed marijuana led to hard drugs. Forty-four percent found marijuana helped them to relax, up from 34 percent in 1993. Partnership members are concerned that marijuana use will continue upward "unless these attitudes change." The study was conducted by Audits & Surveys Worldwide, Inc.

What I hear the PDFA saying is that unless people continue to listen to and believe the propaganda that marijuana is evil, addictive, and poisonous, use will continue to increase. Those earlier high percentages would never have been perceived had people heard the truth to begin with. The more recent numbers indicate that people are learning on their own, without hearing unadulterated marijuana reporting, that compared to alcohol and nicotine, marijuana is relatively harmless.

Is It Time for a New Approach?

New solutions are being studied by European countries, including the Netherlands, Germany, Spain, France, and Italy. The Netherlands appears to be leading the way to sanity. Marijuana use has not been a crime in that country for almost twenty years. The Dutch philosophy is that drugs are a part of life, they will never go away, but they can be controlled. The Dutch see drug use as a health problem, not a criminal problem. By decriminalizing marijuana, the Dutch have successfully prevented young people from experimenting with hard drugs.

Marijuana and hashish are sold in coffee houses and smoked there. Young adults are not in contact with criminal figures who are interested in switching them from nonaddictive marijuana to hard drugs. With twenty years of coffee house experience, the government has learned that marijuana is not a steppingstone to other drugs. Hard drug use has remained stable for more than ten years in the Netherlands. The government believes that the police cannot solve the drug challenge.

Including state and local spending, in the last fifteen years, the U.S. war on drugs has cost $250 billion and produced no reduction in drug use. Could it be time to change strategies? The emphasis in the Netherlands is going after the hard drug dealers, organized crime, and traffickers. Heavy focus is given to getting hard drug users into drug treatment programs.

Our government believes that condoning any illegal drug use will create millions of hard drug users. This assumption does not prove out. All illegal drugs are currently and easily obtained. In over fifty years of contact with marijuana users, I have yet to see one of them seeking out hard drugs when marijuana is available.

Even our own U.S. Department of Justice says that crime would be eliminated by marijuana legalization. The following information is from its own bulletin "Marijuana Digest," 1991:

> The large profits of drug marketing, particularly of marijuana, have also attracted rural groups formerly engaged in other criminal activities such as illegal alcohol production. However, these causes of crime would be eliminated by legalization. There are no studies on record that indicate that significant numbers of people steal to support marijuana dependency. While occasional stories surface of booby-trapped fields, the marijuana trade does not have a violent reputation.[22]

DARE to Tell the Truth?

DARE is the nation's largest drug use prevention program, initiated in 1983 by former Los Angeles Police Chief Daryl Gates. It reaches approximately 50 percent of local school districts nationwide and receives at least $700 million annually from the federal government.[23] DARE presents some accurate data, but it also includes unproven scientific theories and innuendoes that marijuana is extremely dangerous.

The hazard lies in our youth trusting the police to present only honest, scientifically proven information. Instead, police officers present erroneous information that they have been taught, such as the claim that marijuana causes brain and lung damage and sterility. Students have reported that a police officer speaking for DARE remarked, "We can't say for sure that pot causes brain damage, but that's what it does. You just can't tell—yet."[24]

Some of the DARE police officers tell students that illegal drugs are very bad and using them makes you a bad person. The officers ask students if they know anyone who uses drugs. The students feel they can trust the police and may confide in an officer that their parents or siblings smoke pot. In one case in Colorado, a ten-year-old boy called the police to report that his parents smoked marijuana. He identified himself as "a DARE kid."

In another case, Mary, a fifth-grader in Maine, visited the police station following a DARE class and informed them that she knew two people who use marijuana: her parents! The police obtained a search warrant and discovered some pot plants in the parents' bedroom. Mary's parents were arrested and convicted of growing marijuana. Mary has required extensive psychological counseling owing to her guilty feelings of betrayal.[25]

Sadly, when young adults find that they have been deceived, they lose respect for the police, and then they question information presented about all drugs. DARE has had no significant effect on the students' use of any of the substances measured.[26]

Marijuana Must Be Legalized

If we had the opportunity to exchange the thousands of assault weapons on the street for pea shooters, would we be open to such a trade? That's the difference between other drugs and the marijuana "pea shooter."

Intoxication is a fact of life. There will never be a drug-free America. No amount of threats, including the death penalty, no amount of interdiction, no amount of prison sentences have ever worked in reducing the use of drugs. Mankind and animals have used drugs since the beginning of recorded history. Even cats roll, tumble, and "smile" with a hit of catnip, and birds get drunk on pyracantha berries!

As long as human beings are curious and wish to heighten metaphysical or religious experiences, seek a release from poverty or racism, or just relax, drugs will be used whether they're legal or illegal. After thirteen years of alcohol prohibition, the government finally realized that it was glamorizing alcohol use. Unintentionally, it has done the same thing with marijuana.

The best we can do is legalize the least harmful drug, marijuana. When marijuana is finally legalized, at least an additional 100,000 people will be freed up: police employees, prison guards, prison cooks, National Guardsmen, DEA workers, helicopter pilots, parole officers, and secretaries who daily produce thousands of pages of paperwork. We will then have an opportunity to arrest and incarcerate hard drug kingpins, sex offenders, and violent criminals. Prison cells will be available, saving billions of dollars in additional prison construction.

I've known police officers who abhor their jobs because of the marijuana hypocrisy, which is a job requirement. Officers who are able to avoid urine testing often have a relaxing smoke of pot a few times a week in the privacy of their homes. The next day they have to go out and arrest a pot smoker. Consequently, some officers have lost respect for the legal system.

Even during prohibition, alcohol was exempt for religious and industrial purposes. But not pot. It's not about justice; it's about saving face and protecting multinational cartels. When the federal government can think of a good way to save face and ignore pressure from big money, as it finally did with cigarettes, marijuana will be legalized. With enough citizens demanding it, legalization will come to pass, sooner or later.

On May 10, 1994, country music star Willie Nelson, 61, was arrested in Hewitt, Texas, for possession of marijuana. He said he was driving home, encountered heavy fog, and pulled over to get some sleep. Police approached the car to investigate. Searching the car, they found less than two ounces of pot. In a January 1991 *High Times* interview, Nelson said, "I'm not in favor of the war on flowers and herbs. Stress is the greatest killer on this planet, and the greatest medicine for stress is still cannabis."[27]

It's time for Uncle Sam to correct the "marijuana mistake."

The Bill of Rights Is Scrapped

One of my deepest concerns about the marijuana drug war is that not only are we being deprived of a botanical that offers proven medical benefits, but we are also losing our rights under the Constitution. As far as the federal government is concerned, marijuana is illegal for use by anyone, for any reason. For centuries marijuana has been used by people of many faiths for religious purposes as well as by millions of people around the world for medicine. It's criminal that patients who derive proven benefits from pot are subject to arrest, loss of their property, and possibly years in prison. Whether you personally wish to use marijuana or not, consider that when some individuals lose their rights, we all lose. Violations of these constitutional rights are conspicuous and rampant in the war on marijuana:

- First Amendment freedom of religion and peaceable assembly
- Fourth Amendment protection against unreasonable searches and seizure
- Fifth Amendment promise of presumed innocence
- Seventh and Eighth Amendments guarantee of a jury trial and guarantee against excessive fines and cruel and unusual punishments.

Legalize Marijuana Now!

I have, in this book, explained the many reasons that marijuana should be—indeed *must* be—relegalized:

1. There is growing disrespect for the law. Misuse of criminal law to punish peaceful users of marijuana far outweighs any harm caused by the drug itself.
2. Damage is caused to the individual by incarceration, which often also results in rape and suicide. Incarceration causes humiliation from being a convict and an ex-convict, losing employment, losing family and home, and having to rely on government welfare, which costs taxpayers billions more.
3. The illegality of marijuana brings young people and adults in contact with criminal elements, which can lead to hard drugs, violence, or death.
4. The billions of dollars spent on marijuana arrests, prosecution, interdiction, and imprisonment is helping to bankrupt the country for a drug that the DEA's own administrative judge called "one of the safest

therapeutically active substances known to man" and "safer than many foods we commonly consume."

5. The DEA should not make decisions for medical doctors regarding what medicines should or should not be prescribed.
6. Marijuana prohibition encourages the black market and is causing turf wars, violence, death in the streets, and a mockery of law enforcement. Marijuana's bulkiness also encourages the criminal element to concentrate on easier drugs to smuggle such as heroin, cocaine, methamphetamines, and LSD. Peaceful marijuana users are exposed to more dangerous drugs.
7. Marijuana prohibition is resulting in the passage of more anti-marijuana laws, hiring of more narcotics agents, creation of a false sense of security, and further erosion of our constitutional rights.
8. The adults must understand that they have been educated to believe alcohol, nicotine and caffeine are nondrugs, while the pot their children use is evil. Each drug must be graded according to its relative potential for social and personal harm. If people are not honestly educated about marijuana, they will continue to keep it illegal. The "war on drugs" theme should be changed to "The war for *honest drug education*."
9. The grievous miscarriage of justice in the form of entrapment must stop. It causes the worst kind of resentment against law enforcement. Most Americans empathize with the person entrapped. (A valid example was the aftermath of the drug entrapment of Mayor Marion Barry of Washington, D.C.: his landslide election put him back into office in November of 1994.)
10. People currently serving time for marijuana offenses should be set free with a clear record. This would greatly increase respect for our legal system, and it would eliminate billions of tax dollars for never-ending prison construction. (If individual legislators had to pay for

keeping nonviolent people in prison, the odds are that thousands of overcrowded prison cells would be emptied.)

What can we do to hasten the relegalization of marijuana?

1. Speak out against present drug testing. Instead, request impairment testing, which evaluates a worker's competence through a hand-eye coordination test, which is similar to a video game and takes about one minute.
2. Demand an investigation of why marijuana as medicine is not acceptable to the DEA when it's acceptable to medical doctors.
3. Encourage recognized entertainers and other public figures to acknowledge their use of marijuana and to report if it helps them creatively or medically. If you know a screen writer or director, suggest they reveal how marijuana is medicine.
4. Inform your legislators that marijuana relieves stress, is not physically addictive, encourages peace not violence, and is far less dangerous than alcohol.
5. If you have been helped by marijuana as medicine, call radio and television talk shows and write letters to newspaper editors.
6. Demand that medical research on marijuana be allowed.
7. Request a presidential commission to study the medical uses of marijuana, and ask why it has been withheld from our citizens for so long when it has been recognized by the medical community for thousands of years.
8. Contact the president of the United States. Ask him to work for the release of all those who have been put in prison for the use of marijuana. Ask him to work for the restoration of their rights and the return of their property. Ask that marijuana be made available immediately for those patients it would aid medically.

9. Encourage honest education for all in the media by recommending books that present an accurate account of marijuana and why it is prohibited.
10. Join NORML to learn the true facts about both the positive and negative effects of pot. The more you learn, the more you will recognize the tragedy and injustice of marijuana prohibition.

What are the honest possibilities of marijuana being legalized? Let me just say that in 1930, U.S. Senator Morris Sheppard stated that there was as much chance of ending alcohol prohibition as there was "for a hummingbird to fly to the planet Mars with the Washington Monument tied to its tail." Three years later, alcohol prohibition was repealed.[28]

A $50,000 Challenge

My research and personal experience have convinced me of the benefits of marijuana. Even if I have to mortgage my home to pay it, I hereby offer $50,000 as a cash reward to anyone who can scientifically prove that marijuana is not medicine.

Epilogue

> *Cowardice asks the question: is it safe? Expediency asks the question: is it politic? Vanity asks the question: is it popular? But conscience asks the question: is it right? And there comes a time when one must take a position that is neither safe, nor politic, nor popular—but one must take it because it is right. One has a moral responsibility to disobey unjust laws . . . An unjust law is a code that is out of harmony with the moral law.*
>
> Dr. Martin Luther King, Jr.
> "Letter from a Birmingham Jail" (1963)

IN THE WORDS OF PRESIDENT JOHN F. KENNEDY: "The great enemy of the truth is very often not the lie—deliberate, contrived and dishonest—but the myth—persistent, persuasive and unrealistic."

On August 2, 1977, President Jimmy Carter addressed Congress on the harm done by prohibition: "Penalties against possession of a drug should not be more damaging to an individual than the drug itself. Therefore, I support legislation amending federal law to eliminate all federal penalties for up to one ounce of marijuana." An honest mandate by a courageous president.

Appendix I

Transcripts of House Hearings on the Marijuana Tax Act I

Following are excerpts of the hearings of the Committee on Ways and Means, House of Representatives, 75th Congress, First Session on H.R. 6385, April 27–30 and May 4, 1937.

The following were the witnesses: Clinton M. Hester, assistant general counsel for Department of the Treasury; H. J. Anslinger, Commissioner of Narcotics, Department of the Treasury; Raymond G. Scarlett, Wm. G. Scarlett & Co., Baltimore, Maryland; Dr. William Woodward, legislative counsel, American Medical Association, Chicago, Illinois.

Committee members were as follows: Robert L. Doughton, North Carolina, chairman; Fred M. Vinson, Kentucky; David J. Lewis, Maryland; Daniel A. Reed, New York; John D. Dingell, Michigan; and John W. McCormack, Massachusetts.

In April 1937 the U.S. House Committee on Ways and Means of the 75th Congress held hearings for the proposed legislation on the control of marijuana through prohibitive taxation.

Note that William Woodward, M.D., representing the American Medical Association, was against the passage of marijuana prohibition.

> *Chairman*: The Committee will come to order. The meeting this morning has been called for the purpose of con-

sidering H.R. 6385, introduced by me on April 14, 1937, a bill to impose an occupational excise tax upon certain dealers in marijuana, and to safeguard the revenue therefrom by registry and recording. This bill was introduced by me at the request of the Secretary of the Treasury. Representatives of the Treasury Department are here this morning to explain the bill. Mr. Hester, assistant general counsel for the Treasury Department will be the first witness to be heard in behalf of the proposed legislation.

Hester: Mr. Chairman and members of the Ways and Means Committee, for the past two years the Treasury Department has been making a study of the subject of marijuana. A drug which is found in the flowering tops, seeds and leaves of Indian hemp, and is now being used extensively by highschool children in cigarettes. Its effect is deadly. I would like to say at this point that we have with us this morning Commissioner Anslinger, of the Bureau of Narcotics, who has had charge of the enforcement of the Harrison Narcotic act, and who will have charge of the enforcement of this act, if this bill is enacted into law. We also have with us a pharmacologist who is prepared to testify on the effect of the drug on human beings. We also have an expert chemist, and one of the outstanding botanists in the country, who are prepared to testify with reference to the bill, if you desire to hear them. The marijuana cigarette is one of the most insidious of all forms of dope, largely because of the failure of the public to understand its fatal qualities. The nation is almost defenseless against it, having no federal laws to cope with it, and virtually no organized campaign for combating it. The result is tragic. School children are prey to peddlers who infest school neighborhoods. High school boys and girls buy the destructive weed without knowledge of its capacity for harm, and conscienceless dealers sell it with impunity. This is a national problem and it must have national attention. The fatal marijuana cigarette must be recognized as a deadly drug, and the American children must be protected against it.

The purpose of House Resolution 6385 is to employ the federal taxing power, not only to raise revenue from the marijuana traffic, but also to discourage the current and widespread undesirable use of marijuana by smokers and drug addicts, *and thus drive the traffic into channels where the plant will be put to valuable, industrial, medical, and scientific uses* [emphasis added]. In accomplishing the general purpose two objectives should dictate the form of the proposed legislation. First, the development of a scheme of taxation which would raise revenue, and which would also render virtually impossible the acquisition of marijuana by persons who would put it to illicit uses without unduly interfering with the use of the plant for industrial, medical, and scientific purposes, and second, the development of an adequate means of publicizing dealings in marijuana in order that the traffic may be effectively taxed and controlled. In order to obviate the possibility of an attack upon the constitutionality of this bill, it, like the National Firearms Act, permits the transfer of marijuana to nonregistered persons upon the payment of a heavy transfer tax. The bill would permit the transfer of marijuana to anyone. It would impose a $100 an ounce tax upon a transfer to a person who might use it for purposes which are dangerous and harmful to the public, just as the National Firearms Act permits a transfer of a machine-gun to anyone but imposes a $200 tax upon a transfer to a person who would be likely to put it to an illegal use. Although the $100 transfer tax in this bill is intended to be prohibitive, as is the $200 transfer tax in the National Firearms Act, It is submitted that it is constitutional as a revenue measure.

Vinson: What is the fair market value, per ounce, of marijuana?

Hester: In its raw state it is about $1 per ounce, as a drug.

Vinson: I notice in your statement—and I want to say it's a good statement, the gentleman does not have any other kind of statement when he comes before our committee.

Hester: I thank you.

Chairman: Through what channel or agency is this drug in its deleterious form dispensed or distributed? Is it sold by druggists, or at grocery stores?

Hester: I will answer your question, but I hope you will ask the same question of Mr. Anslinger, because he can speak more authoritatively on that phase of the subject. The flowered tops, leaves, and seeds, are smoked in cigarettes.

Chairman: Is it carried generally by druggists?

Hester: I do not think so, for this reason. It is very variable. It may affect you in one way, and me in another way, and then, too, there are many better substitutes.

Chairman: And a deleterious use?

Hester: The smoking of it, yes. You can take the tops, leaves, and seeds and fix them in a way somewhat similar to tobacco. It is just about the same as tobacco. You can smoke it like tobacco.

Chairman: Just as an illustration, suppose I were in the market for some of this drug, where would I find it?

Hester: There are about 10,000 acres under cultivation by legitimate producers.

Chairman: I want to know where it can be bought; where is it being sold?

Lewis: Where do the victims get it?

Reed: I think what the chairman wants to know is how the high-school children are able to get it. Is it true that there are illicit peddlers who hang around the high-school buildings, and as soon as they find out that there is some boy to whom they think they can sell it, they make his acquaintance?

Hester: Yes, I read in the newspapers not long ago that a place on Twelfth Street was raided, where a lady was selling marijuana.

Lewis: Do legitimate companies make these cigarettes, or are they made in an illicit manner, like bootleg whiskey used to be made? Do reputable firms make these cigarettes?

Hester: I would like to refer that question to Commissioner Anslinger.

Reed: I would like to make a statement at this point in reference to this question. Some years ago the committee of the House of which I happened to be chairman held a hearing going into the narcotic problem. This was at the time that there was a great deal of talk about heroin, and we devoted a good deal of time of that hearing to that subject. We had experts there from New York and other parts of the country. At that time they were selling heroin through peddlers to high-school students. Particularly to athletes. The peddler was usually a man of some personality, and he would sell the heroin to these tired boys as they came off the athletic training field. They would say to these boys, "Here is something that will put pep in you." They soon had a lot of these boys in these schools developed into addicts. I assume you have the same thing here.

Chairman: Mr. Anslinger, the committee will be glad to have a statement from you at this time. Will you state your full name and the position you occupy with the Treasury Department?

Anslinger: Mr. Chairman, my name is H. J. Anslinger. I am commissioner of narcotics in the Bureau of Narcotics, in the Treasury Department. Mr. Chairman and distinguished members of the Way and Means Committee, this traffic in marijuana is increasing to such an extent that it has become the cause for the greatest national concern. In medical schools the physician-to-be is taught that without opium medicine would be like a one armed-man. That is true, because you cannot get along without opium. But here we have a drug that is not like opium. Opium has all of the good of Dr. Jekyll and all the evil of Mr. Hyde. This drug is entirely the monster Hyde, the harmful effect which cannot be measured.

Reed: I want to be certain what this is. Is this the same weed that grows wild in some of the Western States which is now called the loco weed?

Anslinger: No, sir, that is another family.

Dingell: That is also a harmful drug-producing weed, is it not?

Anslinger: Not to my knowledge: it is not used by humans.

Chairman: In what particular sections does this weed grow wild?

Anslinger: In almost every state in the Union today.

Reed: Is it not Indian Hemp?

Anslinger: It is Indian Hemp. We have some specimens here.

Vinson: When was this brought to your attention as being a menace among our own people?

Anslinger: About ten years ago.

Vinson: Why did you wait until 1937 to bring in a recommendation of this kind?

Anslinger: Ten years ago we only heard about it throughout the Southwest. It is only in the last few years that it has become a national menace. It has grown like wildfire, but it has only become a national menace in the last three years. It is only in the past two years that we have had to send reports to the League of Nations.

McCormack: What are its first manifestations, a feeling of grandeur and self-exaltation, and things of that sort?

Anslinger: It affects different individuals in different ways. Some individuals have a complete loss of a sense of time or a sense of value. They lose the sense of place. They have an increased feeling of physical strength and power. Some people will fly into a delirious rage, and they are temporarily irresponsible and may commit violent crimes. Others will laugh uncontrollably. It is impossible to say what the effect will be on any individual. Those research men who have tried it have always been under control. They have always insisted upon that.

McCormack: Is it used by the criminal class?

Anslinger: Yes, it is. It is dangerous to the mind and body, and particularly dangerous to the criminal type, because it releases all of the inhibitions.

Dingell: What is the price of marijuana?

Anslinger: The addict pays anywhere from 10 to 25 cents per cigarette. It will be sold by the cigarette. In illicit traffic the bulk price would be around $20 a pound. Legitimately, the bulk is around $2 a pound.

Dingell: How does that compare with the price of opium or morphine? Do the class of people who use this drug use it because it is cheaper than the other kinds?

Anslinger: That is one reason, yes, sir. To be a morphine or heroin addict it would cost you from $5 to $8 a day to maintain your supply. But if you want to smoke a cigarette you pay 10 cents.

McCormack: Just one of them can knock the socks off of you?

Anslinger: One of them can do it.

McCormack: Some of those cigarettes are sold much cheaper than 10 cents, are they not? In other words it is a low-priced cigarette, and that is one of the reasons for the tremendous increase in its use?

Anslinger: Yes. It is low enough in price for school children to buy it.

McCormack: And they have parties in different parts of the country that they call "Reefer parties?"

Anslinger: Yes, sir, we have heard of them, and know of them.

McCormack: Another thing is that they will not be able to get other kinds of dope, but they do have an opportunity to get this marijuana, which causes it to be so much sought after and used in the community.

Anslinger: That is true, and the effect is just passed by word of mouth, and everybody wants to try it.

Chairman: Dr. Woodward, will you come forward and give your name and address and the capacity in which you appear.

Woodward: Mr. Chairman and gentlemen, my name is Dr. William C. Woodward, representing the American Medical Association. The address is 535 North Dearborn Street, Chicago, Illinois.

Chairman: Do you appear in the capacity of a medical expert, a legal expert, or a legislative expert, or in all three capacities?

Woodward: My profession is that of a practitioner of medicine and of legal medicine. I have combined the two. If you want to class me as an expert, you might class me as a medical expert. I have lectured as medical lawyer and doctor.

Chairman: Thank you, Dr. Woodward. Please continue.

Woodward: There is nothing in the medicinal use of cannabis that has any relation to cannabis addiction. I see the word "cannabis" in preference to the word "marijuana," because cannabis is the correct word for describing the plant and its products. The term "marijuana" is a mongrel word that has crept into this country over the Mexican border and has no general meaning, except as it relates to the use of cannabis preparations for smoking. It is not recognized in medicine, and hardly recognized even in the Treasury Department. Marijuana is not the correct term. It was the use of the term "marijuana" rather then the use of the term "cannabis," or the use of the term "Indian Hemp" that was responsible, as you realized, probably, a day or two ago, for the failure of the dealers of Indian hempseed to connect up this bill with their business until rather late in the day. So, I shall use the word cannabis, and I should certainly suggest that if any legislation is enacted, the term used be "cannabis," and not the mongrel word "marijuana." I say the medicinal use of cannabis had nothing to do with cannabis or marijuana addiction. In all that you have heard here thus far, no mention has been made of any excessive use of the drug by any doctor, or its excessive distribution by any pharmacist. And yet the burden of this bill is placed heavily on the doctors and pharmacists of the country, and I say very heavily, most heavily, possibly of all, on the farmers of the country. My interest is primarily, of course, in medical aspects. We object to imposing of an additional tax on physicians, pharmacists, and others catering to the sick: to require that they register and reregister, that they have special order forms to be used for this particular drug, when this matter can just as well be covered by the Harrison Narcotics Act. If you are referring to the particular problem, I object because it is utterly unsusceptible of execution, and an act that is not susceptible to execution is a bad thing on the statute books.

Chairman: If the use of marijuana as a dope has increased until it has become serious and a menace to the public, as has been testified here—and the testimony here has been that it causes people to lose their mental balance, causes them to become criminals, so they do not seem to realize right from wrong after they become addicts of this drug—taking into consideration the growth of its injurious effects and its diminution in its use so far as any beneficial effect is concerned, you realize, do you not, that some good may be accomplished by this proposed legislation?

Woodward: Some legislation, yes, Mr. Chairman.

Chairman: If that is admitted, let us get down to a few concrete facts. With the experience with the Bureau of Narcotics and with the state governments trying to enforce the laws that are on the state statute books against the use of this deleterious drug, and the federal government has realized that the state laws are ineffective, don't you think some federal legislation necessary?

Woodward: I do not.

Chairman: You do not?

Woodward: I think it is the usual tendency to—

Chairman: I believe you did say in response to Mr. Cooper that you believed that some change, or some legislation, or some change in the present law would be helpful. If this is true, why have you not been here before this bill was introduced, proposing some remedy for this evil?

Woodward: Mr. Chairman, I have visited the Commissioner of Narcotics on various occasions—

Chairman: That is not an answer to my question at all.

Woodward: I have not been here because—

Chairman: You have been representing the medical association. If your association has realized the necessity, the importance of some legislation—which you now admit—why did you wait until this bill was introduced to come here and make mention of it? Why did you not come here voluntarily and suggest to this committee some legislation?

Woodward: I have talked these matters over many times with the—

Chairman: That does not do us any good to talk matters over. I have talked over a lot of things. The states do not seem to be able to deal with it effectively, nor is the federal government dealing with it at all. Why do you wait until now and then come in here to oppose something that is presented to us? You suggest nothing whatever to correct the evil that exists. Now, I do not like to have a roundabout answer to that question.

Woodward: We do not propose legislation directly to Congress when the same end can be reached through one of the executive departments of the government.

Chairman: You admit that it has not been done. You said you thought some legislation would be helpful. That is what I am trying to hold you down to. Now, why have you not proposed any legislation? This is what I want a clear, definite, clean-cut answer to.

Woodward: In the first place, it is not a medical addiction that is involved, and the data do not come before the medical society. You may absolutely forbid the use of cannabis by any physician, disposition of cannabis by any pharmacist in the country, and you would not have touched your cannabis addiction as it stands today, because there is no relation between it and the practice of medicine or pharmacy. It is entirely outside of those two branches.

Chairman: If the statement you have just made has any relation to the question that I have asked, I just do not have the mind to understand it: I am sorry.

Woodward: I say that we do not ordinarily come directly to Congress if a department can take care of the matter. I have talked with the commissioner, with Commissioner Anslinger.

Chairman: If you want to advise us on legislation, you should come here with some constructive proposals, rather than criticism, rather than trying to throw obstacles in the way of something that the federal government is trying to do. It is not only an unselfish motive in this, but they have a serious responsibility.

Woodward: We cannot understand yet, Mr. Chairman, why this bill should have been prepared in secret for two years without any intimation, even to the profession, that it was being prepared.

Chairman: Is not the fact that you were not consulted your real objection to this bill?

Woodward: Not at all.

Chairman: That is not it?

Woodward: Not at all. We always try to be helpful.

Vinson: The fact that they took that length of time in the preparation of the bill, what has that to do with the merits of the legislation?

Woodward: The legislation is impractical so far as enforcement is concerned, and the same study devoted to state legislation with 44 state legislatures in session this year would have produced much better results.

Dingell: The impression I gain from your last remark is that it is only the medical profession that is interested in this bill, but what about the 125,000,000 people in this country? This is not only a bill that the medical profession is interested in, or that the AMA is interested in, but all the people are interested in it. Incidentally, I would like to ask, how many doctors are members of the AMA?

Woodward: Approximately 100,000.

Dingell: That many are members of the AMA?

Woodward: Yes, sir.

Dingell: How many doctors are there in the United States?

Woodward: Probably 140,000 or 150,000, or there may be 160,000.

Dingell: Are we to understand that the medical men of the state of Michigan, or the medical profession in Wayne County, or the medical association of Detroit, are opposed to this legislation?

Woodward: I do not know. No medical man would identify this bill with a medicine until he read it through, because marijuana is not a drug.

Dingell: Please tell me this, what effort has been made in my state through the medical association to protect the school children, and the unfortunate people who are falling victims to this habit? I ask that question because we are talking about controlling it through the state. I want to know what has been done by the state of Michigan, and the members of the medical profession to give protection intended by this bill.

Woodward: It is, of course, impossible for me to say just what has been done in any particular state, but in the Michigan laws of 1931, chapter 173, they do regulate the production and distribution of cannabis indica.

Dingell: What kind of regulation is that?

Woodward: I do not have the law here.

Dingell: Can you tell me whether that legislation was at the time sponsored by the medical association of my state?

Woodward: I do not know. I cannot carry all of those details in my mind. You understand marijuana is simply a name given cannabis. It is a mongrel word brought in from Mexico. It is a popular term to indicate cannabis, like "coke" is used to indicate cocaine, and as "dope" is used to indicate opium.

Dingell: We know that it is a habit and is spreading, particularly among youngsters. We learn that from the pages of the newspapers. You say that Michigan has a law regulating it. We have a state law, but we do not seem to be able to get anywhere with it, because, as I have said, the habit is growing. The number of victims is increasing each year.

Woodward: There is no evidence of that.

Dingell: I have not been impressed with your testimony here as reflecting the sentiments of the high-class members of the medical profession in my state. I am confident that the medical profession in my state of Michigan, and in Wayne County, particularly, or in my district, will subscribe wholeheartedly to any law that will suppress this thing, despite the fact that there is a $1 tax imposed.

Woodward: If there was any law that would absolutely suppress the thing, perhaps that is true. But when the law simply contains provisions that impose a useless expense, and does not accomplish the result—

Dingell: That is simply your personal opinion. That is kindred to the opinion you entertained with reference to the Harrison Narcotics Act.

Woodward: If we had been asked to cooperate in drafting it—

Dingell: You are not cooperating in this at all.

Woodward: As a matter if fact, it does not serve to suppress the use of opium or cocaine.

Dingell: The medical profession should be doing its utmost to aid in the suppression of this curse that is eating the very vitals of the nation.

Woodward: They are.

McCormack: Are you not simply piqued because you were not consulted in the drafting of the bill?

Woodward: That is not the case at all. I said, in explaining why I was here, that the measure should have been discussed, and an expression of opinion obtained before the Treasury Department brought the bill before the Congress of the United States, so that it would be in a form that would be acceptable, with as few differences as possible.

McCormack: With all respect to you and for your appearance here, is it not a fact that you are peeved because you were not called in and consulted in the drafting of the bill?

Woodward: Not in the least. I have drafted too many bills to be peeved about that.

McCormack: There is no question that the drug habit has been increasing rapidly in recent years.

Woodward: There is no evidence to show whether or not it has been.

McCormack: In your opinion, has it increased?

Woodward: I should say that it has increased slightly. Newspaper exploitation of the habit has done more to increase it than anything else.

McCormack: Is it likely to increase further unless some effort is made to suppress it?

Woodward: I do not know. The exploitation tempts young men and women to venture into the habit.

McCormack: At any event it is a drug.

Woodward: Cannabis indica is a drug, yes.

Chairman: The public authorities dealing with this evil, the state authorities, and federal authorities, say they need further legislation in order to protect the people from its insidious influence and effects. Under these conditions, do you not believe Congress should try to do something?

Woodward: I think something should be done, but it is only a question of what should be done.

Chairman: You stated a while ago that you believed this law would be ineffective. Of course the law against carrying concealed weapons, designed to protect people against criminals is not entirely effective, but you would not advocate the repeal of the law. The laws against prostitution and murder are not entirely effective, but without legislative control, we would be at the mercy of the criminal class, and we would have no civilization whatever.

> *Chairman*: We thank you for your appearance before the committee. We will now take a recess to meet tomorrow at 10 in executive session.

The House and Ways Committee approved the Marijuana Tax Act and sent it to the Senate Subcommittee, which after one day of hearings also approved it.

On January 14, 1937, the bill came before the full house. Only four congressmen asked for an explanation of the bill's provisions. What they received was an account of the criminal acts perpetuated by marijuana use from a member of the Ways and Means Committee. The act passed without a roll call. The testimony presented by Commissioner Harry S. Anslinger before the Ways and Means Committee was given as fact and accepted as such because his title was Commissioner of Narcotics. The question of whether the American Medical Association agreed with the bill was answered by Congressman Vinton.

> Our committee heard testimony of Dr. William *Wharton* [emphasis added] who not only gave this measure his full support, but also the approval from the American Medical Association which he represented as legislative counsel.

The Marijuana Tax Act was enacted into law in September of 1937.

Appendix II

Excerpts from "Opinion and Recommended Ruling, Findings of Fact, Conclusions of Law and Decision of Administrative Law Judge"

The following are the words of Judge Francis L. Young, September 1988, in the matter of the marijuana rescheduling petition. United States Department of Justice, Drug Enforcement Administration:

> One of the most serious problems experienced by cancer patients undergoing chemotherapy for their cancer is severe nausea and vomiting caused by their reaction to the toxic (poisonous) chemicals administered to them in the course of this treatment. This nausea and vomiting at times becomes life threatening.
>
> Beginning in the 1970s there was considerable doctor-to-doctor communication in the United States concerning patients known by their doctors to be surreptitiously using marijuana with notable success to overcome or lessen their nausea and vomiting.
>
> In about December, 1977, the previously underground patient practice of using marijuana to control emesis burst into the public media in New Mexico when a young cancer patient, Lynn Pearson, began publicly to discuss his use of

marijuana. Mr. Pearson besought the New Mexico Legislature to pass legislation making marijuana available legally to seriously ill patients whom it might help.

Marijuana induces some patients to eat. The benefits are obvious, doctors have found. There is no significant loss of weight. This allows them to gain strength and makes them better able to fight the cancer. Psychologically, patients who can continue to eat even while receiving chemotherapy maintain a balanced outlook and are better able to cope with their disease and its treatment, doctors have found.

For example, in late 1980, a three-year-old boy was brought by his parents to a hospital in Spokane, Washington. The child was diagnosed as having cancer. Surgery was performed. Chemotherapy was begun. The child became extremely nauseated and vomited for days after each chemotherapy treatment. Several standard available anti-emetic agents were tried by the child's doctors. None of them succeeded in controlling his nausea or vomiting.

Learning of the existence of research studies with THC or marijuana, the parents asked the child's doctor to arrange for their son to be the subject of such a study so that he might have access to marijuana. The doctor refused, citing the volume of paperwork and recordkeeping detail required in such programs and his lack of administrative personnel to handle it.

The child's mother read an article about marijuana smoking helping chemotherapy patients. She obtained some marijuana from friends. She baked cookies for her child with marijuana in them. She made tea from marijuana. When the child ate these cookies or drank this tea in connection with his chemotherapy, he did not vomit. His strength returned. He regained lost weight. His spirits revived. The parents told the doctors and nurses at the hospital of their giving marijuana to their child. None objected. They all accepted smoking marijuana as effective in controlling chemotherapy induced nausea and vomiting, and (were all curious about) the cookies.

Soon this child was riding a tricycle in the hallways of the Spokane hospital shortly after his chemotherapy treatments while other children there were still vomiting into pans, tied to intravenous bottles in an attempt to rehydrate them, to replace the liquids they were vomiting up. Parents of some of the other patients asked the parents of this "lively" child how he seemed to tolerate his chemotherapy so well. Of those parents who began giving marijuana to their children, none ever reported back encountering any adverse side-effects. In the words of the mother "When your kid is riding a tricycle while his other hospital buddies are hooked up to IV needles, their heads hung over vomiting buckets, you don't need a federal agency to tell you marijuana is effective. The evidence is in front of you, so stark it cannot be ignored."

The overwhelming preponderance of the evidence in (the record) establishes that marijuana has currently accepted medical use in treatment in the United States for nausea and vomiting resulting from chemotherapy treatments in some cancer patients. To conclude otherwise, on this record, would be unreasonable, arbitrary and capricious.

Glaucoma is a disease of the eye characterized by the excessive accumulation of fluid, causing increased intraocular pressure, distorted vision and, ultimately, blindness. Highly qualified and experienced physicians in the United States have accepted marijuana as having a medical use in treatment for glaucoma. (One) found that large dosages of smoked marijuana effectively reduced Robert Randall's intraocular pressure (IOP) into the safe range over an entire test day. He concluded that the only known alternative to preserve Randall's sight which would avoid the significant risks of surgery is to include marijuana as part of Randall's prescribed medical regimen . . . (In 1984) a questionnaire was distributed which queried . . . ophthalmologists on cannabis therapy for glaucoma patients refractory to standard treatment. Most of the responding ophthalmologists believed that THC capsules or smoked marijuana need to be available for patients who have not benefited significantly from standard treatment.

Irvin Rosenfeld has been diagnosed as having pseudo hypoparathyroidism. This uncommon disease causes bone spurs to appear and grow all over the body. Over the patient's lifetime hundreds of these spurs can grow, any one of which can become malignant at any time. The resulting cancer would spread quickly and the patient would die. Even without the development of a malignancy, the disease causes enormous pain. The spurs press upon adjacent body tissue, nerve and organs. In Rosenfeld's case, he could neither sit still nor lie down, nor could he walk, without experiencing pain. Working in his furniture store in Virginia, Mr. Rosenfeld was on his feet moving furniture all day long. The lifting and walking caused serious problems as muscles and tissues rubbed over the spurs of bone. He tore muscles and hemorrhaged almost daily . . .

One day he smoked marijuana while playing chess with a friend. It had been very difficult for him to sit for more than five or ten minutes at a time because of the tumors in the backs of his legs. Suddenly he realized that, absorbed in his chess game, and smoking marijuana, he had remained sitting for over an hour—with no pain. He experimented further and found that his pain was reduced whenever he smoked marijuana.

Rosenfeld told his doctor of his discovery. There was a drastic decrease in Rosenfeld's need for such drugs as Dilaudid and Demerol and for sleeping pills. The quality of pain relief which followed his smoking of marijuana was superior to any he had experienced before. As his dosages of powerful conventional drugs decreased, Rosenfeld became less withdrawn from the world, more able to interact and function. So he has continued to the present time.

Marijuana has a currently accepted medical use in treatment in the United States for spasticity resulting from Multiple Sclerosis and other causes. It would be unreasonable, arbitrary and capricious to find otherwise . . . the same is true with respect for the hyperparathyroidism from which Irvin Rosenfeld suffers.

Nearly all medicines have toxic, potentially lethal effects. But marijuana is not such a substance. There is no record in the extensive medical literature describing a proven, documented cannabis-induced fatality. This is a remarkable statement. First, the record on marijuana encompasses 5,000 years of human experience. Second, marijuana is now used daily by enormous numbers of people throughout the world.

Estimates suggest that from twenty million to fifty million Americans routinely, albeit illegally, smoke marijuana without the benefit of direct medical supervision. Yet, despite this long history of use and the extraordinarily high numbers of social smokers, there are simply no credible medical reports to suggest that consuming marijuana has caused a single death. By contrast aspirin, a commonly used, over-the-counter medicine, causes hundreds of deaths each year. Simply stated, researchers have been unable to give animals enough marijuana to induce death. A smoker would theoretically have to consume nearly 15 pounds of marijuana within about fifteen minutes to induce a lethal response. In strict medical terms marijuana is far safer than many foods we commonly consume. For example, eating ten raw potatoes can result in toxic response. By comparison, it is physically impossible to eat enough marijuana to induce death.

Marijuana, in its natural form, is one of the safest therapeutically active substances known to man. By any rational analysis marijuana can be safely used within a supervised routine of medical care—based upon the facts established in this record . . . one must reasonably conclude that there is accepted safety for use under medical supervision. To conclude otherwise, on this record, would be unreasonable, arbitrary and capricious.

Notes

Chapter 1. My Introduction to Marijuana

1. E. M. Brecher, *Licit and Illicit Drugs* (Boston: Little, Brown, 1972), p. 414
2. University of Kentucky Agricultural Extension Leaflet, March 25, 1943.
3. "The Leaflet," NORML, March 1993, p. 2.
4. Ronald K. Siegel, Ph.D., *Intoxication, Life in Pursuit of Artificial Paradise.* (New York: E. P. Dutton, 1989), p. 10.
5. Ibid, p. 11.
6. Ibid, pp. 300, 302, 303.
7. Brecher, p. 457.
8. *Freedom @ NORML*, NORML (Washington, D.C.), vol. 2, no. 5, November 1996.
9. Mike Males, "America Wages War on Teen-agers—Not Drugs," *Santa Rosa (California) Press Democrat*, 25 August 1996, p. G1.
10. Chief Jim Anderson, telephone interview with author, 2 December 1996.
11. "State Shuts Down SF Marijuana Club," *Santa Rosa (California) Press Democrat*, 5 August 1996, p. B3.
12. Deb Riechmann, "Soft Money Nearly Triples Since 1991–92," *Santa Rosa (California) Press Democrat*, 2 February 1997, p. A1.
13. Angie Cannon, "Anti-drug Campaign Strategy Shifted," *Santa Rosa (California) Press Democrat*, 26 February 1997, p. A7.

Chapter 2: Marijuana—Medical Miracle Herb

1. "H. Li, "The Origin and Use of Cannabis in Eastern Asia: Their Linguistic Cultural Implications," in *Cannabis and Culture*, V. Rubin, ed. (The Hague: Mouton, 1975), p. 54.

2. Abel, E. L. *Marijuana: The First Twelve Thousand Years.* (New York: Plenum, 1980), p. 14.
3. "Forum Newsfront" *Playboy*, October 1993, p. 44.
4. J. Grigor, "Indian Hemp as an Oxytocic," *Monthly Journal of Medical Science* 15, no. 5 (1852):124-125.
5. V. Robinson, "An Essay on Hasheesh," *Medical Review of Reviews* 18 (1912), pp. 159-169.
6. Ibid.
7. Written permission by *High Times*, Peter Gorman, 18 January 1996.
8. Lester Grinspoon, M.D., and James Bakalar, *Marijuana: The Forbidden Medicine* (New Haven: Yale University Press, 1993), p. 51.
9. "The Leaflet," NORML, March 1993.
10. Ibid.
11. United States Department of Justice, Drug Enforcement Administration, *In the Matter of Marijuana Rescheduling Petition*, September 1988.
12. Ibid.
13. Dean Edell, M.D., on KGO (ABC) Television, San Francisco, February 12, 1991, by permission.
14. "Patients Protest at White House for Medical Marijuana," *Active Resistance*, NORML (Washington, D.C.), Fall 1994, p. 3.
15. Ibid.
16. Ibid.
17. Ibid.
18. Ibid.
19. Ibid.
20. Ibid.
21. Ibid.
22. Ibid.
23. Ibid.
24. Ibid.
25. Ibid.
26. Ibid.
27. Greg Lucas, "Assembly Approves Marijuana as Medicine," *San Francisco Chronicle*, 19 May 1995, p. A21.
28. Ibid.
29. Ibid.
30. Ibid.
31. Ibid.
32. Ibid.
33. Ibid.

34. Ibid.
35. Jack Herer, *The Emperor Wears No Clothes* (Van Nuys, Calif.: Queen of Clubs, 1993/94), p. 27.

Chapter 3: Marijuana Prohibition—Sham!

1. Benson D. Roe, M.D., "The Drug War Misses an Important Mark," *San Francisco Chronicle*, 25 November 1992, p. A19.
2. Lester Grinspoon, M.D. *Marijuana Reconsidered* (Oakland, Calif.: Quick, American Archives, 1994), p. 324.
3. Jack Herer, *The Emperor Wears No Clothes* (Van Nuys, Calif.: Queen of Clubs, 1993/94), p. 27.
4. Ibid.
5. Kichard J. Bonnie and Charles H. Whitebread, *The Mur ihuana Conviction* (Charlottesville: University of Virginia Press, 1974), p. 34.
6. J. H. Hayes and L. E. Bowery, "Marihuana," *Journal of Criminology* 23 (1933): pp. 1086-98.
7. D. F. Musto, *The American Disease* (New Haven: Yale University Press, 1973), p. 220.
8. Derrick Z. Jackson, columnist, *Boston Globe*, "Blame Falls on Blacks," as appeared in *Santa Rosa (California) Press Democrat*,

30 November 1993, p. B5.

9. Ibid.
10. Ibid.
11. Ibid.
12. Herer, *The Emperor Wears No Clothes*, 1993/94, p. 27.
13. Ibid.
14. D. F. Musto, *The American Disease* (New Haven: Yale University Press, 1973), p. 227.
15. "Marijuana More Dangerous Than Heroin or Cocaine," *Scientific American*, May 1938, (reprinted in Jack Herer, *The Emperor Wears No Clothes*, [Van Nuys, Calif.: Queen of Clubs, 1993/94], p. 132).
16. H. J. Anlsinger and C. R. Cooper, "Marihuana: Assassin of Youth," *American Magazine* (1937), p. 124.
17. J. Kaplan, *Marihuana* (New York: Pocket Books, 1972), p. 98.
18. U.S. Congress, House of Representatives, Committee on Ways and Means, *Hearings on H.R. 6385*, 75th Congress, 1st session, 1937, p. 228.
19. H. J. Anslinger, *The Murders: The Story of the Narcotic Gangs.* New York: Farrar, Straus, and Cudahy 1961), p. 38.
20. E. M. Brecher, *Licit and Illicit Drugs* (Boston: Little, Brown, 1972), p. 415.
21. Ibid.

22. Ibid.
23. Ernest L. Abel, *Marijuana: The First Twelve Thousand Years* (New York: Plenum, 1980), p. 228.
24. Ibid.
25. E. M. Brecher, *Licit and Illicit Drugs* (Boston: Little, Brown, 1972), p. 418.
26. Ibid.
27. Ibid, p. 243.
28. Ibid, p. 244.
29. Ibid.
30. Ibid.
31. Ibid.
32. Herer, *The Emperor Wears No Clothes*, 1993/94, p. 28.
33. Ibid.
34. Brecher, *Licit and Illicit Drugs*, p. 418.
35. Ibid, p. 419.
36. Ibid.
37. Ibid.
38. Ibid.
39. Ibid.
40. Ibid.
41. Herer, *The Emperor Wears No Clothes*, 1993/94, p. 29.
42. Ibid.
43. Ibid., p. 30.
44. "Federal Court Ruling in NORML vs. DEA," "The Leaflet," NORML, Summer 1993, p. 1.

Chapter 4: Who Benefits from Marijuana Prohibition?

1. Herer, *The Emperor Wears No Clothes* (Van Nuys, Calif.: Queen of Clubs, 1991), p. 8.
2. "Japanese Tycoon Tops Richest List," *San Francisco Chronicle*, 21 June 1993, p. C2.
3. "The Leaflet," NORML, Fall 1991.
4. Ibid.
5. "The Leaflet," NORML, Summer 1993, p. 8.
6. James Bovard, "The Playboy Forum," *Playboy*, October 1995, p. 45.
7. Ibid.
8. "Civil Forfeiture," *Active Resistance*, NORML (Washington, D.C.), Summer 1993, p. 8.
9. Ibid.
10. Herer, *Emperor Wears No Clothes*, 1993/94, p. 35.

11. Dr. Earl Mindell, "The Inside Story," Winter 1994, pp. 4–7.
12. Herer, *The Emperor Wears No Clothes*, 1993/94, p.35.
13. Excerpts from Anheuser-Busch Companies, Inc. *Report of First Quarter 1992 & Annual Meeting of Shareholders*, pp. 9, 10.
14. "Record Jump in Prison Population," *Santa Rosa (California) Press Democrat*, 4 December 1995, p. 1.

Chapter 5: Are We Being Protected from Evil—or Honesty?

1. Peter Passell, "Less Marijuana, More Alcohol?" *New York Times*, 17 June 1992, p. 9.
2. Michael Dunham, "When the Smoke Clears," *Reason*, March 1983, pp. 33-36.
3. "Myth: Marijuana Prohibition Improves Public Safety," *NORML Reports*, NORML, Junc 1994.
4. "The Junk Science of Anti-Marijuana Claims," "The Leaflet," NORML, Summer 1993, p. 2.

Chapter 6: Our Legal "Killer Drugs"

1. James Bennett and Thomas J. Dilorenzo, *Official Lies, How Washington Deceives Us*. (Alexandria, VA: Groom Books, 1992), pp. 12, 13.
2. From the soundtrack of the original motion picture *The Burning Question (Reefer Madness)*. Produced by George Hirliman. An Albert Dezel Production, 1936.
3. Robert O'Brien, M.D., Sidney Cohen, M.D., and James Fine, *Encyclopedia of Drug Abuse*, 2nd ed., (New York: Facts On File, 1992), p. 178.
4. Ibid.
5. Curt Dewdes, *Listen*, February 1991, pp. 16-19.
6. Ann Landers, "Pulling Out Baseball's Tobacco Habit at Its Roots," *Santa Rosa (California) Press Democrat*, 10 October 1993, p. D2.
7. Philip J. Hilts, "Tobacco Execs: No Addiction," *Santa Rosa (California) Press Democrat*, 15 April 1994, p. A2.
8. Robert O'Brien, M.D., and Morris Chafetz, M.D., *The Encyclopedia of Alcoholism*, 2nd ed. (New York: Facts on File, 1991), p. 51.
9. Ibid., p. 104.
10. State Farm Insurance, *Good Neighbor News*, 1992.
11. Richard Glen Boire, *Marijuana Law* (Berkeley, Calif.: Ronin Publishing, Inc., 1992), p. 92.
12. "The First 20 Years," broadcast on KLSX 97.1 (Los Angeles, California) and other stations of the Westwood One radio network (January 29, 1990).
13. Brecher, *Licit and Illicit Drugs*, p. 432.
14. Ibid.
15. Ibid.

16. Fans often remember songs by their actual titles or their incipits (their opening words) or their nicknames. The ones noted here fall into all three categories.

Chapter 7: *Marijuana Alert* Madness

1. Peggy Mann, *Marijuana Alert* (New York: McGraw Hill, 1985), p. 4.
2. Ibid., p. 10.
3. Ibid., p. 32.
4. Herer, *The Emperor Wears No Clothes*, 1991, pp. 82-83.
5. Ibid., p. 79.
6. Mann, *Marijuana Alert*, p. 10.
7. Ibid., pp. 30-31.
8. "The Merck Manual of Diagnosis and Therapy, 1992," *Active Resistance*, NORML (Washington, D.C.), Summer 1993, p. 2.
9. Mann, *Marijuana Alert*, p. 183.
10. Ibid., pp. 145-146.
11. "Facial Shape and Perennial Exposure to Marijuana, Alcohol and/or Cocaine," *Pediatrics*, January 1992, p. 67.
12. Mann, *Marijuana Alert*, p. 231.
13. Ibid., p. 160.
14. Ibid., pp. 162, 163.
15. Ibid., pp. 160, 161.
16. Ibid., p. 136.
17. *California NORML Reports*, April 1992. (Based on a study originally published in *Drug and Alcohol Dependence*, 1991, vol. 28: pp.12-28.)
18. Mann, *Marijuana Alert*, p. 139.
19. Ibid., p. 171.
20. Ibid., p. 190.
21. Ibid.
22. Herer, *The Emperor Wears No Clothes*, 1993/94, pp. 82-83.
23. Mann, *Marijuana Alert*, p. 4.
24. Ibid., pp. 218-228.
25. Ibid., p. 221.

Chapter 8: Marijuana Is Medicine—and More

1. Fay Flam, "Scientists Find Sleep Chemical," *Santa Rosa (California) Press Democrat*, 9 June 1995, p. B3.

Chapter 9: Hemp is Not Marijuana!

1. H. Li, "An Archeological and Historical Account of Cannabis in China," *Economic Botany* 28 (1974):437-48.
2. Roger A. Roffman, *Marijuana as Medicine* (Seattle: Madrona, 1982), p. 33.

3. Eric Steenstra, "Hemp Rediscovered," *Active Resistance.* NORML (Washington, D.C.), Spring 1994, p. 13.
4. Portions of the forgoing uses for hemp are from "Energy Farming in America," by Lynn Osburn and the Business Alliance for Commerce in Hemp. For more information on the many uses of hemp, send $1.00 and a self-addressed, stamped envelope to BACH, P.O. Box 71093, Los Angeles, CA 90071-0093.
5. Ibid.
6. Ibid.
7. To purchase a copy of *Hemp for Victory*, the United States 1942 Department of Agriculture's pro-hemp film, on video, send $22.00, which includes shipping, to: H.E.M.P., 5632 Van Nuys Blvd., Suite 210, Van Nuys, CA 91401.

Chapter 10: Pot/Drug War Atrocities

1. "Drug-license Bill Advances," *Santa Rosa (California) Press Democrat*, 21 February 1997, p. B3.
2. "Legislature Kills `Smoke a Joint, Lose Your License,'" *California NORML Reports*, September 1995, p. 1.
3. *Active Resistance*, NORML (Washington, D.C.), Summer 1994, p. 15.
4. Ed Rosenthal, William Logan, and Jeffery Steinborn, "Defeating the Spy-Tech Search Warrant," *High Times*, October 1995, p. 53.
5. "Marijuana, Medicine, and the Cops," "The Leaflet," NORML, Fall 1991, p. 2.
6. "Life in Prison for Wild Hemp," "The Leaflet," NORML, Winter 1992. p. 2.
7. Ibid.
8. Howard Troxler, Columnist, *St. Pete Times*, November 1991, p. 4.
9. "Report from the Front: South of the Border," "The Leaflet," NORML, Spring 1992, p. 10.
10. "The Leaflet," NORML, Winter 1992.
11. "The Leaflet," NORML, Winter 1992, p. 3
12. Ibid.
13. "The Leaflet," NORML, Fall 1991, p. 2.
14. Ibid.
15. Ibid.
16. Tom Cahill of Fort Bragg, California, a photographer and journalist. By written permission.
17. E. M. Brecher, *Licit and Illicit Drugs* (Boston: Little, Brown, 1972), p. 471.
18. Ibid.
19. James Bovard, "Oops—You're Dead," "Playboy Forum", *Playboy*, December 1994, pp. 50-51.
20. Ibid.

21. Ibid.
22. Ibid.
23. *Active Resistance*, NORML (Washington, D.C.), Summer 1994, p. 7.
24. *Active Resistance*, NORML (Washington, D.C.), Fall 1994, p. 16.
25. "Boston Globe Readers Overwhelmingly Support Medicinal Marijuana," *Active Resistance*, NORML (Washington, D.C.), Fall 1994, p. 17.
26. Ed Vaughan, "National Guard Involvement in the Drug War," NORML (Washington, D.C.) *Active Resistance*, Summer 1993, p. 7.
27. Ibid.
28. Ibid.
29. Ibid.
30. Ibid.
31. Dan Morain, "Assembly Revives 3 Strikes," *Santa Rosa (California) Press Democrat*, 10 July 1996, p. A3.
32. "Cops' View of the 'Drug War,'" *San Francisco Examiner*, 9 April 1995, p. C16.

Chapter 11: Drug Testing

1. "Urine Testing," Public Education Brochure by the National Organization for the Reform of Marijuana Laws, 1995.
2. Ibid.
3. Ibid.
4. Richard Glen Boire, *Marijuana Law*. (Berkeley: Ronin Publishing, Inc., 1992), p. 144.
5. "The Leaflet," NORML, Winter 1992, p. 9.
6. Ibid.
7. Ibid.
8. "The Leaflet," NORML, Winter 1992, p. 9

Chapter 12: Marijuana in Hawaii and on the Mainland

1. "Carroll Ponders Bill to Make Pot Legal," *Honolulu Advertiser* 9 February 1973, p. A10.
2. "Survey of Hawaii's War on Drugs," Hawaiian Hemp Company magazine, February 1993, p. 2.
3. E. M. Brecher, *Licit and Illicit Drugs* (Boston: Little, Brown, 1972), pp. 369, 441, 442.

Chapter 15: Relegalize Marijuana

1. Sabin Russell, "U.S. Drug Czar Visits Haight, Denounces Medical Use of Pot," *San Francisco Chronicle*, 16 August 1996, p. A8.
2. R. Engs, *Alcohol and other Drugs: Self-Responsibility* (Bloomington, Ind.: Tichenor, 1987), p. 293.
3. Ibid.

4. Ibid.
5. Ibid.
6. Ibid., p. 294.
7. Ibid.
8. E. M. Brecher, *Licit and Illicit Drugs* (Boston: Little, Brown, 1972), pp. 453, 454, 455.
9. Ibid., p. 457.
10. Ibid., pp. 460, 461.
11. Ibid., p. 463.
12. Ibid., p. 465.
13. Jack Herer, *The Emperor Wears No Clothes* (Van Nuys, Calif.: Queen of Clubs, 1993/94), p. 89.
14. Jennifer Mann, "Unforgettable Peggy Mann," *Reader's Digest*, January 1992, p. 96.
15. Fred Barns, "Bennett the Drug Czar: An Agenda," *The American Spectator*, vol. 22, no. 4, April 1989, pp. 14, 15.
16. Bernard Gauzer, "Should Marijuana Be Legal?" *Parade, Register Guard* (Oregon), 12 June 1994.
17. "Gingrich Drug Proposal," *Santa Rosa (California) Press Democrat*, 15 July 1995, p. A6.
18. *Active Resistance*, NORML (Washington, D.C.), Spring 1994.
19. PRIDE, *Parent Primer*, 1994.
20. Herer, *The Emperor Wears No Clothes*, 1993/94, p. 81.
21. Ibid., p. 76.
22. Bureau of Justice Statistics, United States Department of Justice, *Marijuana Digest*, 1991, p. 3.
23. *Active Resistance*, NORML (Washington, D.C.), Fall 1994, p. 16.
24. Herer, *The Emperor Wears No Clothes*, 1991, p. 75.
25. Richard Glen Boire, *Marijuana Law* (Berkeley, Calif.: Ronin Publishing, Inc., 1992), p. 39.
26. Kristina Marlow and Steve Rhodes, "Study: DARE Falls Short of Goal," *Santa Rosa (California) Press Democrat*, 6 November 1994, p. A8.
27. "Willie Busted," *Active Resistance*, NORML (Washington, D.C.), Summer 1994, p. 3.
28. NORML membership letter received by author, September 25, 1995.

Index

READER QUESTIONNAIRE AND ORDER FORM

To order copies of *Marijuana: Not Guilty As Charged,* an outstanding gift, phone toll-free 1-800-507-2665.

We encourage and welcome your messages to the author. Please feel free to forward a note to David R. Ford, c/o Good Press, P.O. Box 1771, Sonoma, CA 95476. Those of you on the Internet can write him directly at drford@vom.com.

In addition, Good Press welcomes your comments regarding future editions of *Marijuana: Not Guilty As Charged.* Feel free to include information on your experiences and/or opinions about any of the following matters on a photocopy of this page or on a separate sheet:

I would like to submit my

(1) medical experience with marijuana.

(2) experience as to how marijuana reduced stress in my life.

(3) experience as to how marijuana improved my life.

(4) opinion as to why marijuana should be legalized.

(5) opinion as to why marijuana should not be legalized.

__ You have my permission to use my name, city, and state.

____

Please print your name, city, and state, if okay to use.

__ You may use my city ________ and state _______ only.

Other comments ______________________________________

____

How I first heard about this book:

__ Bookstore __ Word of mouth __ Newspaper __ Radio/TV __ Other

What I liked most about this book:

____

____

____

____